Inside
Learning Network
Schools

Marilyn Herzog
General Editor

Richard C. Owen Publishers, Inc.
Katonah, New York

Library of Congress Cataloging-in-Publication Data

Inside learning network schools / Marilyn Herzog, general editor.
        p.   cm.
    Includes bibliographical references and index.
    ISBN 1-57274-129-5 (pbk.)
    1. Language arts (Elementary)—Arizona—Phoenix—Case studies. 2.
English language—Composition and exercises—Study and teaching (Elementary)—Arizona—Phoenix—Case studies. 3. Classroom management—
Arizona—Phoenix—Case studies. 4. School management and organization—
Arizona—Phoenix—Case studies. I. Herzog, Marilyn, 1951- .
LB1576.I64 1997
372.6'09791'73—dc21   97-20344
                                                               CIP

RICHARD C. OWEN PUBLISHERS, INC.
PO Box 585
Katonah, New York 10536
914/232-3903

Production management H. Powers Communications, Inc.
Project editor Amy J. Haggblom

Printed in the United States of America

9 8 7 6 5 4 3 2 1

To Jan and Peter Duncan

Table of Contents

Foreword
Richard C. Owen

Who could have known the significance of that meeting in St. Louis during the NCTE conference in November of 1988? Margaret Mooney, Mike Hagan, and I spent most of two days in the lobby of a convention hotel talking about a design for a summer workshop experience for teachers.

We had come together because Richard C. Owen Publishers, Inc. was charged with marketing the national reading program of New Zealand, and we had concluded that we needed to offer teachers some exposure to the theory on which the program was based.

Margaret had been sent by the New Zealand Department of Education and Mike was an American teacher and educator from California. We came up with a design, the very best one we could produce at that time, and we took the first steps toward what was to become Literacy Learning in the Classroom, a robust four-day experience that has now energized more than 30,000 American teachers.

Margaret was to offer the keynote address at nine workshops scheduled for the following summer. A group of American facilitators invited by Mike and me were to engage participants in discussions over the three days that followed, introducing them to the ideas about teaching reading and writing that had evolved in New Zealand over a period of thirty years. Two weeks before the first workshop in Portland, Oregon, I received a worried call from Margaret. Her health was delicate and her doctor had told her not to travel. We had lost our keynote speaker at a most inopportune time.

My contact in the Department of Education was Barbara Mabbett, a no-nonsense manager. She acted immediately, agreeing to send two replacements for Margaret, both of whom were Reading/Language Advisors for the Department of Education. Margaret Hayes came for the first six workshops; Jan Duncan replaced her for the last three.

Both Margaret and Jan did a credible job under adverse circumstances. They entered a foreign, almost alien, environment where teachers were struggling to make sense of a new paradigm for teaching. American teachers were attempting to shift from the role of technician to the role of professional. They were trying to move away from a curriculum controlled by a basal manual to a curriculum that is child centered.

After the workshop in Portland I bought T-shirts for the facilitators that said "We survived Portland." We not only survived Portland, we survived the summer. It was a summer of learning–about workshops, about management, about teaching and learning. I found it stimulating and exhausting, a pattern those of us involved with summer institutes have come to experience year after year.

What does this description of Literacy Learning in the Classroom have to do with The Learning Network? Quite simply, this is where we come from. The plan for The Learning Network emerged from many late-night discussions with the workshop staff about how to support change over time.

We knew that the four days of the summer experience were evolving into something quite powerful, but we were troubled by the lack of support during the school year for helping teachers make changes over time. Every day that passed after a teacher attended the workshop, that experience receded one day into the past. Very few participants could be expected to draw sustenance from the workshop after the first few weeks. In that situation very little real change would likely occur.

Little did we know that Jan Duncan had a spouse in New Zealand who had insights into change in schools. Jan and Peter offered a wonderful combination. Jan had a deeply embedded understanding of the theory of teaching and learning that had evolved in New Zealand; Peter had a slightly broader view that encompassed elements of change in educational organizations. Together they were keenly interested in creating a mechanism to support change in American schools.

By 1992 Jan was coming to the United States for extended periods of time during the school year. She agreed to take a leave of absence from her job in New Zealand to spend ten months with us. Peter decided that it was time for early retirement so he too could be involved.

The ten months stretched to five years, during which they were both intimately involved in the development of The Learning Network. The Network reflects the efforts of many people, some directly in the design and implementation of the two-year commitment schools make and others less directly through the contributions they have made to the refinement of the summer institute. But all who have had a hand in The Learning Network will agree that the resource we have developed represents the heart and soul of Jan and Peter Duncan. I am grateful for their unflagging commitment to help all of us become learners in ways we never thought possible.

There have been many events along the way that have given shape to The Learning Network, but the single most defining moment in my memory occurred in Memphis, Tennessee in July of 1991. We were into the third summer of the institute and we were conscious that the experience participants had during the four days differed depending on who was their facilitator. Facilitators differed in their interpretation of concepts and in the value they placed on particular behaviors.

Is it important to communicate a consistent message to participants? If so, what is the message? And how do we establish consistency? We grappled with these questions nightly. We argued about the model and over time we came to describe the argument as "Do we *adapt* what we call the New Zealand model or do we *adopt* it?" As you will see in the Prologue by Marilyn Herzog, the structure of the model was articulated at that time as Knowing the Learner, Knowing the Resources, and Knowing the Approaches.

Honest people can forever disagree on the answer, but for those of us involved with The Learning Network, resolution came in the form of "adopting the model." I had learned from those New Zealanders who mentored us that this model offers a consistent, cohesive theory of teaching and learning and that the impact in a school is heightened significantly when all teachers work together to develop common understandings and practices.

The decision to focus on adopting what is now referred to as the Literacy Learning model created a rift within the workshop that disappointed some people. As an organization we regrouped and began to move forward, refining our plan for The Learning Network.

The transition from a focus on the four-day experience to a focus on long-term school development has taken years. More of our energy is now devoted to working at multiple levels of change within schools. We started by exploring ways to provide direct support for teachers in the classroom. We revised our position as we came to recognize the importance of building the mechanism for sustained growth into the school community. The structure that we endorse is the critical triangle–that set of relationships among the principal, the site-based teacher leaders, and the program coordinator, the professional staff person from The Learning Network who is on campus to provide support.

We have become more deeply invested in helping principals make the shift from manager to instructional leader. We have become more deeply invested in helping teacher leaders develop the understandings and skill of conducting instructional dialogue. We have become more deeply invested in helping prepare other teachers in the school for change.

The circles ripple outward. Every year it seems our experience with The Learning Network introduces yet another component of change that we need to consider. But at the root of it all is the idea of supporting the professional growth of teachers, helping each of them develop a theory of teaching and learning that drives their practice. That theory is still explored and articulated in the summer institute, Literacy Learning in the Classroom.

In the chapters that follow you will be introduced to the ideas and the structure of the theory and to the way in which The Learning Network supports changes in the attitudes, understandings, and behaviors of teachers. The authors of the chapters are deeply involved in their own change and in supporting changes in colleagues.

No one will tell you that the task is simple. The authors are practitioners engaged in the effort at the school and district level. They are committed to building on theory rather than focusing on methodology. What we do reflects what we know and understand. The question you will hear asked repeatedly throughout this book is "Why am I doing what I am doing?"

There are three parts to this book, framed by a Prologue and Epilogue written by Marilyn Herzog, a trainer of program coordinators for The Learning Network. Part I explores the structure of The Learning Network–the way in which The Network works within the school to support change.

Part II looks at literacy learning, which is the content area we use as a vehicle for helping teachers develop their theory. You will discover an emphasis in these chapters on appropriate instruction. I use the word "instruction" to mean planned efforts on the part of the teacher to influence learning outcomes of children. In other words, in our view the role of the teacher is to teach.

In Part III we expand our focus from the individual classroom to the school as a whole and to the larger community. Supporting changes in individual teachers has significant impact, but it pales next to the idea of an entire school of teachers who share a common vision, develop common understandings, and work together to put children onto a continuum of learning.

Imagine the impact on the life of a child when teachers use the same tools to gather data, when that data is evaluated in a consistent way, and when that evaluation is used to plan for instruction. Imagine the impact on the life of a child when teachers are able to organize that data to share with the teacher in the next grade. What the teacher "knows" about the learners makes it possible to begin teaching on Day 1 of the new school year. Imagine the impact on the life of a child when she knows what to expect from the teacher in her new classroom. Her learning starts immediately and is substantive. She is going to get the very most she can from her school experience.

We do not have to imagine these things happening in schools. They exist now in The Learning Network. Might we have gotten to this point without the involvement of Jan and Peter Duncan? Maybe. But I can't believe that it would have occurred this quickly, and I know that it would not have been with the vigorous challenging of ideas and practices that have been the hallmark of their work.

We expect that work to continue, but at a greater distance. Their move back to New Zealand marks not an end but a beginning. I know that both Jan and Peter believe fervently in the idea of teachers and schools being "self-winding," an image reminiscent of watches that predate quartz batteries. The idea applies also to The Learning Network. To what extent are we able to continue our growth independently?

We cannot expand any faster than we can train competent and confident program coordinators, and we cannot train program coordinators without skillful trainers of program coordinators. Marilyn Herzog and Mike Shelton have the awesome responsibility for continuing the training that Jan started.

We have learned that the training of program coordinators mirrors the training of teacher leaders. We start with support that helps the program coordinator to improve practice in her classroom based on a consistent and cohesive theory. The trainer goes to the classroom of the program coordinator, takes an observation based on an action plan, and engages the program coordinator in instructional dialogue. The theory that drives the classroom practice of the program coordinator is as important to the program coordinator as it is to the teacher leader and the classroom teacher.

We continue that support in two week-long class meetings at Learning Network sites during the first school year and work at five institutes as part of a facilitator team, building understandings during the summer. The curriculum has 41 days of contact built into it prior to the program coordinator beginning to work in schools.

The second year of program coordinator training involves an additional 30 days of support, including four site visits, a winter program coordinator meeting at a Learning Network site, and professional development work at the summer institutes. The third year involves an additional twelve days of support along with some professional development work at the summer institutes. Thereafter we envision continuing contact.

We are adding about six new program coordinators each year. The curriculum for their training continues to evolve as we learn more about what constitutes competence. The professional development of the program coordinator never ends. The professional development of the teacher leaders never ends. The professional development of The Learning Network never ends.

Are there key lessons we have learned from Jan and Peter that relate to our ability to continue the work? One that comes to my mind is vigilance. We have to be ever alert to maintain rigor, lest we water down the process. A second lesson is to remember that we are not developing experts but rather professionals able to determine the needs of the learner and able to focus on providing the appropriate level of support so that learner can take his or her next learning step.

This book is a marker of progress. It brings to mind a favorite quote from Margaret Hayes: "It's not how far we have gotten; it's how far we have come from where we started." Our progress is significant and substantial, but we all recognize that we have a long way to go.

Acknowledgments

Throughout this book you will find references to individuals who have been influential in the creation and shaping of The Learning Network. In addition to the contributions of Jan and Peter Duncan, there have been many people whose insights have made a difference.

Barbara Mabbett, the general manager at the Schools Publication Branch of the New Zealand Department of Education, had the foresight to see value in supporting an educational experience in the United States. Margaret Mooney and Mike Hagan worked to create the original design for the summer institute. Margaret Hayes, who with Jan Duncan came from New Zealand the first summer (and for several summers thereafter), offered general sessions at the summer institute, and worked closely with the first group of fifteen American teachers who were risk-takers willing to experiment with a different way of running a workshop.

Two facilitators in particular became active in working with us in the early stages of The Learning Network. Donna Byrum and Leslie Swanda Willey left secure teaching jobs to live the role of the program coordinator. Through their experience and the experience of Jan Duncan, who was involved in the same work, we made changes and revisions that redefined The Learning Network. The teachers and principals in the schools where Jan, Donna, and Leslie carried out their work provided critically important assessment samples.

The first group of six program coordinators began their training in the fall of 1995. From them we learned a great deal about the understandings needed for an educator to become a program coordinator and about the forms of support needed to help widely scattered individuals see themselves as part of a cohesive group. We continue to learn from the first class and from the classes who have followed.

Marilyn Herzog had the temerity and the courage to follow in the footsteps of Jan. Her sense of herself as a learner and her skillfulness in working with others is a key to the continued growth of The Learning Network. And within the New York office, the dedication and organizational capacity of Phyllis Greenspan and the RCO staff has kept the whole system functioning. Marilyn and Phyllis have taught all of us about how to maintain equilibrium when disequilibrium seems to be standard.

To all who have had an involvement in developing and implementing The Learning Network, I offer my thanks and appreciation.

RCO

Prologue
From New Zealand to the U.S.: Making the Model Our Own
Marilyn Herzog

*"The end of all our exploring is to arrive where we have
started, and see that place for the first time."*

T.S. Eliot

In 1988, I was searching. I was a successful primary classroom teacher
in Phoenix, Arizona who had been at the business of teaching for about
fourteen years. I was a "gourmet omnivore" (Joyce and Showers 1980)
when it came to learning new things about the teaching of reading and
writing. I attended every workshop that came to town in my quest to be
the best teacher that I could be. I would attend the workshop on Saturday, learn "how to" be a better teacher of reading and writing, and go
into the classroom on Monday morning, ready to make big changes. I
was also a reader. One book that impressed me was Donald Graves'
Writing: Teachers and Children at Work (1983), which enabled me to
dive into Writer's Workshop with enthusiasm. I became enamored
with what I began to hear and understand about reading instruction in
New Zealand. I read the reading handbook *Reading in Junior Classes*
(Ministry of Education 1985), glossing over the content and pouring in
depth over the colored pictures. I tried to make my classroom look like
the rooms in those pictures. In my quest to understand how to teach
children to read, I bought *The Early Detection of Reading Difficulties*
(Clay 1979). I struggled through *Foundations of Literacy* by Donald
Holdaway (1979) and began to play with the approach of shared reading.

I was a good teacher during these years. I was challenged by and enjoyed my job. The students in my classroom thrived and learned. But early on I subscribed to the belief that "Where you are is an okay place to be, but not an okay place to stay" (Davis 1991). It was no surprise when the brochure arrived in the mail in the spring of 1989 that I would be first to sign up for a summer workshop, then called Whole Language in the Classroom, presented by Richard C. Owen Publishers. And the dangling carrot in front of my nose was that there would be a "real" New Zealander at that workshop. It was promised that I would learn everything that I needed to know in order to teach just like they did in New Zealand. I wanted to know how to do it; at this point I felt I was already familiar with the theory.

What do I remember about those four days? I remember that the New Zealander spoke on Sunday evening. I remember that she had a really wonderful dress and I remember that she had beautifully colored overheads of the classrooms in New Zealand. I took copious notes of everything that she said because I was convinced that I would be able to make the changes necessary in my classroom so it would look and be just like a classroom in New Zealand. We met in small groups with American teachers who decorated the walls with stuff that looked like it came out of these New Zealand classrooms.

The drive home from Tucson with my colleagues was non-stop talk about what we could do to put this New Zealand model in place. We would "do" reading to, shared reading, and guided reading in our classrooms. We would do all the suggested activities that would make children readers and writers. When I look back at the resource book from that summer institute, I'm surprised to see how much of an impact it really had on the changes that were to occur in my classroom. Not only did it have an impact on the physical look of the classroom, but it provided the beginnings of a journey into understandings that would eventually bring me back to where I began.

How did the classroom change that year? We had a shared book experience every day with a big book and the whole class. The teaching objective was determined by what I *thought* the students needed. My students were writing daily. They were choosing their own topics and we were "celebrating" the student's writing. Indeed, my classroom began to look like those classrooms in the photographs. I saw engagement and enthusiasm with many learners involved in the process.

I knew that I was doing a better job teaching reading and writing than I had previously. I understood the power of students reading real books and choosing their own topics for writing. I was seeing growth in many of the learners in my classroom and there was no doubt that they thought school was a good place to be. But I continued to experience a measure of "intellectual unrest" (Johnston 1987). There were still a significant number of students in my classroom who did not exhibit the kind of growth that I wanted to see. They read the little books for emergent readers and writers and memorized them, but didn't seem to get much further. The children wrote daily, but I did not see marked growth in the content or mechanics of their writing pieces. I was pretty sure that I was the missing link—but I didn't really know what I needed to do next.

I received a call the following winter from Richard Owen, asking if I would be interested in applying for the role of a facilitator for the summer workshop that I had attended. I was surprised and pleased, because this would be my opportunity to connect myself more directly with this New Zealand model as well as having the opportunity to learn directly from the New Zealand facilitators. I replied to the questions that were asked concerning my philosophy about teaching and learning, my experience working with adults, and my depth of understanding about the New Zealand model.

I attended the facilitator training in California in the springtime and quickly realized that the "depth" of understanding I had about the New Zealand model amounted to nearly no knowledge at all. I was quickly quieted and overwhelmed by the American teachers who had been facilitators before and especially by the presence of the New Zealanders. My brain was overloaded by the knowledge of what I didn't know and I decided that no matter what, I really wanted this experience and if I kept really quiet, Richard Owen wouldn't know the big mistake he had made.

It was at this meeting that I met Jan Duncan. Jan was a Language and Reading Advisor for the Ministry of Education in Wellington, New Zealand. When she spoke, everyone listened. She spoke with the strength of understanding that not only impressed people, but also intimidated them. She asked questions and demanded answers. She seemed unbending in her beliefs. She asked us to challenge our understandings when we were pretty sure that we didn't have any. She asked us to examine our classroom practice with a microscope.

The summer was a huge challenge. The days were filled with the institute experience, where I was the one who was supposed to know what this was all about. We were no longer American presenters that summer, but rather facilitators of dialogue. That presented a huge challenge for me, as I didn't even know what dialogue was supposed to look like. In addition to that huge challenge, we had very lengthy meetings following the institute. These meetings were facilitated by Jan

Duncan. I listened to the conversations going on at those meetings. I made the decision that I would not speak unless I had something to say that was worth saying, or unless I had a good question to ask. I hardly said a word all summer.

But I listened and I learned. I learned that there was no magic to this New Zealand model. I learned that this was not a model driven by cute ideas or glossy pictures; it was a model that was driven by teachers who possessed a strong theory base in their heads about reading and writing. I learned that I was not going to be told how to do this; that the importance did not lie in being able to tell people what I was doing, but in the ability to answer the question, "Why am I doing what I'm doing?"

The workshop talked about Knowing the Learner, Knowing the Resources, and Knowing the Approaches. The New Zealand presenters talked about using running records and writing samples to get to know your learners, about the supports and challenges in the texts and learning experiences, and about *Reading To, With, and By Children* (Mooney 1990) as instructional approaches. I wrote down every word that came out of the mouth of the New Zealanders at all those institutes that summer. I was sure that if I just listened hard enough and long enough, I would be able to put this literacy model in place when I got back to my classroom in the fall.

For the next few years, I was "playing at the model." My room continued to look as if this model were in place. My daily plan showed times for reading and writing to children, shared and guided reading and writing and time for students to use what they know. I was asking the right questions as I played at guided and shared reading: Does it make sense? Does it sound right? Does it look right? I was talking about supports and challenges in text and searching for them. I was beginning to take running records but did not have the knowledge to analyze them; I had no idea of what to do with the analysis. I dived into the New Zealand handbook for writing, *Dancing with the Pen* (Ministry of Education 1992), looking for all the clues to support my teaching of writing. I was doing well with the understandings I had at that time.

In fact, I was very good at "talking the talk" but I knew that in reality, I was not "walking the walk." I was like a stretched rubber band. I would get so far, then snap back, unable to continue. I depended on the summer institutes, the facilitator training, and our meetings at night to get me through the next year.

I was not alone in my frustrations. Groups of facilitators would sit up until the early hours of the morning having deep discussions that usually ended with, "What is it that we are supposed to understand and how in the heck can we put it all in place in September?"

Call it fate, luck, or determination: in 1993, at the same time that a new school was opening in my school district, The Learning Network was beginning to emerge as an opportunity for long-term teacher development. Kay Coleman, the newly appointed principal, looked at this as the opportunity to bring the New Zealand model to Phoenix. Bonnie Rhodes and I, already facilitators for the summer institute, would be trained as teacher leaders at the brand-new Las Brisas Elementary School. Jan Duncan would work alongside us eight times during the year as our program coordinator. We embarked on our journey as teacher leaders and our school embarked on the journey of The Learning Network.

The institute structure changed a bit the summer before we began The Network experience. We began to talk about the teaching and learning cycle shown in Figure 1. I began to understand that all decisions I was to make about my students were based on this cyclic nature of teaching and learning. Assessment was the collection of data and evaluation was what I did with that data. Planning involved knowing the results of that evaluation and selecting the appropriate resources

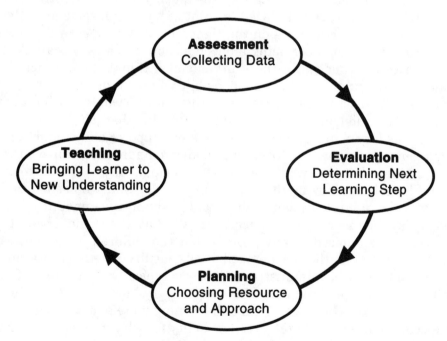

Figure 1. The teaching and learning cycle.

and learning experiences for teaching. And teaching was a highly skilled focused activity that would result in learning for all students. The stakes were high and my expectations were higher.

I can remember the last institute of the summer before we began this journey. I had spent the summer feeling rather comfortable with participants and challenging them to not worry about how they would do something, but focus on why they would be doing it. Meanwhile, at every opportunity, I would ask facilitators more experienced than I about the *how*. How did you organize your language arts block? How long was this block? Did you have guided reading groups with children every day? How many groups did you see per day? What were the other kids really doing? How long did the kids write? Did you really publish everything your students wrote? I was trying to get enough information to make it through the first day at least.

Keeping that teaching and learning cycle in mind, I began the year by bringing my children into school for the Observation Survey (Clay 1993a) two weeks before school started. I spent thirty minutes with each six-year-old and promptly fell in love with my kids. In knowing them as learners, I was able to see the strengths they brought into this classroom. I remember Nathaniel, when asked to write a dictation sentence, putting down his pencil and saying, "I think I should just say it for you." I can recall watching Chelsea quickly and confidently breeze through every text that I placed in front of her. I can remember Ryan beginning all of his writing on the right side of the paper and going to the left. I can remember being amazed at how much they really knew in such a short time on Earth. I can remember thinking how much they had to learn and what a huge responsibility I had undertaken. I can remember the trust in their eyes. I was the one who would teach them to read, write, and learn. I was committed to doing that job.

I was fortunate to have several major supports as I embarked on this journey. One was a strong and dedicated administrator who was determined that this would work. As principal, Kay Coleman took it upon herself to allow us the opportunity to do what we needed to do: learn to be skillful teachers. She spent a significant amount of time each day in the classrooms learning all that she could about this process. She rejoiced in any growth that the children made and was just as excited as the teachers. She held faculty meetings to a minimum and all of the administrivia that was typically the content of faculty meetings appeared on a blue memo every Monday in order to allow us to devote the meeting time to learning more about literacy. She expected that we would take responsibility for what needed to be done in order for the school to run smoothly. By being so supportive, by being a pillar of strength, by being able to see the vision of what could be, Kay allowed us to do what we needed to do–teach and learn.

Another support for me on this journey was the other teacher leader at this school. Bonnie Rhodes' fifth-grade classroom was next door to my first-grade classroom. Between our rooms was a moveable wall. We kept one section open at all times. The open door provided instant communication between the two of us. It also allowed the students to move back and forth as the need arose. Most importantly, it allowed both of us to see that when theory drives your practice, you are continuously asking "why am I doing what I'm doing?" Consistency and learning on a continuum became very evident, even with a span of early primary to late intermediate grades. We would continually question ourselves aloud in front of each other. Sometimes we wouldn't reply to the questions, but just saying them helped us resolve them. We would argue in a very Socratic way. We would pose questions to our faculty and the conversations were amazing. We were saturating ourselves with our teaching and reflecting. We couldn't get enough.

The most significant support to the change in understandings were the visits from the program coordinator, Jan Duncan. She brought to this process all of her understandings and expertise from her years of teaching and work as an advisor to teachers in New Zealand. She would observe in my classroom for half of each day that she was on campus. We would engage in instructional dialogue, where Jan would question me about the understandings that were driving my practice. She would provide both the pressure and support that would promote my growth as a teacher leader.

Jan came into the classroom and, to my surprise, immediately focused her attention on the children. She watched them plan for their language arts block and asked them questions. She dug into draft writing books and asked the children questions. She sat down beside them as they read and asked questions. She watched their involvement in projects and asked them more questions. It took a long time for me to realize that she knew that my understandings would manifest themselves in the behaviors of the children. Through the children, Jan was able to get a window into what I was thinking and where the gaps in my understandings might lie.

I remember one morning early in the school year. I was always impressed with the level of concentration Jan exhibited when in my classroom. She provided wonderful demonstrations of reflection by continually trying to figure things out. This day was no exception. She stood behind a bank of three computers with her arms folded and brows furrowed. She asked me, "What are the students doing on these comput-

ers that has to do with reading or writing?" As I watched the kids playing computer games, I realized that what they were doing would provide little opportunity for their development as life-long readers, writers, and learners. I dug into the resources that were available, so that
when I stood behind that bank of computers I could say that what they
were doing definitely would aid in their development as learners.

From that point, for a very long time, I would look at my practice
and my next thought would be, "What would Jan think and say if she
saw me do that?" There was the shadow of that program coordinator on
the shoulder of this teacher at that time in my teaching.

The evidence of my growing understandings caused me to revisit
the teaching and learning cycle frequently. I began to see the real reason for taking and analyzing running records; they enabled me to know
where my students were and where I needed to take them next. I
ended each day with a pile of 29 draft books on either side of me. I
looked daily at the progress that the students were making and made
decisions for the next day based on what they could do and needed to
do. My daily planning sheet, shown in Figure 3, was in front of me, and

Figure 2. Using the computer as a life-long learner.

Tuesday date <u>April 26</u>

Attendance/Lunch

Read To <u>Nightmare In My Closet</u> Objective <u>dem. real story w/twist</u>

Write To <u>Imaginative Story</u> Objective <u>plan for Imag. story</u>

LAB Time / Planning

Rove <u>✓up on Zack, Kate, Grace</u>

Ali

Allie — <u>Spelling: Jonathan, Tyler E.</u>

Briana

Chelsea

Emily — Small Group <u>Rosie At The Zoo</u> (Guided)

Grace — Obj. <u>confirm/rej. pred. thru text</u>

Greg — <u>Marcus   Kurt   Ian</u>

Ian — <u>Allie   Nathaniel</u>

Jeffrey — Rove <u>Teresa: Plan publication of</u>

Jonathan — <u>pop-up book</u>

Katie — <u>Spelling:</u>

Kelley — <u>Hayley, Michael, Kelley</u>

Kurt

Makayla — Small Group <u>Handwriting</u>

Mallory — Obj. <u>letter formation p,g,q,y,j</u>

Marcus — <u>Mike, Stephen</u>

Matthew — <u>Matt, Ali</u>

Michael — Rove

Nathaniel — <u>Editing conf:</u>

Pete — <u>Emily - format friendly letter</u>

Ryan — <u>Grace - commas in series</u>

Stephen

Teresa — Small Group <u>Flies</u> (shared)

Timmy — Obj. <u>using index to access info.</u>

Tyler — <u>Makayla   Zack   Chelsea</u> Tyler M.

Tyler E. — <u>Pete   Kate   Jeffrey</u>

Zachary — Rove

<u>Running Record</u>

<u>Ali</u>

<u>Jeffrey</u>

Small Group <u>Maui & Sun.</u> (Guided)

Obj. <u>Holding story in head ~ what will happen next?</u>

<u>Greg   Timmy   Mallory</u>

<u>Briana   Ryan</u>

Rove

Reflections (What did you read, write or learn today?)

<u>Teresa - share pop up</u>

<u>Pete - share info. gathering</u>

<u>Grace - commas</u>

Figure 3. Teacher planning sheet.

provided the road map for tomorrow based on what I had seen today. I selected the resources for my daily instruction based on those assessment samples I had evaluated. I struggled with the selection of the resources. Did the texts contain enough supports for this group of students? Would there be too many challenges? How much background knowledge would the readers need to bring to the text?

I realized that I was beginning to bring my knowledge of the reading process and writing process to the decisions that I was making. And the teaching ... the days that I was able to bring the child, the resource, and the teaching point together and feel real success did not happen that often, but when it happened I knew how it felt. And it felt good! I knew that learning had occurred.

I began to look at my students, who were unfolding in front of my eyes. The children were embracing reading and writing with the same joy and enthusiasm that I was. They came to school expounding about what they were going to write about that day and where their ideas had come from. Teresa confided that she kept a little notepad by her bed in case she woke up in the middle of the night or early in the morning with a great topic. Pete worried that he had so many "I wonder" questions he didn't think he would have time in his life to answer them. Emily wrote a poem about an accident involving her father, shown in Figure 5, that stilled the heart of anyone who read it. This little classroom was developing into a community of learners. They re-

Figure 4. Small group reading instruction.

My Dad Got Hurt

My dad got hurt.
He was standing under an awning
And it fell on him.
The next night I had a bad dream;
I went into my mom and dad's room
There instead of my dad was Joyce,
A friend of ours.
I wondered in my heart where my Dad was...
He said he would be home this night
I went over to my mom's side
I asked where dad was
Then we went over to Evan's room
My mom said, "Dad is hurt"
I felt scared because I couldn't
See him in California.
It felt like I was being forced down a
Dark, dark, real dark hole
I cried like a waterfall
I was so scared.
I thought that I'd never see my Dad again
He missed a lot while he was hurt;
My sixth birthday,
The first whole book I ever read.
But he got
Better
and
Better
and
Better

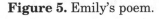

Figure 5. Emily's poem.

joiced in each success and bolstered each other when challenged. And they did the same for me.

Jan's frequent visits prevented me from sitting on my accomplishments for longer than a minute. Her responsibility was to take me further, no matter what growth had occurred since the last time she had been there. I was assured that new learning would occur for me as a result of these visits. The confidence I began to develop in my own beliefs became more apparent. My action plans looked very different from the action plans at the beginning of the year. I no longer was concerned with showing her my best teaching or my work with the most proficient students. I demanded that she observe me grappling with my biggest challenges. I showed her what I believed were some of my biggest mistakes and expected that I would learn from the dialogue that would follow.

It was a rather insignificant incident that made me begin to believe that the New Zealand model was becoming my own. It was close to Mother's Day. I was late, as usual, with the construction of the annual Mother's Day gift. I went to my trusty file cabinet, looked under "Mother's Day," and pulled out the tried-and-true Mother's Day book that children had constructed in my room for the past ten years.

As I looked at it, I asked myself, "Why am I thinking of doing this book? What is the theory that would be driving this practice? Is this

Figure 6. Modeling writing.

something that life-long readers, writers, and learners would do?" Then I began to think what I do as a life-long reader and writer on Mother's Day. I write my mother a letter. The next morning, I wrote my mother a letter in the daily modeled writing in front of my students. I talked aloud about all the memories I share with my mother. I talked about the times we had together that made me laugh when I remembered them. I talked about the times when she had been ill and I had been really frightened that I might lose her. I talked about the things I really wanted her to know and that I sometimes forgot to tell her. I organized these thoughts in a plan, then used my plan to write a sensitive, genuine letter to my mother that I later published and mailed. As a result of that demonstration, some of my students wrote lovely, poignant letters to their mothers, as Chelsea did (Figure 7), some wrote a story, as Theresa did (Figure 8), some chose to just make a little card, and some chose to express themselves in a totally different way, as Hayley did (Figure 9).

In reflection, I realized that this was the first time that I had made a significant decision based on my understandings and had not once thought, "What would Jan think?" I was developing a conviction of beliefs that belonged to me. They did not belong to the New Zealand

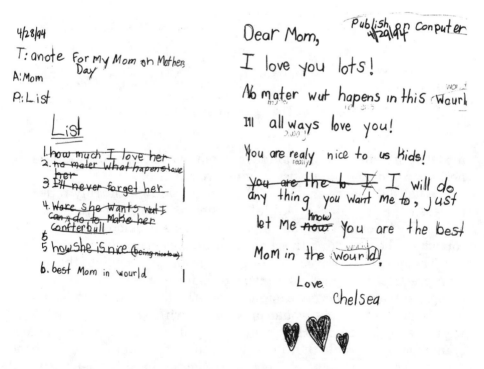

Figure 7. Chelsea's Mother's Day piece.

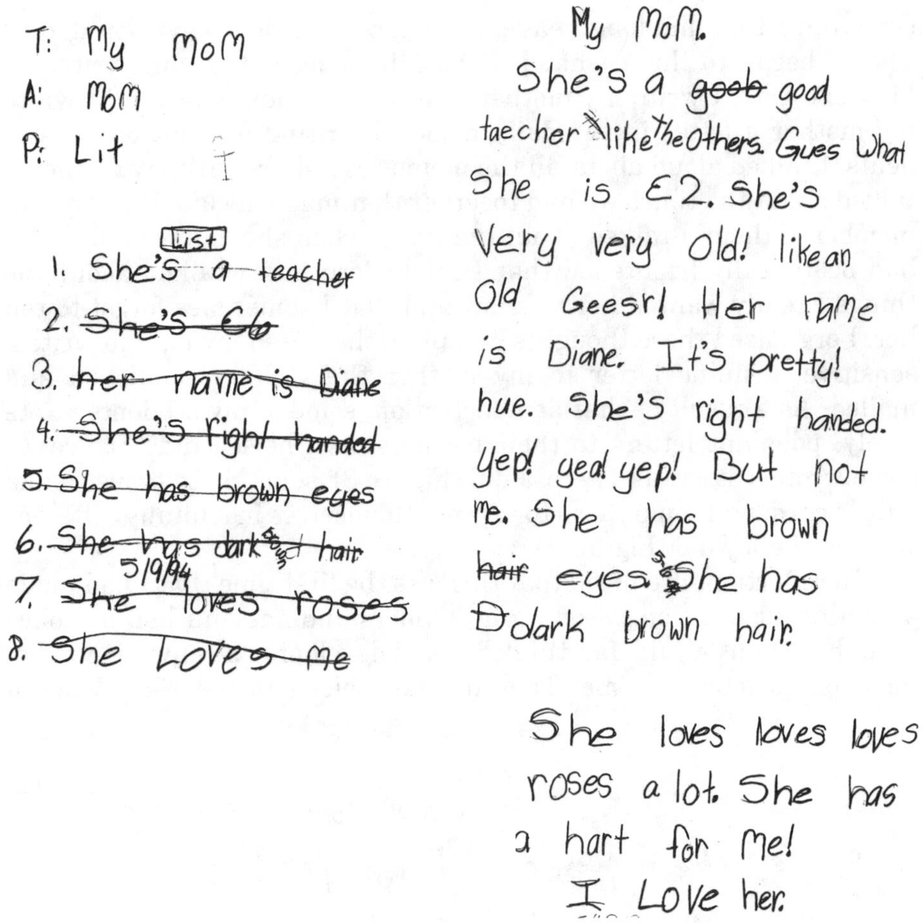

T: My mom
A: mom
P: Lit

List
1. She's a teacher
2. ~~She's 66~~
3. ~~her name is Diane~~
4. ~~She's right handed~~
5. ~~She has brown eyes~~
6. ~~She has dark hair~~
    5/9/94
7. ~~She loves roses~~
8. ~~She Loves me~~

My mom.
She's a ~~good~~ good
taecher like the others. Gues what
She is E2. She's
Very very Old! like an
Old Geesr! Her name
is Diane. It's pretty!
hue. She's right handed.
yep! yea! yep! But not
me. She has brown
hair eyes. She has
dark brown hair.

She loves loves loves
roses a lot. She has
a hart for me!
I Love her.

Figure 8. Theresa's Mother's Day piece.

model or to a single New Zealander. From that moment on, I knew that nothing could stop the theory driving my practice.

What did I learn that year? I learned that to be a truly reflective professional educator–a skillful teacher–someone has to start the process by asking us the hard questions. This develops within us the capacity to begin asking those hard questions of ourselves.

The next year proved to be significant in my growth of theory driving practice. In my job as a teacher leader in Year 2, I was working alongside teachers on my campus. Just as I had done the year before with Jan, the teachers would provide me with an action plan. What were they going to do? How were they going to develop their understandings? How would they know when they were there? I would spend twenty to thirty minutes in their classrooms observing. Then we would

Figure 9. Hayley's Mother's Day song.

have another thirty minutes for instructional dialogue. The instructional dialogue forced me to come to greater depths of understanding as I questioned teachers about their understandings. I had to develop a "filing cabinet in my brain" and know which drawer to open as I searched for the right question.

What was the role of the program coordinator in this new challenge? Jan was there to support my growth as a teacher leader working with teachers. She would observe alongside me, listen to the instructional dialogue with the teachers, then dialogue with me, digging into my understandings as well as my ability to bring the understanding of the teacher to a new level.

These days were challenging. I was teaching children and teaching teachers. Sometimes I couldn't see where one ended and the other began. The strength of my conviction about what I was doing with children was spilling into my work with adults. If I had to know my learner in the classroom through assessment and evaluation, then I had to know the teachers in the same way. My assessment sample for teachers became their action plans and my observations. The notes I took formed the basis of my evaluation. I could see their strengths and next steps. My understandings about reading, writing, and the conditions for learning provided the basis for planning the instructional dialogue. The dialogue itself provided the basis for my teaching.

I was reminded constantly of what Marie Clay said: "Teaching is likened to a conversation, where you listen carefully to the speaker before you reply" (1979, 6). I had to listen very carefully to the teachers as they were coming to grips with their new learning. I also had to think ahead of them. It was not unusual to find that my action plans matched their action plans. Did I really understand the theory driving the practice? It forced me back to my classroom, testing those constructs in my own practice.

As a result of this reflection, I was listening more carefully to the children in my classroom. As I began to listen more carefully, opportunities for learning just popped out at me. When Michael wanted to know how to find information on cheetahs, I would ask him, "Where would you find information about cheetahs?" and off he would go to the media center. I encouraged investigations and by ending each small group reading opportunity with the question, "Do you wonder anything after reading this book?" a world of opportunities for learning opened up for these children. Michael, Tyler, Marcus, and Ian wondered, "Why aren't there any polar bears at the South Pole?" and researched to find the answer. I rejoiced when Tyler came bursting into the room one morning saying, "You'll never guess what! My last name is the same as my dad's, even every letter!" knowing that he had made an important connection: print carried a message. I listened to Chelsea wonder why there was no longer a salad bar in the cafeteria, and instead of giving her the answer, led her to an investigation that taught her the skills of interviewing and reporting information (Figure 10).

At this same time, we were moving as a school from dependence on the program coordinator to independence. At the beginning of the school year we made lists of questions to ask Jan each time she came. How are we to do this? What if this situation arises? How should we handle this problem? What we soon began to realize was that she was not providing us with the answers. Instead, she was providing us with the capability and confidence to answer our own questions. As the year came to an end, we still had a list for Jan, but the list contained the important decisions we had made. Instead of answers, we asked for her opinion in how we had handled the decisions.

Funny how, at this point, the words "New Zealand" did not seem to frequent my vocabulary as often. I continually made reference to the books and people that I admired and respected, but my self-confidence

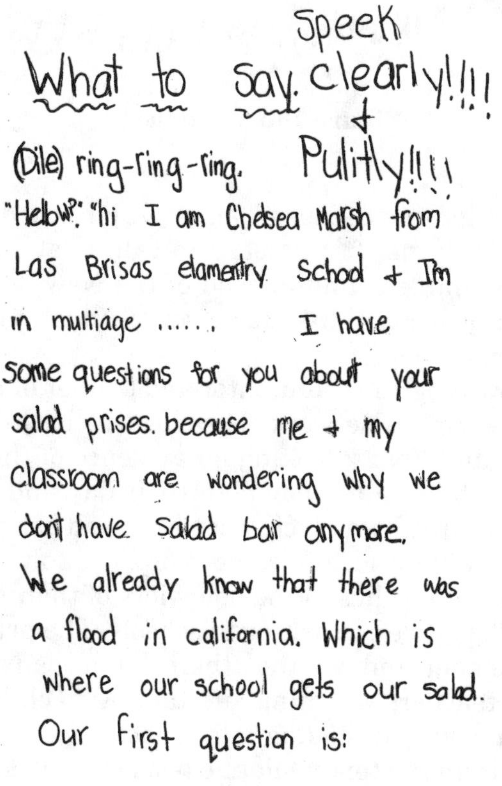

speeĸ
What to Say. clearly!!!!!
+
(Dile) ring-ring-ring.   Pulitly!!!!
"Helbw?" "hi I am Chelsea Marsh from
Las Brisas elamentry School + Im
in multiage ...... I have
some questions for you about your
salad prises. because me + my
Classroom are wondering why we
don't have Salad bar anymore.
We already know that there was
a flood in california. Which is
where our school gets our salad.
Our first question is:

Figure 10a. Salad bar investigation.

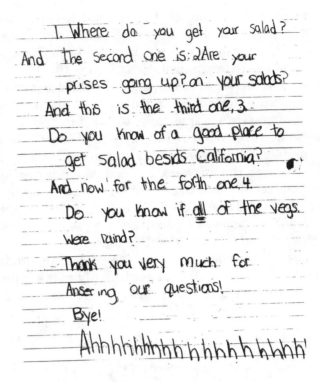

1. Where do you get your salad?
And the second one is: 2Are your
prises going up? on your salads?
And this is the third one, 3.
Do you know of a good place to
get salad besids California?
And now for the forth one, 4.
Do you know if all of the vegs.
were raind?
Thanks you very much for
Ansering our questions!
Bye!
Ahhhhhhhhhhhhhhhhh!

Figure 10b. Continued

in what I was doing came because I knew why I was doing it. The beliefs now belonged to me. It was easy to call what I did each day a model of teaching and learning instead of the New Zealand model. It was no longer an abstract thing, but a set of understandings that we would continue to develop.

My role is now program coordinator and trainer of program coordinators for The Learning Network. I walk into classrooms of teacher leaders in Year 1 and Year 2 looking for evidence of their understandings. I sit next to children as they plan their day and ask them what they are doing and why. I watch children read and ask them questions. I watch children write and ask some more. I know that the key to teachers' understandings lies in the behaviors of their students.

I rejoice in what I see happening in schools. The principal and I observe a teacher leader and see that there are already three teachers and two student teachers watching and talking to children. I listen to seven children in a shared reading talking actively about the meaning they are making from the text while the teacher smiles and takes monitoring notes. We watch the teacher read and write to her students, the

Figure 10c. Continued

focus being on accessing nonfiction books for information on scorpions. She naturally thinks her way through the use of these texts and how they were selected. She looks at the questions she wants to answer and checks the table of contents or index that will lead her in the direction she wants to go. The children are deeply engaged. They look closely at her and quietly offer their suggestions and assistance. I look at their faces and I feel a warmth in knowing that learning is occurring.

The five teachers accompany the teacher leader and me to the instructional dialogue. We explain what will be happening during the instructional dialogue and ask if they would leave their questions until after we have finished our discussion. The teacher leader takes me through the teaching and learning cycle as she describes the assessment sample that prompted the reading and writing to, how she planned by selecting the nonfiction resources, the focused learning outcome she had selected, and where she sees the children's learning going from here.

We open up the discussion to the group. The teachers talk about their amazement at the level of conversation that had occurred in the shared reading group. They knew those learners were a diverse group and couldn't believe that the students all looked and sounded so successful in that group. One teacher states that she had never seen anything like it in all her years of teaching. Another teacher remarks about the knowledge and skills the students seemed to be acquiring as a result of their investigations. The conversation among the group changes to a discussion of how they could support all learners in the school in their growth in this direction. One teacher states, "We have to get together and talk about what we want for these kids. If we do, then we will own it."

As I sit and listen and comment from time to time, I think of a few things. I can't believe that it's Friday afternoon at four o'clock and these teachers seem in no hurry to go anywhere. They just want to talk about teaching and learning. I see in their eyes and hear in their voices the beginning of that development of conviction of beliefs. I hear the teacher leader talk about the strengths of the learners that she works with and what she knows about where they are and where they need to go next. I revel in the word *ownership* with these teachers. I know already that the model they are describing does not belong to New Zealand, to the Literacy Learning institute facilitators, or even to me, but to the teachers themselves. I see the sparkle in the principal's eyes as she listens to this discussion. I know we are moving in the right direction.

What has enabled us to make the model our own? First, it took a large number of teachers who knew that there was more we could be doing for children and were determined to find it. It took American teachers deciding that rigor was of extreme importance, and that as educators, we needed to find out what our students knew and what they needed to know and then we needed to teach it and have the highest expectations that learning would occur.

It took a publisher named Richard Owen, who began to see that anything was possible in public education; that with a big enough vision and a group of skillful educators, we could make amazing things happen.

It took Peter Duncan, who brought with him a wealth of experience in systemic change. Peter quietly and confidently provided incredible ideas and always asked the most significant questions in order for this dream of The Learning Network to flourish and grow.

And it took a New Zealand educator, Jan Duncan, who enabled us to make the model our own. She challenged and continues to challenge our thinking. She saw the great possibilities that were within us, just waiting to be awakened. What was often perceived as a hard, inflexible approach was exactly what we needed to develop the strength of belief that we now have. Jan developed within us a strong knowledge of why we do what we do. And with that knowledge we are able to provide the ebb and flow of learning experiences based on the needs of the individuals with whom we work. Jan gave us the solid conviction of beliefs that encouraged within us the independence and ability to go at it alone.

It's summer again and the brochures have been printed and distributed for the summer institute; Literacy Learning in the Classroom. The brochure looks very different from the first one printed in 1989. The most significant change is that most of the general session facilitators are American teachers. As American facilitators, we pride ourselves on the strength of our commitment to this model of teaching and learning. It belongs to us. The examples of student work in the resource book are all from children in classrooms across the United States. As we work our way through the four days, we realize that we have indeed come back to where we began and each time we come back, we see that place for the first time. The process of learning has begun again, and it looks very good.

MARILYN HERZOG *is a program coordinator and trainer of program coordinators for The Learning Network. She was a teacher leader at Las Brisas Elementary School, a Learning Network site in Glendale, Arizona. She has been a teacher for 24 years, working with learners from early childhood to adult. Her experience includes the positions of reading coordinator, staff development specialist, and preschool director. During the summer Marilyn works as a facilitator for the Literacy Learning in the Classroom institutes.*

PART I

The Learning Network

CHAPTER 1

The Change Process

Kathy Kussy

"Getting ready for next year always used to mean starting over. Now it will just be adding to what I know. I used to worry about planning for time to set up my classroom. Now I'm planning what I'm going to read this summer to increase my understandings."

JoAnna Wright
Teacher Leader, Phoenix, Arizona

As superintendent of Easthampton Public Schools, a district of six schools, over 2,000 students, and over 200 teachers in suburban Massachusetts, I believe that I am our district's educational leader as well as its administrator. The process of learning about and selecting The Learning Network as a staff development model in Easthampton began in 1993. In that year a group of Title I teachers and I had been working on a mission statement and goals to guide the district to better learning outcomes for our students. What surfaced were haunting questions relating to power, professional relationships, what it means "to know," and how to build a community. To answer those questions, we began to read and learn together about change in education. We read many books and articles related to the theories behind "whole language" that supported us and helped our thinking, but the practices we read about and observed did not support the proposed theories. We became increasingly concerned that a change in this direction, supported by many people on our faculties, was not meeting our goals. We were committed to engaging all students as active readers and writers who see literacy as a meaningful part of their lives. We wanted to make this happen in classrooms throughout the district, but we were struggling.

It was no surprise to me when a group of teachers called me one day and asked me to come to a workshop they were attending. They said that a New Zealander, Jan Duncan, was talking about the same things we were. The next day I attended a workshop by Jan for administrators with three principals. We were all excited to hear about how others were implementing research-based practices to shift relationships in classrooms and engage all students as life-long readers, writers, and learners. The teachers began to share their excitement with their peers and prompted the curiosity of others. As a result, a group of staff members asked me to pursue the possibility of bringing Jan to work with teachers in their schools. I began to explore the possibility of bringing The Learning Network to Easthampton.

Through meetings and conversations with Richard Owen and Jan Duncan I came to know more about The Learning Network. What drove me forward was the match between our own goals for the district and the theory of teaching and learning guiding the educators involved in The Network, especially Jan. The teachers and administrators in my district were all eager to place the learner as paramount in classrooms and schools and to learn how to enable the learner–whether child or adult–to engage in a process of constructing individual meaning for new learning and growth. I knew that changing the culture of the schools had to begin with our own beliefs and understandings about teaching and learning and that the best opportunity for meaningful change was to begin in classrooms, with on-going, in-depth professional development. We were all willing to work together to make this happen. I could not let this opportunity for the teachers in Easthampton to work with Jan Duncan to pass us by.

I began by organizing resources. Our system had experienced a number of years of declining budgets and resources were scarce. There was no staff development budget for the year, so we applied for various grants. A web of funding sources was created.

With some budget items under control, I moved forward with implementation by focusing on communication. I worked with teachers and administrators to plan three professional development days and an evening meeting with Jan so that all staff, parents, and community members would have an opportunity to listen, share, and ask questions about the initiative. An invitation was then extended to anyone interested in working with Jan for the next two years in the role of teacher leader. Building meetings and meetings with individuals provided everyone with the opportunity to clarify their questions and concerns.

It became clear that teachers considering engagement in this process were concerned about resources, support, and assurance of a

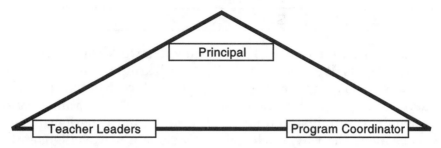

Figure 1.1. The critical triangle.

safe environment for learning. The critical triangle (Figure 1.1) formed by the principal, the teacher leaders, and the program coordinator was a new and somewhat threatening concept. They did not want the process of working closely with their principals, and possibly exposing weaknesses in their practice, to turn into an opportunity for formal evaluation and criticism. To alleviate this concern, the administrators and I used a goal-setting process to meet the criteria for evaluation and provide the freedom for exploration and risk. The teachers would be assessed and evaluated when necessary based on what they were trying to achieve in their individual growth as educators and how they were doing in reaching their goals.

Although we had some funding in place, another concern was about adequate resources. I explained to the teachers how the funds we had procured, although limited, would be used to support their needs. I also promised to support their efforts and to solve other problems as they arose.

While many teachers wanted the opportunity to work with and learn from Jan, some were not comfortable with a staff development model as intense as the on-going classroom observations and instructional dialogue that this model required. These teachers preferred holding monthly staff development activities outside their classrooms. However, two elementary teachers and two middle school teachers committed to the training. Later, a Reading Recovery® teacher also came on board. Many of the other interested teachers decided to wait a year and see how it went. To accommodate the various preferences of teachers, we asked Jan to schedule general monthly meetings so that anyone wanting her assistance in a more traditional way would have that opportunity. Over the summer of 1993, 35 teachers and administrators from Easthampton attended the four-day Literacy Learning in the Classroom institute and in the fall Jan began working alongside the teacher leaders in their classrooms.

BECOMING LEARNERS

Our entire first year in The Learning Network was a great challenge to all of us. We had accepted that our learning would be a continual process—a journey over time. We just didn't realize that the course would be so rough. I have often described it as a roller coaster ride—climbing to highs, falling to deep lows, and experiencing some plateaus along the way. Each time we took on a new challenge, there was a period of decline followed by an uphill climb of personal learning. We came to understand that this process was one of real learning and that, as learners, we had to learn to live with ambiguity and anxiety. We also learned how necessary it was to take small steps toward accomplishing our own personal goals and the importance of learning how to work together. We learned that, with time, our hard work resulted in confidence in our new understandings and practice.

Two days each month Jan worked with the teacher leaders, observing in their classrooms and holding instructional dialogue. Each teacher leader's action plan provided the focus for the observation and instructional dialogue. The building principal and I accompanied Jan on her visits. One afternoon a month, Jan met with all the teacher leaders in the district. This was followed by a meeting with the teacher leaders and administrators together in which they focused on common concerns. Between Jan's visits and these monthly meetings, the teacher leader class had their own focus meetings. Substitutes were provided to allow them time to attend.

At our first meeting together, Jan shared the criteria for being a skillful teacher (Figure 1.2) (Richard C. Owen Publishers 1997a, B-5)

The skillful teacher is one who:

- considers him- or herself a learner;
- ensures that the conditions for learning are in place;
- understands the processes of creating meaning in reading and writing;
- knows the learner, evaluates to identify a learning step;
- knows resources and learning experiences, can make a selection that best meets the needs of the learner(s);
- is able to identify the supports and challenges within the resource or learning experience, can determine the appropriate approach to reach a learning outcome;
- has a well-defined theory about teaching and learning which is translated into classroom practice.

Figure 1.2. The skillful teacher.

and the selection of effective teacher leaders (Figure 1.3) (Richard C. Owen Publishers 1995a). She emphasized the importance of our growth as a community of learners and the need to create the critical triangle between herself, the teacher leaders, and the principal in each school. She clearly articulated high expectations that we would succeed. Teacher leaders left that meeting feeling somewhat overwhelmed, but we started right in.

When Jan began to work alongside the teacher leaders in their classrooms, she sometimes surprised them. Instead of focusing exclu-

---

Two teacher leaders will be chosen from each school. Two teacher leaders ensure the continuity of the learning process. They support each other throughout the process; given sufficient release time, each can work with up to eight teachers per year starting in Year 2. The Learning Network registration fee for working with two teacher leaders is the same as the fee for working with one.

The successful teacher leader:

- has respect for and is respected by colleagues;
- is a competent classroom practitioner with three to five years of classroom experience;
- has responsibility or permanent partial responsibility for a classroom during Year 1 and beyond;
- sees him- or herself as a learner; is open to new ideas and new learning;
- displays leadership qualities and works comfortably alongside adults;
- can motivate others to take responsibility for their own personal/professional growth;
- is able to stay focused on and committed to a set of beliefs, even in the face of resistance and challenge from others;
- seeks professional challenge.

Identifying the best people for the position is important for the success of The Learning Network. The principal makes the final selection of teacher leaders with the support of the program coordinator and the entire faculty. However, this is not a popularity contest. We are looking for qualities in people that inspire confidence and lead to long-term change in the people with whom the teacher leader works. The above criteria will help the principal determine who can do the job effectively.

Figure 1.3. The selection of teacher leaders.

sively on what the teachers were doing, as in a formal evaluation, she would talk to the children. "What are you doing?" "Why are you doing it?" "What are you going to do next?" It was a bit threatening to the teachers for Jan to be asking their students these questions. Even more challenging was that during subsequent instructional dialogue with the teachers, Jan would ask them, "*Why* are you doing what you're doing?" This process was very frustrating, not only for the teacher leaders, but for all of us. We all discovered that we didn't have the "right" answers—or any answers, for that matter. We didn't really *know* why we were doing what we were doing. We couldn't articulate the understandings that were driving our practice.

Our meetings were equally frustrating. We came together with an expectation that Jan would tell us what to do. We wanted a recipe. We were looking for answers, not questions. We had not yet learned that the model we were throwing ourselves into didn't have pat answers. Jan did give the teacher leaders tasks for their focus meetings, but even with direction they described their first times together as chaotic. In their discussions about what they valued in readers, writers, and learners, they were jockeying for position and arguing over words. They were not yet working together as learners.

These first few months were a time of great unrest for all of us. We were engulfed in looking at all that we didn't know and overcome with the challenge. Numerous times teacher leaders remarked that if Jan asked "why" one more time they'd scream. We quickly learned the meaning of the word "disequilibrium." We had plenty of it. Feelings of being "out of control" or "like a fish out of water" were articulated often, and almost every teacher and principal came to me and stated that he or she must be "a slow learner." After all, we had all attended the four-day institute introducing us to the Literacy Learning model, so why didn't we "get" it? Some people who came to me expressed feelings of frustration so strong that they didn't know whether they could continue. I wondered on a day-to-day basis who the players were and for how long they would be around.

Ultimately, however, and somewhat to our surprise, we found that we had begun to internalize the disequilibrium. We knew that it would not go away, but we also began to understand that wasn't a bad thing. I remember asking a couple of people, one a principal with a letter of resignation in hand, whether they could really walk away from this process and forget it, or if this unrest and need to learn would go with them. Rather than give up, we all dug in. Knowing that we would have support from Jan and the opportunity to learn together, we began to examine new ways to support one another and to take new risks.

We were coming to see how personal and difficult the process of learning really was and how important it was to personalize learning in our classrooms. As teacher leaders dug into their own learning, resources become critical. I began to look at new ways to provide the instructional and professional resources they needed when they needed them. In the world of schools, budgets and allocation processes are not always the most flexible systems. Still, I was able to open accounts for the teacher leaders at local bookstores and work out ways for them to access funds. The duties of one of our staff were altered so the teacher leaders could have assistance in videotaping their classroom practice.

While I worked out the means for acquiring resources, teacher leaders were learning in their classrooms. They began to develop new ways of coming to know their learners and for recording and monitoring reading and writing progress over time. They became familiar with the teaching and learning cycle (Figure 1.4), which, supported by an understanding of the reading process, the writing process, and the conditions that need to be in place for learning to occur, forms the Literacy Learning model. It was a significant shift for them to use assessment and evaluation as ongoing processes to *inform* their practice. Understanding evaluation as a process of analyzing assessment samples to determine the next learning step for individual learners challenged

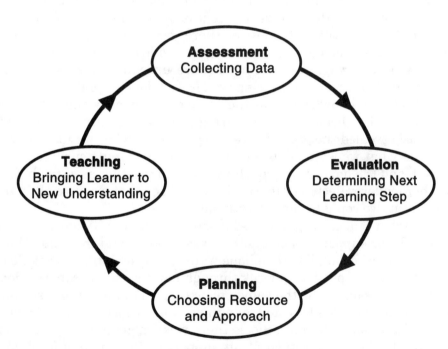

Figure 1.4. The teaching and learning cycle.

their past classroom practice and required new skills. As they began to share their monitoring books with each other they noticed that their observation notes reflected book titles, page numbers, and very general terms such as "good" and "excellent." They realized that this sort of documentation told them nothing about how each child was learning. The teacher leaders began to focus on documenting what each child was doing. As they came to know their learners they began to understand the importance of planning instruction based on what each learner was close to doing. There was no "one size fits all" answer.

Everyone involved in The Learning Network became an avid reader and was immersed in their own learning. As the process of learning became more comfortable, the teacher leaders were ready to take on the next challenge. Then Jan introduced a new element to the teacher leader meetings. She asked teacher leaders to begin bringing the videos of their classroom practice to focus meetings so that they could share their practice and learn together. The first video experience is one that we will all remember for years to come as a philosophical, life-changing experience. Jan asked teacher leaders to view the video with an eye toward finding evidence that the learner and the construction of meaning were paramount in the classroom and that learning had occurred. In the videotape, we identified that the content of the lesson was paramount, the learners were not engaged, the teacher's questions were not directed at the creation of meaning, and since there was no clear objective to the lesson, there were no meaningful learning outcomes. The teacher leader sharing this video described the experience as devastating. The rest of us were uncomfortable as well. Although most of us were reflecting on a lesson done by one of our peers, we all had the knowledge that the same conclusions would have been reached if it had been any of us sharing a video of our practice. This experience revealed the great discrepancy between what we *said* we valued and what we were *doing*. It was pivotal in shaping our individual growth and the purpose for which we came to together as a group. One teacher leader reflected that "When we realized that we were all in the same boat, we could be honest with one another."

Teacher leaders began to feel a sense of community among themselves. Their support of one another was ongoing and frequent. Many hours after school and on the phone were spent pondering an article or book to gain perspective and talk through new ideas. It became evident that there needed to be the same opportunity for support and sharing between teacher leaders and administrators. Since teacher leaders represented four different schools there was fragmentation just by location. They were concerned about support at the building level, and principals were concerned that they were being left out of some of the theory-building process necessary for them to support the teacher leaders. We were all concerned about a mystique and sense of mistrust growing among some of the other teachers. To resolve this sense of unease, I started monthly meetings of all system administrators and teacher leaders to plan, share, provide support, and learn in a structure that we affectionately referred to as "the literacy club." As our meetings progressed, I observed that the behaviors I expected–digging in, challenging, taking risks, taking responsibility, and applying theory to new situations–were not surfacing in all of us. There was a lack of healthy questioning, an unwillingness to admit to problems, and in some instances a lack of engagement. I realized that we all, as administrators, needed to develop the same skills that the teacher leaders were learning to facilitate the learning of groups, and that it must begin with me.

I had been making some critical shifts in my own thinking as I worked with teacher leaders and watched as they met their new challenges. I began to think about what I knew about my learners, how we used assessment in the school system, and how the process of evaluating assessment samples is essential in planning. I realized that I had a lot to learn. I began to think and plan my interactions, primarily with this group but also with others, in the same way that teacher leaders were designing their interactions in the classroom. I started writing my own action plans and engaged in my own learning. I began to think of this group as my classroom and to examine my own practice in relation to the expectations of the skillful teacher. As the superintendent, I recognized my need to be an engaged learner and teacher just as I expected other administrators to become. And so we moved forward together. What we now held in common was a need to know, a need to really engage and to learn, and a need to ask and be asked "Why am I doing what I'm doing?"

BECOMING TRULY REFLECTIVE

The teacher leaders continued to view and discuss videos of their classroom practice. At first Jan modeled the kinds of questions we needed to ask ourselves and each other to become reflective. As time went on the teacher leaders took over the dialogue and Jan would reflect on the questions they asked one another. It proved difficult to focus on the understandings driving the practice rather than on the lesson and the students. Jan would continually refocus us by modeling the questions that would help us to probe deeper into our own under-standings. Each time, she would zero in on a new piece of learning, and each time we would leave with new questions.

In the spring of 1994 the teacher leaders presented a typical, un-rehearsed video session for an audience of interested educators. The observers indicated that the questions the teacher leaders were asking of one another were "why" questions. "You're really probing for infor-mation," and "It was obvious that the intent was not to fix the lesson," were specific comments. Another observer expressed a sense of awe at "the willingness of the teacher leaders to expose and explore their un-derstandings in front of a large group of strangers and their willing-ness to engage in discussion occurring at the leading edge of their un-derstandings." The teacher leaders were thrilled that what they were learning how to do was evident in their practice.

To Jan's skilled eye, however, there was always a next step to be taken. She continually brought the group back with a new question; a new challenge. This process allowed us to see the importance of risk taking and to work from our own strengths while learning from one an-other. We were able to challenge each other in order to take our next steps. This process required real honesty and trust, which did not hap-pen overnight.

Teacher leader focus group meetings played a critical role in build-ing the trust essential to our development as learners. As teacher lead-ers began to identify their own challenges, they no longer expected or needed Jan to assign tasks. What they were working on in their class-room practice, their action plans, and the videos provided direction. Each meeting became very focused and, because they were driven by a real need to know, there was engagement. Over the year the teacher leaders shared their assessment and monitoring practices, gained ex-perience writing clear objectives, developed questions that probed for meaning, prioritized the skills they valued in life-long learners, dug into developing deeper understandings of the reading and writing processes, and questioned the meaning of authentic response. They came together to share stories, to get other people's perspectives, and to learn from one another. They read and shared many professional re-sources and began to develop a common vocabulary based on shared meaning. It was exciting to be a part of this group, but it wasn't always easy.

I vividly remember the meetings in which we identified the skills we valued in life-long learners and wrote action plans for addressing those skills. The words I heard most frequently that day were "This is hard." And it was. In the past we had all been dependent on moving students through a sequence of skills identified by publishers of textbooks or school and district mandates. We learned how crucial it was for teachers to develop an understanding of what a fluent reader and writer does, to have that repertoire of skills in their heads, and to teach the skills when the students demonstrated that they were ready for them. The skills themselves didn't change. The shift came from understanding the importance of teaching skills that the learners would use for the rest of their lives and to teach them at the point of need through an authentic context.

Focus meetings helped us all to develop our understanding of content, but even more importantly, the actual process that we were going through together was invaluable. We moved through the process of developing common understandings together. The most powerful transformation we experienced as a group, however, was our ability to ask questions and to challenge. When we asked questions, we knew that the purpose was to gain understanding, and we accepted that if we were to be learners, our understandings would be challenged. Challenges were not personal, but rather a means of seeking clarification and further exploration. We began to feel secure in sharing with colleagues what we were still not clear about, and we came to trust one another. Teacher leaders indicated that this was a real move away from the old system, in which they didn't let anyone know what they didn't know. They came to feel that they were all on the same learning journey and that it was all right to take risks, to experiment, and to approximate. We valued being able to share our successes and our problems. This open and honest relationship between the teacher leaders and myself was key to my learning. I could ask them for feedback on my practice, share what I was struggling with, and expect that they would challenge my understandings. What we were learning to do and how we were doing it was no different than what we were looking for in our classrooms.

A CYCLE FOR PROFESSIONAL GROWTH AND DEVELOPMENT

Change and growth also occurred away from the group, in individual classrooms. At first the cycle of writing action plans, being observed by the program coordinator, and being questioned in an instructional dialogue put real pressure on the teacher leaders. At the same time, this process, shown in Figure 1.5 (Richard C. Owen Publishers 1996a, 10), provided them with the opportunity to focus on what they

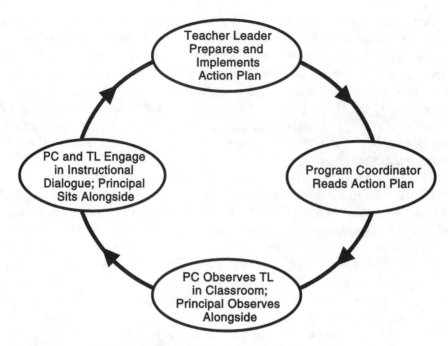

Figure 1.5. The cycle for individual growth and development.

were personally engaged in learning and to be continually supported and challenged to take their next steps. I began to observe the most enthusiasm and passion for personal learning in the classrooms when teachers observed their students doing things that wouldn't have happened before. Teacher leaders started to look forward to Jan's visits. They were beginning to appreciate having someone with whom to discuss practice and to help them reflect on why they were doing what they were doing. It helped to talk to someone who expected an answer. Jan valued them as learners. They came to view this process as the most professional experience they had ever had. As one teacher put it, "To have someone to reflect with was wonderful."

Action Plans

What gave focus to the change process was each teacher leader's action plan (Figure 1.6).Writing these plans was difficult at first. It was a real transition to move from thinking about product, or what they did, to process, or how they would learn. Teacher leaders' first action plans were aimed at fixing everything. Learning to take small steps took time. Eventually the teacher leaders were able to set goals

The Learning Network

ACTION PLAN

Name _____ School _____

Grade _____ Date _____

What am I going to do?

How am I going to develop my understandings?

How will I know when I'm there?

Figure 1.6. An action plan.

for themselves that provided a balance between the known and the un-known. They didn't try to move to something totally beyond their un-derstandings. Their risk taking became "do-able" and therefore a bit more comfortable. At first the teacher leaders were writing their action plans for Jan, but as they increased their skill in identifying their own next learning steps, they began to write them eagerly. They no longer waited for Jan to focus their actions because they were no longer writ-ing them for her, or for anyone else. They were writing them to further their own learning.

Observation

Jan continued to ask the students questions. The teacher leaders now understood that their understandings were manifested in their learners' attitudes, understandings, and behaviors. By talking with and observing students, she could come to understand the practice that was in place. She would often sit with a teacher leader during a read-ing or writing conference, listening as the teacher probed for meaning and guided the students to new learning. Sometimes she would model questions or take a quick running record.

Instructional Dialogue

The focus of instructional dialogue was always on the teachers' un-derstandings about what drove their practice, rather than on the prac-tice itself (Figure 1.7). Jan still asked "Why are you doing what you are doing?" That never changed. Each time the teacher leader would take away a new bit of learning and each time new questions would formu-late their next action plans.

The opportunity for personal learning over time and in classrooms was a unique and critical element to a real change in practice. The cy-cle of action plans, observation, and instructional dialogue provided the opportunity for teachers to reflect. This resulted in each partici-pant gaining the competence and confidence necessary to meet the di-verse needs of all the students in their classes. It also enabled them to become better able to contribute to and work cooperatively with a group. As one teacher leader noted:

Each time we had a conference with Jan, she would ask why we were doing what we were doing and give us questions to think about. She made us articulate our theory and, as we ar-ticulated it, we refined it. When we came to meetings, we be-

The Learning Network — INSTRUCTIONAL DIALOGUE

Name _____ School _____

Teacher Leader ☐   Teacher ☐   Date _____

Key points discussed:

Understandings developed:

Signed _____ PC ☐
                                 TL ☐

Figure 1.7. An instructional dialogue form.

gan to have more things in common. We had a common language, our belief systems came closer and, therefore, we were able to take a look at a little part of what was bothering us.

TAKING TIME TO LEARN

Sometimes, significant changes in practice were avoided for awhile, but as the teachers shared their stories with one another, they came to see that as long as they held off, they were holding out on students. It took time to use new practices efficiently and effectively. Falling back on old ways was discouraging, but it happened. Jan understood this and accepted our need, on occasion, to fall back until we could regain our momentum. She knew what each teacher leader was still learning to do and assured them that this would take time.

Time and the opportunity for practice and refinement of new understandings is essential to new learning. A teacher leader shared that if she hadn't had time to develop understandings she "would have been this rote person spinning off what someone else was saying." They came to see that no one could tell them the answers. They had to search within themselves.

Supervising Change

The strength of The Learning Network, for teachers, teacher leaders, and administrators, is that it is universal. Whether one is working with students or adults the understandings about good teaching and learning are the same. I've come to view the processes of teaching and learning as synonymous with the process of change and professional development. What I learned from teacher leaders and from their students enabled me to look at my role as an educational leader in a new way. Knowing that my understandings were manifested in the behaviors of my learners caused me to take new responsibility for what I know and my actions. My own action plans gave focus to what I was trying to do. I began to design my meetings as demonstrations and to share my thinking. I used resources in new ways, and I organized my time so that I could get alongside each person and find out what understandings were in place for them and how I could help further their growth. The building administrators I worked with reflected that it was different to have the superintendent in schools and classrooms, challenging their thinking. Teacher leaders indicated that the engagement of the superintendent was a real asset. It provided the opportunity to develop theory district wide. I continuously asked *myself* why I was doing what I was doing, and why others were doing what they were doing. At first I had questioned at great length my belief in approximation. I wanted these changes to happen *now*; I was sometimes impatient. But what I learned amazed me. By setting clear, focused outcomes for myself and others, I began to identify small shifts in our behaviors. I became excited when I saw understandings taking shape in practice. I knew that there was no quick fix. I began to feel confident that this process not only allowed shifts to occur, but that these were shifts that would endure and which we could continue to build upon.

I also came to understand how difficult it is to give up behaviors that have become a part of us. As we examined our practice in classrooms and in professional development forums in relation to our goals, we discovered that many of our behaviors were actually prohibiting the development of independent, life-long learners. We recognized that many of the shifts we had made in our practice in the past had been aimed at changing just the resources or the surface procedures. We had to unlearn some of the old notions in our heads and give up outdated practices.

Each month when we visited the teacher leaders in their classrooms, Jan and I would remark how we could not only *see*, but *feel* the change in these classrooms. There was a sense of learning and a sense of excitement as students became more and more engaged in their learning. It no longer mattered which student Jan talked with because *all* students could articulate what they were doing, why they were doing it, and what they were going to do next. They were engaged in meaningful, purposeful activities and they were self-motivated. They were no longer doing their work because the teacher told them to. They began to articulate their reasons and processes for learning.

MOVING THE CHANGE OUTWARD

At the end of Year 1 the teacher leaders, building administrators, and I felt good about the progress we had made. We had come to know what a community of leaders and learners was like because we were becoming one. We better understood the skills of life-long learning because our own learning taught us how. We were empowered by our own understandings and professional practices developed through inquiry and discovery and a new level of trust for one another and for the outside change agent.

This message began to permeate the system. This process was no longer about five teacher leaders working in their classrooms. We began to share our learning with the entire community–parents, school councils, district councils, support teams, and school committees. We sent out a strong message about the necessity for change. Judson Brown, a reporter for the local newspaper, tagged along during one of Jan's visits. A few days later I complimented him on the article he had written. He responded, "Well, that was the most professional thing I have ever seen happen in my entire life." Later I learned that he had also stated that it was the most moral thing he had ever seen (Kussy 1994). Parents confirmed that they saw carry-over at home. Younger children were assisting older children with their reading and writing and asking each other questions.

Over the course of the year, I had kept school committee members informed and involved in our work. Through stories about our discoveries and the effect on our learners we were able to share our progress with them. In the spring of 1994 the teacher leaders made a formal presentation about The Learning Network to the school committee. Committee members stated that this process addressed the concerns they had about traditional education. They were impressed with the focus on teaching students how to learn, the importance of reading and writing for meaning as opposed to memorizing facts or filling in ditto sheets, and the ability of the teachers to assess and articulate where each child was and to personalize learning. They not only expressed support for the program, but they joined us as learners. Many of them began visiting classrooms and talking to teacher leaders and students. They committed funds to The Network and began to articulate the importance for all teachers to become a part of this professional development model.

MOVING FROM YEAR 1 TO YEAR 2

At our final meeting for the year with Jan, the teacher leaders reflected on where they were by means of a self-assessment tool based on the "Benchmarks and Indicators for Teachers" (Richard C. Owen Publishers 1995b) that program coordinators in The Network use to assess growth. Here was a very humbling experience. They articulated those understandings they had, and they discovered that there was still a whole lot of learning to do, but instead of feeling threatened or overwhelmed, as they had in the beginning, they were excited and energized by what they still had to learn. More importantly, they immediately began to plan how they might best continue. They identified topics to explore together and the strengths of individuals so that they might use each other's expertise and experience to their best advantage in the year to come.

We all had been nervously anticipating Year 2 since about November of Year 1. Knowing that deep understandings would be necessary to effectively assist others heightened our expectations and fueled our need to know. During Year 1, some teachers had met with Jan after school to continue their learning. These teachers were eager to have teacher leaders in their classrooms in the coming year. For them our demonstrations and stories were a source of inspiration and hope for their own practice. For others, however, the teacher leaders were a threat. Teacher leaders had begun to be subjected to less-than-professional interactions from some of their peers. We tried to find comfort in the story of the tall poppy—when someone sticks his or her neck out, there is always someone there to cut it down.

Jan had modeled for us the skills we needed to assist others in reflecting on their practice, but we lacked confidence. We knew that we would begin again with a great amount of uncertainty, anxiety, and disequilibrium, but this was a process we had learned to accept. We knew that there was no real mystery to what we were doing and that the way to engage others was to make it safe for them to join us. Our role was to come to know them as learners, to know their strengths, and to assist them in taking their own next steps. We would have the responsibility to ask "why." We also knew how threatening this process could be. We would still have Jan to assist us in this new process. We would still have one another. But most importantly we had ourselves. We had become reflective practitioners. We had lived the journey and knew what it took. We had come to know that we cannot mandate new learning, but we can accept the responsibility to assist others to ask their own questions and create their own understanding.

In Year 2 each teacher leader began to read action plans, observe, and hold instructional dialogue with a number of teachers. Once a month, Jan, the principal, and I would observe in the teacher's classroom alongside the teacher leader. We would listen as the teacher leader dialogued with the teacher. Then Jan would engage the teacher leader in tiered dialogue, guided by the teacher leader's action plans related to his or her work with each teacher. She asked the teacher leaders questions, which enabled them to reflect on whether they had come to know what understandings the teachers had in place. She assisted them in examining whether their questions were clearly focused. We all strived to identify appropriate teaching points and struggled with how to provide the support necessary to help each teacher make connections. Sometimes Jan modeled this process, guiding a teacher to his or her next learning step with ease and confidence. She continuously demonstrated the process of handing over responsibility for learning while offering support for that next learning step.

Working alongside others in their classrooms has proved to be a real challenge. In an effort to build safe, trusting relationships we often found ourselves walking on eggshells and worrying about pushing people too hard. Finding the balance between pressure and support is difficult. Our greatest challenge has been in digging deep enough with teachers; moving beyond the surface level of practice and getting to their understandings. We have a responsibility to ask "why" to find out what they know and to develop challenging questions that will enable them to move forward. Early in our involvement in The Learning Network we referred to observation and instructional dialogue as a mentoring process. We have learned that it is so much more than traditional mentoring or coaching. No one in The Network tells anyone else "one best way to do things." This is especially difficult when they are looking for answers and asking for recipes, just as we did not too long ago.

BECOMING A SELF-WINDING DISTRICT

In the 1995-1996 school year, our third year of involvement with The Learning Network, Jan remained active in our district working with new teacher leaders. As we begin our fourth year together and our three new teacher leaders are beginning to assist others, we face many of the same challenges we did in Year 1. As more and more of our faculty comes on board, we have found that the process of managing change requires a considerable amount of time and effort. Each year there is a greater need to develop flexible schedules to provide teacher leaders and the teachers they are working alongside with time for this process. Creative teaming approaches have been developed in lieu of substitutes or additional staff members. Resources continue to challenge us; there are just never enough. Professional resources for teachers and authentic student resources with charm, magic, impact, and appeal are a necessity. What we have found, however, is that when teachers know the resources they make well-informed purchasing decisions and that money that was once spent on workbooks and dittos can be used for high-quality children's literature and other materials.

Each year the investment of time and funds in The Learning Network is challenged. We counter this by pointing out that because it is an initiative driven by the development of understandings, we are becoming self-winding. Each time we come together we learn. We are developing a core group of people who will be able to continue growth within the district. We are no longer spending money on the latest materials, nor are we wasting funds by moving from program to program and workshop to workshop, discarding what came before.

Our understandings have influenced all aspects of our system. As teachers and administrators become skillful teachers and responsible learners they are exploring new topics. Curriculum development has been a major focus and reflects the importance of designing instruction for the needs of learners and the development of essential life-long learning skills. The work of school councils, building support teams, and special education teams reflect the need for ongoing assessment and evaluation as a means for planning and implementing effective practices and programs for students and teachers. Teacher leaders and principals work closely together to plan staff meetings and to assist others in working together to improve learning outcomes for all students.

CHANGES FOR THE FUTURE

This change is still ongoing. Working with a teacher leader is a choice for teachers to make. We have lost a few teachers along the way for a variety of reasons. Often we hear "been there, done that." Many have stated that no one can find fault with the understandings behind our practice, but it just isn't how they teach. Others, particularly at the upper grade levels, aren't engaged because they don't yet see the validity of the teaching and learning cycle in content areas. For some who would like the support of a teacher leader, the pressure from others to avoid this professional development model is too intense.

I worry not only about the fate of this professional development model, but about our own. Each of us, whether teacher or administrator, has had to face open hostility and personal pain. I have read about different types of people and how they react to change. I have also read about the strength of the status quo and how difficult it is to implement real change. Those who work to sabotage the change process can be as powerful as those who promote change. In our district there seems to be a strong voice for the right of teachers who do not wish to participate in The Learning Network, but not for those who do.

As educators we have to make decisions. Are we going to teach our students how to learn and to keep on learning? Are we going to individualize teaching so that all students will experience learning success? Are we going to create learner-centered schools and classrooms where teachers are responsive to and responsible for the needs of students? Are we going develop communities based on collaboration and trust? Most educators know that real change must begin in the classroom with teaching and learning, and that for real change to occur we must focus on teachers' understandings. Evidence suggests that traditional professional development activities that take place outside of the school never lead to real changes in practice. In Easthampton we are beginning to make changes in our understandings that are leading to increased learning for our students.

I remember that everyone involved in The Learning Network in Easthampton School District used to say, "Jan said ..." a lot. I don't hear that anymore. What I hear now is "My understanding is ..." We have a process for learning in place. Our own expectations drive us forward and make us accountable to all of our learners. We no longer need to wait for a program coordinator to ask us "why." We recognize the importance of articulating why we do what we do, and through reflection we are able to refine and redefine our understandings. We understand that to be learners we must be willing to challenge and to be challenged. Jan didn't give us answers. Instead, she gave us the greatest gift of all–questions. Learning to question has helped all of us work and learn collaboratively. We have become reflective practitioners responsible for our own continued development and the development of others. Jan helped each of us to search within ourselves and to take responsibility for what we do and to know why we do it. Change isn't something that someone else gives or does. Change isn't an event. Change is a personal journey which we each must commit to embark upon if we are to improve teaching and learning. Those wishing for change must be willing to begin first with themselves and to continuously keep digging into and reflecting on why we do what we do. We have changed. Our reward is evident in our students. Our vision of classrooms and schools where all children do learn has become a reality. We have new hope that we can meet the needs of all of our learners and the passion to see it through. We have become empowered professionals. We believe that by achieving common understandings about teaching and learning we can initiate and sustain effective educational change for all students in all classrooms.

KATHY KUSSY *has been superintendent of Easthampton Public Schools, a Learning Network site in Easthampton, Massachusetts, since 1989. She was associate superintendent from 1989 to 1991, and prior to that was a curriculum coordinator, school development program consultant, reading consultant and teacher, and classroom teacher. Kathy holds an Ed.D. in Educational Administration from Columbia University Teacher's College, New York, New York.*

CHAPTER 2

Action Plans, Observation, and Instructional Dialogue

Angel Stobaugh

"Learning to do effective instructional dialogue is like learning to speak a foreign language."

Dianne Kotaska
Program Coordinator

What do you think Dianne Kotaska means by that opening quote? I asked her, and this is what she said:

For a long time all you can do is "parrot" the language, but you mispronounce words, stress the wrong syllable, use the wrong verb tense, attach the wrong article, fracture the structure, fumble and stutter, and make repeated attempts to get it right.

Even while struggling to find the right words, you strive to make sense, and you usually communicate with the help of others more fluent. With practice and support your pronunciation improves, verb tense clears up, and you become more fluent and more flexible. Finally, there is a point at which you "cross over" and take on the rhythm, the intonation, the subtle nuances. You begin to think in the new language.

I am striving to think in the language of instructional dialogue!

I am striving too. When asked to write this chapter on observation and instructional dialogue I said, "Write about it? I'm still figuring it out!" That's when I realized that I was where I wanted to be. I'm a learner who will always question my practice, who will always look to improve my skillfulness, and who thrives on being challenged. This growth happened because a change agent called a program coordinator came into my classroom to observe my practice and challenge me to reflect on what I knew about literacy instruction through instructional dialogue. This involved applying the use of the teaching and learning cycle to an adult learner—me. Instructional dialogue is a central concept of The Learning Network and an element that distinguishes The Network from all other types of teacher development.

My growth continues as I am now a program coordinator who visits schools to observe teacher leaders in their classrooms and conduct instructional dialogue. I have learned through my experiences how focused observations and instructional dialogues help teachers explore theory and connect it with effective practice.

When I became involved with The Learning Network, I was a Title I teacher in Boulder Valley Schools in Colorado. I had six years of classroom experience and had worked one year as a Title I teacher. Throughout these years students seemed happy to be in my classroom. I prided myself in teaching the curriculum outcomes in a variety of ways, in having students design projects of all kinds to show the knowledge they had gained from our units, and in never having sent a student to the office for discipline. I felt confident with my knowledge and skills as a teacher. My administrator and the students' parents were happy with the progress being made so I knew learning was occurring, but I couldn't point to any precise instructional practice of mine as the cause.

Through my involvement with The Learning Network, I began to realize that much more learning should have been taking place. Students in my classroom were motivated to read and were developing fluency, yet they showed little sign of being constructive or strategic readers. I was planning reading activities, such as reading novels in small groups and having students discuss the plot or character development throughout the book. I was asking students to respond in writing after they read by either completing a story map or using sentence starters such as: "If I were (main character) I would have ..." and "I like the way the author ..." These activities kept students on task so I could monitor the amount of text they were reading. The activities spurred excitement and reasons to read, but they didn't teach students more about the process of creating or recreating meaning through reading. Through observation and instructional dialogue I realized that, although I was giving my students the time and opportunity to explore books, I was not teaching reading.

In writing, my students were moving through what I understood the writing process to be, yet not improving the quality of their writing or increasing their knowledge of the writing process with each successive piece. Again, through observation and dialogue I realized that they were doing many different kinds of activities using writing, but not using or learning about the writing process through these activities. I wasn't teaching writing. I was scheduling activities that included writing.

THE CHALLENGE OF NEW LEARNING

Jan Duncan came to my school in the mountains of Colorado to observe me working with children. Her objective was to help me develop the theory that was driving my practice. It was through her focused observations and instructional dialogues that I began to learn what I thought I knew. She would read my action plan and observe my classroom practice. Then in instructional dialogue she would ask me difficult questions that I couldn't answer. The first few observations and instructional dialogues brought me to tears because up to this point I considered myself to be a good teacher. I was the best teacher I knew how to be. Then Jan comes along with all of these questions that made me describe and analyze my practice. She challenged me and helped me to construct new understandings, which changed my practice.

I will never forget the questions Jan asked during our first few instructional dialogues:

♦ "Angel, why does this student have this book for independent reading? How do you know it is or isn't appropriate for her continued growth?"
♦ "What challenges were in this guided reading text that students could use for new learning?"
♦ "What was your teaching point?"
♦ "Did learning occur?" "How do you know?"
♦ "What evidence do you have that learning occurred?"

- "Why is the students' writing the same this month as compared to last month?"
- "What new learning is occurring for this child specifically?"
- "Does everyone in this classroom need to learn about spaces between words? So why are they all doing the same activity?"

I came to understand that as a teacher, meeting the needs of all learners happens when I understand and apply my knowledge of the teaching and learning cycle. I realized that I didn't need to have all the answers. I needed to be open to take on new and deeper understandings, which in turn would help me to teach and my students to learn. Coming to this realization created a major change in me. I had to investigate the reading and writing processes and the various types of assessments that I was using. I had to move away from using assessments to determine the learning I *thought* was taking place to using assessments to determine the learning that *needed* to take place. I learned about supports and challenges inherent in texts and came to recognize the importance of matching the child with the right books and appropriate teaching approach. These shifts in my understandings were a direct result of my instructional dialogues with Jan. Without them, I would have continued to be a good teacher rather than a skillful, reflective practitioner.

As American teachers, we are accustomed to staff development being someone showing or telling us how to incorporate an activity into our practice. This knowledge usually comes from experts who teach college courses or provide inservices. We rarely question these practices or consider how they will benefit our learners. When we copy a practice, we are using someone else's understandings. If we adapt what we are shown, we are adapting someone else's understandings. However, when we make attempts on our own, question ourselves, and are willing to have someone else question us, we are developing our own theory. It is when we look inside ourselves and take responsibility for our own professional growth instead of imitating others that we start to make long-lasting changes in our practice. This is the goal of The Learning Network and this happens through the use of action plans, focused observations, and instructional dialogue.

ACTION PLANS

Action plans are tools that help teachers to focus on their own learning. Teacher leaders and teachers write action plans weekly. To assist teachers in identifying areas in which to write action plans, indicators of a skillful teacher have been identified, some of which are shown in Figure 2.1 (Richard C. Owen Publishers 1995b). These action plans center on understandings about the Literacy Learning model.

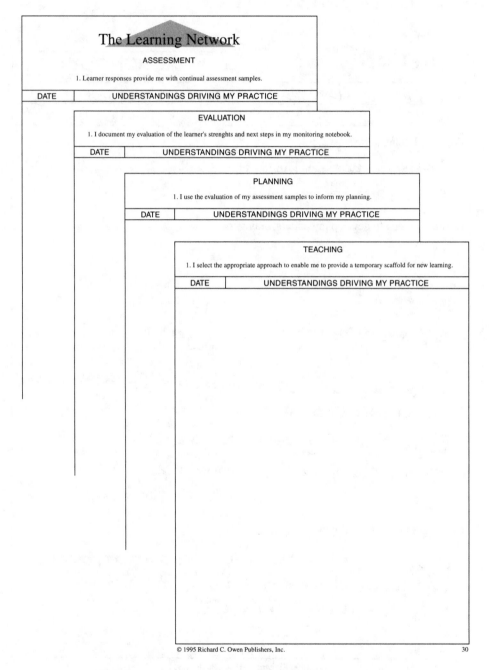

Figure 2.1. Some indicators of skillful teachers.

Often when teachers become involved with The Learning Network, they write action plans only because they've been asked to. But, as time goes on these action plans become the driving force for their individual learning. This shift in thinking is apparent in the action plans shown in Figures 2.2 and 2.3.

The Learning Network	ACTION PLAN

Name __Denise Larsen__   School __Crawford__
Grade __Title I__   Date __September 29, 1995__

What am I going to do?

• Develop a better understanding of the approach of writing to students.

How am I going to develop my understandings?

• Read:
   Dancing with the Pen   pages 108-109
                                 pages 26-84

   Resoure Notebook   pages B-88 – B-89

• Question my present practice as I talk to students about the process as I write.
• Begin to identify students who would benefit from the approach at this time.

How will I know when I'm there?

• When I can articulate why that approach has been chosen for the next learning step for these children.

Figure 2.2. Action plan from the beginning of Year 1.

The Learning Network

| ACTION PLAN |

Name **Denise Larsen**   School **Crawford**

Grade **Title I**   Date **August 12, 1996**

What am I going to do?

· Develop a better understanding of the approach of shared reading and how the teaching of skills does or does not become included in this approach.

How am I going to develop my understandings?

· Resource Notebook pg H-8
· Developing Life-long Rdrs 24-25
· Rdg in Jr Classes 57-61, 101-102, 105-107, 110-111
· Rdg To, With & By 25-30

· Becoming Literate 197-199, 226
· Inside New Zealand 24, 71, 99, 112, Classrooms 131-132, 168, 14, 27, 70
· Learning to Read in 35, 37, 81-82 New Zealand

· Question if skills are taught using this method.
· Use the teacher's role to entice students to books & seeing themselves as readers.
· Pleasure is paramount & specific skills should not interfere with that pleasure. So when are skills taught?
· First reading is for meaning and enjoyment. 2nd reading is used for attention to skill focused on a difficulty within the text. But do you read twice?
· Questioning empowering or depowering students through shared rdg.
· Skills are taught when children need them. Do they need them as shared rdg with the teacher's voice support?

How will I know when I'm there?

· When I can articulate to others my understandings of the shared reading approach. When I feel successful implementing a shared reading group and feel confident in my understandings and practice.

Figure 2.3. Action plan from the beginning of Year 2.

The action plan in Figure 2.2 discusses a general topic, writing to students. Writing to students is an approach that encompasses the entire writing process, conditions for learning, and the teaching and learning cycle. The teacher leader has followed the prescribed format, yet has written the plan with very little personal voice. Because they have never been asked to focus on their learning in this way, many teachers and teacher leaders view action plans as an assignment for the program coordinator. It is clear that the purpose of this action plan was to have something to turn in to the program coordinator on her next visit. I've been asked numerous times at the onset of working with teachers why action plans need to be written weekly if I'm only visiting the school once a month. This tells me that when starting out the teachers place little value on action plans and they are not viewed as tools for professional growth.

The value of action plans is acquired over time. The action plan in Figure 2.3 was written by the same teacher leader one year later. It shows evidence of how this teacher leader began to value the action plan process. The topic is narrowed to understanding the teaching of skills through shared reading. This teacher read a variety of resources and listed statements or questions raised by the readings. This action plan shows an increased level of personal voice and is clearly being written by this teacher to focus her learning. These changes in the action plans occur as teachers move to directing their own areas of growth and as they develop their skills of reflection.

The action plan is divided into three sections: What am I going to do?; How am I going to develop my understandings?; and How will I know when I'm there?

The first question, "What am I going to do?," helps the teacher to focus his or her thoughts on one part of this teaching and learning model. In the example shown in Figure 2.4, the teacher is focusing on developing a deeper understanding of the purpose and selection of books for independent reading. Rather than looking at independent reading in general, this teacher will concentrate on just the purpose and selection of books as she conducts her research.

The second question, "How will I develop my understandings?," directs teachers to list how they plan to gain more information about their narrow topic listed in the first question. The example shows five different resources to be explored as well as reflections the teacher has made to express her current understandings. It also contains questions and thoughts the teacher developed as a result of reading. Often the questions and new learning prompt further investigation, which causes the teacher to return to the research. Articulating this informa-

The Learning Network

ACTION PLAN

Name   Denise Larsen   School   Crawford

Grade   Title I   Date   Sept. 3, 1996

What am I going to do?
Develop a deeper understanding of the purpose for and the selection of books for independent reading baskets.

How am I going to develop my understandings?

Reading To, With, and By Children pgs 11-12; Ch 9

Learning to Read in New Zealand pgs 39-42

Reading in Jr. Classes 75-77, 104-105, 109-110, 112-113

Developing Life-long Readers 23, 27-28

Institute Resource Book (1996) H-9, H-13, H-17--H-26

-Independent reading occurs at all stages of development so children can practice attitudes, understandings, and behaviors while assuming responsibility and control.

-Books available to children should include previous read to's, shared and guided reading (which do not provide too many challenges), unseen text with plenty of support, and self-chosen library books.

-Books for independent reading baskets should reflect students' interests as well as content areas covered in the curriculum.

-Independent reading from self-chosen texts is a habit we want children to develop as life-long readers.

-The teacher's role is to provide texts and then observe and respond to children.

-Anecdotal notes from observation during independent reading will inform the teacher's practice.

-I understand that all approaches are used every day and often within each lesson (to, with, by).

-Are all independent reading books introduced by the teacher in a small group setting? No, but it is one possibility with the weaving of the approaches.

-Independent reading develops life-long readers who choose books and enjoy reading.

-Independent reading can be done alone or with friends, because learning is social.

-Reading skills are improved with practice. Independent reading provides time to practice.

-Texts are selected for independent reading baskets based on supports, which greatly outweigh the challenges.

-Classroom procedure must be in place so independent readers know what to do if they meet a challenge and need assistance to maintain meaning.

-The teacher creates a comfortable environment to enjoy independent reading.

-In another action plan I will dig into reader response activities to follow independent reading.

How will I know when I'm there?
When I have a clear purpose for selecting independent texts and can articulate that purpose with my colleagues. When my independent reading baskets have texts that match my learners' abilities. When I observe my learners rereading and talking with others with enthusiasm about their independent reading books.

Figure 2.4. Completed action plan.

tion forces a teacher to stop and reflect, and to really delve into what he or she knows and is learning about the topic.

The third question, "How will I know when I'm there?," focuses on teacher behaviors. An understanding of The Learning Network is that a teacher's knowledge drives his or her practice. Therefore, as that teacher's knowledge changes, so would his or her classroom practice. In this part teachers describe how they believe their practices will change. It is the accountability section of an action plan. Notice that in Figure 2.4 the teacher describes three different behaviors that she will incorporate into practice: 1) she will articulate to colleagues her clear purpose for selection of texts; 2) she will choose texts that match learners' abilities; and 3) she will show her understandings of independent reading by noting observations of her learners using texts independently. The behavioral changes listed are teacher behaviors rather than the expected behavioral changes of students. It is safe to state that when teacher behaviors shift, student behaviors follow.

This action plan has been well thought out. It will assist the teacher in staying focused and the program coordinator in identifying a next step for the teacher. The program coordinator uses the action plan as one assessment tool in determining the teacher's zone of proximal development. This action plan, along with the observation, will form the basis of the instructional dialogue.

FOCUSED OBSERVATION

To be effective, classroom observations and instructional dialogues must be structured around the action plan. There is so much happening in a classroom at any given time that without focus the observation and instructional dialogue could cover any number of items. This could lead to little or no new learning and as a result cause high levels of frustration on the part of the teacher and the program coordinator.

When I was beginning my work as a program coordinator, my instructional dialogues included many teaching points. I was not yet skillful enough to find my adult learner's zone of proximal development, and I was also developing competency in using questions to move these teachers to one new piece of learning. Through guidance by Jan Duncan, a woman of high expectations and great patience and now a trainer of program coordinators, I developed more skillfulness in the art of observation and instructional dialogue, but as I stated in the opening of this chapter, I'll always feel like I have a lot to learn.

As mentioned earlier, the use of the action plan is vital in assisting a program coordinator in determining a focus for observations. The action plan serves as one assessment tool that the program coordinator evaluates. When evaluating the action plan in Figure 2.4, I would read each section and consider how the teacher's statements relate to the major constructs of the Literacy Learning model (teaching and learning cycle, conditions for learning, reading process, and writing process), then consider what understandings a teacher must have as I observe in the classroom.

For Denise's action plan, I would think through these understandings:

◆ The teacher would need to understand characteristics of readers in all three stages of reading development (emergent, early, fluent)–reading process; teaching and learning cycle; child development.

◆ What does this teacher understand about the use of running records on independent texts and the use of seen and unseen texts?–teaching and learning cycle for assessment and evaluation; reading process.

◆ To what extent does this teacher have knowledge of supports and challenges?–teaching and learning cycle for planning.

◆ What level of value does this teacher place on use, or practice, responsibility, and immersion?–conditions for learning.

When I'm observing in the classroom, this list in my mind will guide the monitoring notes I take. I use these understandings as a filter when I sift through what the teacher and students say and do. From this I can determine the strengths and possible next steps for the teacher in relation to her action plan. When observing in any classroom, I ask questions of students and note their responses because I have learned that teacher understandings manifest themselves in student behaviors. While observing in Denise's classroom, I asked her students why they were reading certain books and where they got them. I wanted to determine how she had divided up the texts and if the students understood that reading was to create meaning rather than to call out words. I asked how often books were changed and if they read other books from different places around the room. This was to learn about the value placed on immersion, responsibility, and practice. I also completed a few running records to determine the types of texts chosen for each student and the appropriateness based on reader characteristics displayed and amount and types of errors made.

Using the observations I made surrounding the understandings I generated from the action plan, I determined two possible teaching points for Denise. One was the use of running records on unseen texts to determine what strategies students have incorporated and apply independently to overcome challenge in text. Another teaching point was that independent texts for students should contain some challenge in order for students to practice reading skills they are learning through instruction.

Now that the observation is complete and I have two possible teaching points to assist this teacher in learning, I begin to read over my monitoring notes, shown in Figure 2.5, which I took throughout the observation to plan for instructional dialogue.

INSTRUCTIONAL DIALOGUE

It seems to be a part of human nature to both seek out and resist change. Change within the boundaries of The Learning Network involves a process of questioning through instructional dialogue. Many teachers find this to be a difficult phase in the process, although once beyond the initial scare of change it becomes difficult to stop their momentum and desire for change through challenge. We can easily make a comparison to Newton's law of inertia:

> [There is a] tendency of a mass at rest to remain at rest and for a mass in non-accelerating motion to maintain that state of motion unless acted upon by an outside force (Gibilisco 1993, 228).

Teachers continue to do as they always have due to the difficulty of resisting momentum. Once the direction of that momentum has been changed, it becomes very difficult to change it back. The involvement of a program coordinator or teacher leader in instructional dialogue is the force that assists in the process of change.

An example of the level of difficulty in beginning this change process comes from a written statement by a teacher leader after her first dialogue session. "This deeper understanding of my necessary next steps with students brought out thoughts on how I am being treated as a learner .... I get lots of questions and challenges to my present way of thinking, which I know is to create 'pleasing tension' and 'deepen understandings.' I only wish there was some human kindness in the challenge." After more involvement with observation and in-

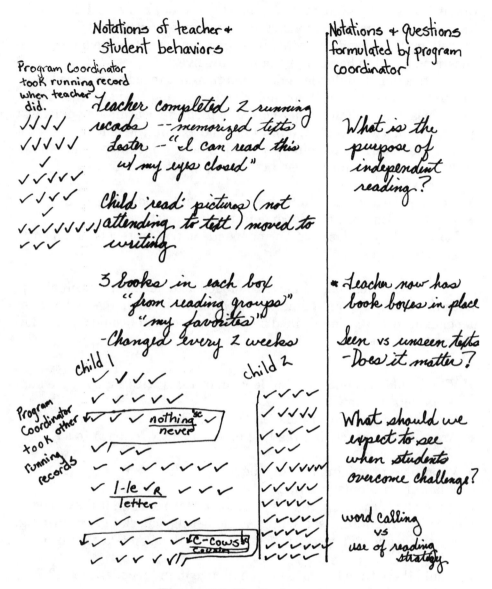

Figure 2.5. Monitoring notes.

structional dialogue, this teacher wrote: "I am feeling like a learner and a leader .... This is the most powerful learning I have ever done, and for the first time in my teaching career I am certain that what I am changing and implementing will help my kids get smarter. I am feeling good." Another teacher wrote: "I hated it. I couldn't sleep at night. I worried constantly, and now I've come to look forward to it. I depend on it." These statements demonstrate the power of instructional dialogue as well as the struggle within ourselves to open up to colleagues, to be questioned, and to begin questioning ourselves.

Instructional dialogue is designed to assist teachers in developing the ability to reflect on their understandings and to make changes in their classroom practice. Therefore, the program coordinator must ask questions that will challenge thinking and extend the teacher's knowledge. I use questions to help me to understand what the teacher knows about a topic. In Denise's case I could ask questions such as:

♦ How do you know that a text is at a student's independent level?
♦ What determines an independent reading level?
♦ How would you describe an independent text in terms of supports and challenges?

I also use questions to move the teacher to her next learning step. With the teaching point being the need for some challenge to be in independent texts (as determined by running records) I could ask the following questions:

♦ Why would students need independent texts with many more supports than challenges?
♦ What is the purpose of independent reading?
♦ Are students practicing reading independently to learn to say each word correctly?
♦ What does practicing reading mean?
♦ What are students practicing?
♦ If they are practicing reading wouldn't that mean that they need to practice attending, searching, anticipating, checking, confirming, rejecting, and self-correcting? Can that be done on text that is memorized?
♦ Would there then be a need for challenge in independent texts? Why or why not?
♦ What types of assessments can be done to determine independent texts for students?

This questioning during instructional dialogue provides the scaffold to take teachers to new learning. These questions are provided to illustrate the importance of questioning being focused on the teaching point, which came from the observation, which was determined by the action plan. There is no prescribed set of questions to ask during an instructional dialogue session because each one of these professional conversations is based on assessments (action plan focus, observations of teacher interactions, interviews with students, responses of the teacher) that the program coordinator or teacher leader working with teachers evaluates. This assessment and evaluation even occurs during the instructional dialogue. The program coordinator or teacher leader must listen to the teacher's responses as he or she continually searches for the teacher's zone of proximal development. The zone of proximal development is that distance between what teachers currently understand and demonstrate in their practice and the next layer of understanding needed to increase their skillfulness. More knowledgeable others support growth within this zone. With teachers, the program coordinators and teacher leaders act as the more capable peers.

When working with students, Lisbeth Dixon-Krauss listed three supportive elements in *Vygotsky in the Classroom*:

1. The teacher mediates or augments the child's learning. She provides support for the child through social interaction as they cooperatively build bridges of awareness, understanding, and competence.
2. The teacher's mediation role is flexible. What she says or does depends on feedback from the child while they are actually engaged in the learning activity.
3. The teacher focuses on the amount of support needed. Her support can range from very explicit directives to vague hints (1996, 16).

As we apply these understandings about working within the zone of proximal development with children to working with teachers, we can make these comparisons:

1. The dialogue is the social interaction where professionals work together to "build bridges of awareness, understanding, and competence."
2. There can be no recipe or prescription for instructional dialogue because the program coordinator's (or teacher leader's) statements, demonstrations, and questions will depend on the responses of the teacher. He or she must be flexible and ready to make shifts based on the feedback from the teacher.

3. The amount of support needed to bring a teacher to new learning
    will vary from explicit demonstration or mirroring of teacher ac-
    tions to starting a question that the teacher can finish with a
    knowing smile.

Here is the instructional dialogue that resulted between the program coordinator (PC) and the teacher leader (TL) based on Denise's
action plan:

PC: Your action plan states that you want to develop your understandings of the purpose and selection of books for independent reading. Why did you choose this focus?

TL: I've been giving students books to read after we read them together in a reading group, so I know they know the words. I wanted to
explore other ways of giving students books for independent reading
and yet be sure they are able to read them.

PC: What do you see as the purpose of independent reading?

TL: It is time when students review the books that they have read
and they practice them.

PC: What does "practice" them mean? What are they practicing?

TL: They practice reading the books so that they can read them to
each other.

PC: So, you are saying that students are practicing independent
reading to correctly say each word?

TL: No. Well, yes. Well, I'm not sure ... I know that reading is the
creation and recreation of meaning, so why are students practicing
reading ? What would they be practicing? I guess they would be using
their reading skills to make sense of the texts.

PC: How is that different than practicing words?

TL: With practicing words, they really don't have to do any reading work. They will just be memorizing the words in the book. Practicing independent reading means they should be attending, searching ...

PC: When you did the running record on Lester, he said, "I can
read this book without looking at the words!" What is that telling you?

TL: He had memorized the words. He wasn't really reading.

PC: I jotted down some observational notes while students were
reading independently. One student read through his books quickly
and went on to writing within five minutes. There was another student
I watched for some time. I also did a running record on him. Let's take
a look. Notice how he was able to move through the text, and look here
how he self-corrected both of these errors. This could be an independent text for this student.

TL: I see.

PC: So how would you describe independent texts?

TL: In the past, I would have said that students would have needed to know almost all the words, but now I'm thinking that students would not need to be familiar with the whole text. Maybe there would need to be more challenge in the texts than what I thought?

PC: Why?

TL: So that students could actually do some reading work.

PC: So in an independent text there would be challenges that the student could overcome on his own?

TL: Yes.

PC: What types of assessments would you use to determine independent texts for all of your students?

TL: Observation and running records would work. I understand now that the student wouldn't have to have all checks. I would expect to see the reader come across some challenges and see them overcoming those challenges ... so possibly re-reading, self-corrections ...

PC: With these new understandings, how will your classroom practice look different?

We continued to discuss practical implications of this teacher leader's new and deeper understandings of independent reading. We closed the session with:

PC: Okay, let's summarize this dialogue session. Using your notes of the key concepts discussed, what new understandings are you taking away?

TL: When students are reading independently they need to be practicing reading, which means using what they have learned through reading instruction. There would need to be challenges that students can overcome in independent texts rather than texts with no challenge. I'm rethinking again about reading as the creation of meaning and not the memorizing of words. I know this, but I wasn't putting this knowledge into practice. I can also see that running records can be used as a tool for determining the level of texts for each student.

We brought closure to the dialogue by completing the instructional dialogue sheet shown in Figure 2.6. Then the teacher added appropriate indicators of a skillful teacher as shown in Figure 2.7.

During every instructional dialogue, we must remember the use of the teaching and learning cycle to determine the learner's zone of proximal development. That is what guides program coordinators, teacher leaders, and teachers to their learners' next steps. Knowing our

The Learning Network | INSTRUCTIONAL DIALOGUE |

Name _Denise Larsen_   School _Crawford_

Teacher Leader ☒   Teacher ☐   Date _November 1996_

Key points discussed:

- Independent reading
  - practice
  - memorizing/ working to overcome challenge

- Running records
  - self-correction
  - rereading

Understandings developed:

- Practicing reading is using knowledge learned from instruction on texts.
- Independent texts have challenges readers can overcome on their own -- familiar and unfamiliar texts.
- Reading = creation of meaning.
- Evaluate running record assessments to determine independent texts for readers.

Signed _Angel Stroubaugh_ PC ☑
                            TL ☐

Figure 2.6. Instructional dialogue sheet.

The Learning Network

EVALUATION

6. I analyze the running record and summarize the information gathered.

DATE	UNDERSTANDINGS DRIVING MY PRACTICE
10/2/96	• I understand that I have to analyze a running record for meaning, structure, and visual information. • I ask myself: Does it make sense? Does it sound right? Does it look right?
11/8/96	I look for patterns of what the reader can do.
11/22/96	• I analyze other behaviors (what comments the reader makes) to determine what he understands. • When I take a running record I am looking for evidence of what I have taught students.

15

Figure 2.7. Indicators of a skillful teacher developed over time.

learner and being aware of their goals is what we need to focus on rather than memorizing a set structure or list of questions to ask. That is what makes instructional dialogue so profoundly different from other forms of collegial coaching and so effective in creating reflective, skillful teachers.

As I close this chapter on observation and instructional dialogue, I want to again caution the reader that there is no formula to follow. Through these pages, I've attempted to illustrate various aspects of action plans, focused observations, and instructional dialogue, not to create a recipe that must be followed.

There are key components that provide a framework, which allows this new learning to occur:

♦ Use action plans to focus the dialogue.
♦ The action plan is focused on the development of teacher understandings rather than the development of a practice.
♦ Clarify any part of the action plan before proceeding to observe a teacher. This will provide for an accurate assessment sample and ensure a progressive, relevant experience for the teacher.
♦ Consider the major constructs of the Literacy Learning model. This will assist in moving from the narrow, microscopic focus to the macro-, more global understandings that can be transferred to other instructional situations.
♦ Throughout the observation, make observational notes that relate to the topic of the action plan to develop possible teaching points.
♦ Through instructional dialogue, new learning needs to occur. The program coordinator or teacher leader must have a focused outcome for dialogue.
♦ The outcome is reached through the use of questions as a scaffold.
♦ At times it is necessary to describe actions during the observation; to be a mirror for the teacher to see his or her actions so those experiences can be used as a link to new understandings.
♦ Instructional dialogue is the time to make connections to the theory of teaching and learning.
♦ These dialogue sessions should not be "psychiatric sessions." They are short and to the point of new learning.
♦ Reference materials can be used any time throughout the dialogue to clarify or challenge thoughts.
♦ It is helpful to use concrete examples, which can come from these resources to develop abstract concepts with teachers.

- At the end of each instructional dialogue, summarize the session.
- To bring closure to the dialogue, teachers complete an instructional dialogue form. Key concepts discussed throughout the dialogue are used to articulate and write the new understandings developed. These understandings can be transferred to the teacher's skillful teacher indicator sheet.
- These instructional dialogue forms are kept and referenced by program coordinators and teacher leaders in future sessions to make connections and build upon what has been previously learned.

ANGEL STOBAUGH *is a program coordinator for The Learning Network. She has worked with schools in Colorado and Texas. She was a classroom teacher for six years in Bennett and Aurora, Colorado and a Title I teacher for three years in Boulder, Colorado. She has a Master's degree in curriculum and instruction with an emphasis in literacy.*

CHAPTER 3

Fragile Relationships

Kathy Itterly

"Much of the year, I have felt as if I had one foot on the dock and one foot in the boat. It's hard to be the learner."

JoAnna Wright
Teacher Leader, Phoenix, Arizona

Michael Fullan stated,

> *Change is difficult because it is riddled with dilemmas, ambivalences, and paradoxes. It combines steps that seemingly do not go together: to have a clear vision and be open-minded; to take initiative and empower others; to provide support and pressure; to start small and think big; to expect results and be patient and persistent; to have a plan and be flexible; to use top-down and bottom-up strategies; to experience uncertainty and satisfaction (1991, 350).*

These words ring so true to our experiences in Northampton, Massachusetts since 1993.

PRIOR TO IMPLEMENTATION

I am a second-grade teacher in Leeds School in Northampton School District, Massachusetts. I have been a teacher leader with The Learning Network since 1993. I have always considered myself to be one of those people in life who welcomes change and challenge. Everett

49

Rogers, in developing a set of adopter types, would have described me to be an "innovator: eager to try new ideas, open to change, and willing to take risks: usually perceived as naive or a little crazy and therefore, not well integrated into the social structure" (as cited by J. Mirman-Owen 1995). Innovators are generally found to be approximately eight percent of the population at large. Other adopter types include: leader, 17%; early majority, 29%; late majority, 29%; and resister, 17%.

Having identified myself as an innovator, I understand my willingness to become one of four teachers from my district to be trained through The Learning Network in the Literacy Learning model in my school system. During the spring of 1993, the principal of R.K. Finn Ryan Road Elementary School announced at an impromptu after-school meeting that he had to know *that afternoon* if two teachers from our school would be willing to be trained in the "New Zealand Literacy Model." He admitted that he was not clear about the details but he did know that: 1) there would be direct involvement with Jan Duncan, the program coordinator; 2) Jan would be spending time in classrooms working side-by-side with the teachers being trained; 3) volunteering meant a two-year commitment; and 4) this training could lead to training other teachers "down the road." I had met Jan one year earlier when she spoke to our elementary school staff , and I held her in high regard.

IMPLEMENTATION IN YEAR 1: THE 1993-1994 SCHOOL YEAR

The training began with attendance at the four-day Literacy Learning in the Classroom summer institute. Unfortunately, our union agreed to a "work to rule" policy that summer, so we were unable to attend. However, by September of 1993 a contract had been agreed upon and the four teacher leaders from my school had a special two-day condensed institute with Jan.

Challenge and Support

In those two days Jan Duncan continuously described an approach to teaching literacy that "puts the learner at the center of the classroom." I sincerely believed that I already had a learner-centered classroom and, having obtained my master's degree in reading, I also thought that I would be merely refining some of my practices regarding literacy acquisition. Since I held these beliefs, I entered the institute sessions confidently, primarily seeking affirmation. By the end of the second day, however, I was feeling somewhat overwhelmed.

It was at this point that Jan began to describe the theoretical base for spelling acquisition in the Literacy Learning model. I experienced my first stirring of resistance. My colleagues teased me about my body language: I sat back, arms folded, questioning why I should abandon what was already in place and "working" in my classroom. I was being challenged to rethink my practice, and I was feeling inner tension because the new spelling theory did not fit into my belief system. Although this was the first time I noticed unease as I challenged my personal beliefs, I was to become very familiar with this emotion over the next three years.

My fellow teacher leaders, who would also describe moments of tension at various stages during the two days, told me not to even *think* about spelling. My colleagues and I were already beginning to know each other in a new way, supporting each other at various moments during those two days. We all agreed that we were feeling overwhelmed, exhausted, and somewhat vulnerable. The training ended with Jan patiently suggesting that we choose just one small piece of our curriculum to begin our "digging in," and to complete our first action plans.

I had not yet internalized the *purpose* of an action plan beyond indicating what I wanted Jan to observe and discuss. My only experiences with observation had been for evaluative purposes. I believed I should be primarily demonstrating my good classroom practices, so I chose to begin in the area of writing, the subject in which my current practices and philosophies matched most closely to the Literacy Learning model (or so I thought). I had no intention of changing my *beliefs* about writing because I thought they already matched what had been presented.

Bussis, Chittenden, and Amarel, in their research study on teachers' perceptions of open education, described this experience: "It is possible to change 'on the surface' by endorsing certain goals, using specific materials, and even imitating the behavior *without specifically understanding* the principles and rationale of the change" (Bussis et al. 1976, emphasis theirs). This was certainly true for me. I had begun working on the writing component of this model in September. By January of 1994 I was still protesting the need for one of the essential elements: a written plan. I rationalized my resistance to the written plan based on my own experiences with writing and the fact that my students were now using webs and there did not appear to be much change in their ability to structure written work. After all, I contended, I had made it this far in my own life without writing out plans before writing. By February the program coordinator *directed* me to start making a written plan any time I needed to write even though I didn't agree with it. Since my other colleagues-in-training supported the practice, I reluctantly agreed.

It was through both the experiences as a learner implementing the steps of the writing process and as a teacher monitoring and assessing student outcomes that I finally came to value and understand the written plan. Without the opportunity to work with a mentor and colleague, I would possibly never have made this shift in my beliefs and practices. Jan's pressure and my three colleagues' support provided the perfect combination that enabled me to move out of my comfort zone.

Through this new understanding I came to realize that many of the beliefs I held previously would be challenged, and that I welcomed these challenges! We four teacher leaders began to ask each other after Jan's visits, "What new understanding do you have after talking with Jan today?" I began to write action plans for my *own* growth, not for the program coordinator. As I re-read sections of books and articles, I began to notice that I had missed quite a lot of information. I would wonder how could I possibly have missed such big ideas! Never before in my twelve years of teaching had anyone ever questioned me about my practice and educational theories. I felt challenged, yet exhilarated.

During those nine months of 1993 and 1994, I was one of a team of nine teacher leaders from two neighboring school districts who would have focus meetings twice each month to discuss teaching and learning using the Literacy Learning model. We four teacher leaders in my school would also meet periodically to discuss our new understandings. The most challenging experience for all of us that initial year was working out a respectful, supportive dialogue group between the two neighboring groups of teacher leaders. It seemed that many discussions got "bogged down" in semantics and led to frustrating meetings. We began structuring our sessions with a written agenda and an assigned facilitator. Although our interactions improved, the four teachers from my school began to value the smaller group dialogues we had among ourselves. We began seeking each other out for support and guidance as needs arose. This seemed to be more frequent as our school community grew more and more aware of our activities. Two of the teacher leaders served on the school council and educated this group of people about the model. We were so busy grappling with the changes going on in our understandings and practices plus our own meetings that we were feeling somewhat removed from the rest of the faculty. We began to realize that we needed to begin the process of informing our colleagues about our experiences and removing some of the mystique.

Our first staff meeting regarding this literacy model occurred in December of 1993. We asked our principal to allow us to do the talking. The four teacher leaders placed all the chairs in a large circle (a revolution in itself) and simply talked informally about our personal experiences using this model of teaching and learning. We had agreed to end the meeting at four o'clock, a prerequisite for establishing trust with our more skeptical audience members. The meeting was well received; however, we did not have answers to some of the questions regarding the district's vision of this professional development model. Our administrators in the district office, particularly the superintendent, were relatively new and had not personally initiated this form of professional development. They seemed to be in a state of exploration. Our principal became very invested in the model and began to fully support its implementation. In the early spring of 1994, we began to meet with the administrators to discuss how the 1994-1995 school year would be structured. Near the end of the school year, teacher leaders presented The Learning Network model to the school committee, a nine-member board consisting of seven elected officials, the mayor, and the school district superintendent.

In the spring of 1994 we decided to initiate another staff meeting to discuss the plans for expanding the training to other teachers. By the end of our meeting, six teachers had agreed to begin training the following summer. This staff development model became the "hot topic" throughout the entire district as plans for the second year's implementation became public. By the end of the school year, 26 teachers from our school had agreed to attend the four-day summer institute, and also to weekly observations and instructional dialogues with a teacher leader. Some of the teachers who would be participating were very skeptical, but our principal could be persuasive. Only three teachers in the school would not be participating during this second year of implementation. It was still unknown just how supportive the new associate superintendent and new superintendent would be in terms of Year 2. Funds became an enormous concern, but our principal was determined to proceed with the implementation.

We finished our first year of training excited and somewhat anxious about moving into the next phase as "teacher educators." Collectively, the four of us were proud and encouraged by what we had seen happening within our classrooms for the students in our school. There seemed to be no turning back now, although at times we would find ourselves shaking our heads, realizing that this was much more of a commitment than any one of us had realized at the onset!

IMPLEMENTATION IN YEAR 2: THE 1994-1995 SCHOOL YEAR

During the second year of implementation, the teacher leaders in my school agreed to record and study the process of change. We inter-

viewed each other three times throughout the year, kept personal journals of day-to-day occurrences, and, in February of 1995, surveyed the
teachers with whom we were working. At the end of the year we examined our transcriptions and journals, allowing categories to emerge as
we tried to understand and describe our various experiences. As we
stepped back and reviewed the year, four themes emerged: stages of
development, roles, supports, and challenges. We also discovered that
we did not yet have our own model regarding the teacher leader/
teacher learner relationship. We had followed Jan's model of our training in Year 1 and expected that what had worked for us would work for
the other teachers. This expectation led to several erroneous assumptions, including: 1) with enough support, all teachers would be capable
of successfully implementing this model of teaching and learning; 2) all
teachers would feel safe with the program coordinator and other observers viewing this learning process; and 3) all teachers would eventually get as excited as we and become self-directed learners. These assumptions had a direct impact on the stages we traveled through.

In retrospect, we were quite naive regarding the change process itself. I personally believed that if I could do my job as a teacher leader
well enough, teachers would feel safe and energized by this learning
model. We were about to embark on a journey without the most important road map: a clear understanding of the change process in educational settings. We had only our own experiences to draw upon, and being risk-takers and innovators, we had no prior experience with
resisters. The only preparation we had came from Jan, who forewarned
us about the disequilibrium. Her words echoed in our minds: "The
change process could be likened to the grieving process." But what did
that actually mean?

Stages

As teacher leaders, when we examined the data in retrospect, we
were able to label five stages in our process of becoming teacher leaders.

Stage One: Naive Optimism

The summer institute experience occurred in August of 1994. In
addition to the 26 teachers from our school, our two principals, the associate superintendent, one principal from another elementary school,
and groups of teachers from throughout the district who would not be

working with a teacher leader at this stage of the implementation attended. Whenever the general sessions broke into smaller dialogue groups, our school's dialogue groups were led by Jan Duncan. The teachers had already been placed into "focus groups," which would remain throughout the school year and were arranged by teacher leader assignment. Two teacher leaders were assigned six teachers and two teacher leaders were assigned seven teachers. Although there were signs of discomfort by some of the group members, the institute was inspirational and people seemed quite enthusiastic.

Teacher leaders began the school year with some anxiety, wondering if we were truly ready to work with our colleagues. Jan Duncan had been a wonderful role model and her skills would be hard to emulate. Still, there was a sense of optimism. At this time, we were working under the assumption that with enough support, all teachers would be capable of competently implementing the Literacy Learning model. This model of teaching and learning requires active teaching and decision-making in the classroom all day long. The Learning Network model expects that a teacher is willing to become a learner within the classroom walls, articulating the metacognitive process during classroom demonstrations. In short, both models assume that professional teachers are life-long learners and risk-takers.

In a study on school change by Bruce Joyce, Carlene Murphy, Beverly Showers, and Joseph Murphy they learned that "least competent teachers learn both subject matter and teaching practices more slowly than do the others" (1989). The Learning Network model of professional development is very threatening to those people who do not feel confident in their teaching and learning process. Jan kept pushing the teacher leaders to bring her into the classrooms of the teachers for whom the process was most difficult. It was those very teachers who were most reticent to be observed. We were working under the assumption that all teachers would feel safe with the program coordinator and other observers viewing this learning process. Teacher leaders had had much experience articulating our understandings to a variety of audiences by our second year in this model. We had also gotten comfortable with the idea of being observed both in our classroom practices and in our dialogue sessions. We felt strongly that our classrooms should be laboratories of learning for all who entered, adults included. Jan encouraged us to keep this entire process out in the open.

Everyone working with a teacher leader had been told that Jan would be observing the practices of the teacher leaders during this school year, thereby entering *all* classrooms at least once. Even though we assured teachers that it wasn't evaluative and that it was the teacher leader whose practice Jan was observing, it caused much discomfort. When I informed one teacher that Jan would be coming into her classroom the following week, she replied, "I'd rather be observed by the superintendent." Because of this reaction, we teacher leaders began to question this practice. However, Jan encouraged us to keep this process open. Her exact words were, "Stop pussyfooting around. Don't ask teachers if it's okay." Since we held Jan in such high regard, at that time we continued to allow open visits. This "push" caused problems as early as November of Year 2.

Stage Two: Discouragement and Uncertainty

By midyear, we teacher leaders realized that there had been a missing piece in our training, and we were working under the assumption that all teachers would eventually get as excited as we and become self-directed learners. This assumption was patently false. We began to notice that some of the teachers appeared "stuck" on one aspect of the model. Several teachers seemed to stay with the same action plan for very long periods of time *if* they even took the time to write one. We began to question our own practice as teacher leaders. Were we not "pushing" hard enough? Jan also seemed impatient with the progress of some of our learners and this heightened our feelings of self-doubt. We felt overwhelmed. Through our continuous reflection and dialogues, we accepted the uncertainty we felt as a team of teacher leaders and drew strength from the acknowledgment that we alone could not assume responsibility for the progress or success of this model of professional development. The questionnaire that we distributed to our teachers in February of 1994 confirmed what we had already suspected: the resistance was growing, rather than abating. We were also still struggling with the issue of open classrooms. Finally, at about the same time, after another emotional experience with one of my teachers, I declared that I would not allow any future observations without prior approval by the teacher. The other teacher leaders agreed and that became our policy. We had learned some very important lessons about respecting our learners and we were beginning to trust our own intuitions as learners and leaders. We recognized that a professional development model could not be applied to all school cultures in the same way. Our teachers needed to feel safe and we felt obliged to make that happen. We began to make decisions with our principal as a site-based team.

Rumors began circulating throughout our entire school system as disequilibrium grew. Jan assured us that this was to be expected and advised us to stay proactive. We all smiled as she said, "Put on your steel corsets and give them a tug." We continued our work, a bit discouraged but strongly committed to the theories that we now valued about teaching and learning.

I shudder to think of how little I truly understood about teaching and learning at this point. We realized later in the school year that Jan's ability to question and "push" us could not be easily replicated with many of the teachers we were working alongside. We have since learned that teacher leaders were more comfortable with change than many of our colleagues. We could be nudged into unfamiliar territory more easily. When Jan questioned the progress of our learners, we said, "Yes, but *you* were supporting *us* last year. We are different than some of our peers."

Stage Three: Crisis Intervention

Although focus groups had been meeting weekly since the beginning of the school year, in February of 1995, we began to meet as a faculty to develop common curriculum goals during our monthly curriculum day meetings. Finally, in mid-March, tensions peaked when a group of teachers in a focus team sponsored a forum to discuss their experiences with interested teachers from other schools. Although all teachers were invited, only those teachers feeling positive about their experience chose to participate. Teacher leaders arrived and were asked to leave by some of the teachers from other schools. We complied and later heard from teachers in our building that a direct, honest, and generally positive dialogue took place.

Up until this point most negativity and discomfort from our teachers had been directed toward the Literacy Learning model itself or toward Jan Duncan. A crisis followed when personal attacks began against one of the teacher leaders. At this time we decided to release one of the most resistant teachers from the process. Without knowing what the consequences would be for this action, it seemed to alleviate much of the unrest at our school.

Stage Four: Rejuvenation

In May of 1995, after attending a professional development conference and hearing the keynote speaker, Robert Evans, discuss the change process, new understandings provided much needed renewal for the teacher leaders. Hearing about other school reform efforts was very affirming for us. We realized that we really were making progress and that change doesn't occur as quickly or smoothly as we had anticipated. We began reading and discussing current research about the change process. Our new perspectives proved to guide us through the final months of school with renewed enthusiasm.

Stage Five: Realistic Optimism

By the end of the school year, plans were made to continue implementation of this professional development model throughout our entire elementary school system. In school year 1995-1996 six additional teacher leaders would work with Jan Duncan and the other teacher leaders would continue to work with new teachers. This expansion continued and continues to have its opponents, with funding as the most cited concern.

Teacher leaders all agree that, through research and experience, we have become much more informed about the change process. We are better prepared to meet the challenges that we know await us. We have "toughened up," but most importantly, we have become more knowledgeable. We have learned not to personalize so many of the setbacks, which are inevitable. We have, in fact, added the element of realism to our optimism.

Wee Steps

I have written in depth about the experiences of the four teacher leaders during that first year (Itterly 1995). We celebrated many successes and grieved over many failures. It was like being on a roller coaster ride blindfolded. We were never able to predict where the highs and lows would be—they just happened. I continued to question my own classroom practices and never felt completely satisfied with my implementation during the entire second year. Sometimes I felt like an impostor trying to help my colleagues come to new understandings when I was still wrestling with some of the practices and theories myself.

Marris provides insight into what was actually happening with many of our learners during Year 2: "Reformers have already assimilated these changes to their purposes, and worked out a reformulation which makes sense to them, perhaps through months or years of debate. If they deny others to do the same, they treat them as puppets dangling by the threads of their own conceptions" (as cited by Fullan 1991, 31). As teacher leaders grew to know and respect the teachers as learners, we became more relaxed about the measurable weekly progress of each teacher.

Supports

The Critical Triangle

The Learning Network describes one of the primary supports for on-going teacher development to be the critical triangle as described in Chapter 4. This refers to the concept of principals, an outside change agent (the program coordinator), and the teacher leaders working together. Through our experiences, the teacher leaders in our school unanimously agreed that these three supports were crucial to our success throughout this implementation phase.

Teacher Leaders

Although our bimonthly focus meetings with the two teams of teacher leaders continued to provide theoretical dialogue, it was our weekly after-school sessions with just the four of us that became our salvation. After a critical bonding experience early in the school year, weekly scheduled meetings emerged. At these sessions we shared many emotional experiences: laughing, crying, comforting, complaining, rejoicing, and sometimes just sighing. Among the four of us, a bond was created that was unlike any other professional relationship I had ever experienced. Honesty and directness were valued by each of us and our meetings became a refuge from all of the external forces.

Administrators

The Learning Network was introduced into our school system by an interim superintendent and an acting associate superintendent. Their long-term strategic goal was described through the delivery of training programs: two elementary schools would have Reading Recovery® training and two elementary schools would have The Learning Network training. The initial plan was to establish these two models in each of the respective schools and then to offer the identical training opportunities in the opposite sites, thereby having all four schools trained in both models. It was later acknowledged that this plan was not presented to teachers in any formal way. This caused a disparity between teachers who had the information and those who did not. The situation was further complicated when the new superintendent and associate superintendent came on board in the middle of this process. Our principal developed many new understandings as the school year progressed. After a rocky start, we teacher leaders began inviting him to our weekly meetings. Here we eventually developed trust and began problem-solving together with his full support. This proved to be extremely valuable as the year progressed.

The Program Coordinator

Because we had four teacher leaders, Jan Duncan, the outside change agent, came to our school for two days each month. She provided us with new fuel for our learning development, held us to very high standards, and helped us troubleshoot when needs arose. She also represented an objective point of view and was often the target of angry teachers in our building. Observing Jan as a life-long learner was a constant source of inspiration to us as we developed new understandings together. Her dedication and energy were limitless.

Journal Writing

In addition to the supports of the critical triangle, my colleagues and I found strength in our own journal writing. Although the frequency of journal entries varied with each teacher leader, we all agreed that the data provided for later reflection was extremely valuable in our process. The entries enabled us to be mindful of our actions and reactions and helped us continue learning from each of our experiences. Writing helped us to organize and clarify our thoughts as we worked through emotional reactions.

Personal Conviction

Reading and discussing current research and publications continued to provide support for each of us as we worked to develop deeper understandings of literacy development, teaching, and learning. We noticed students were becoming more engaged in their learning. We drew strength from our passion and commitment to our beliefs and values.

Challenges

Although teacher leaders experienced many challenges throughout the school year, five major themes seemed to pervade the process: personalities, time constraints, professional limbo, expectations, and resources.

Personalities

There was not consensus in our school that change needed to occur. Each of the teachers on our focus teams had varying levels of commitment to the adoption of this teaching and learning model. Some teachers felt very threatened having colleagues in their classrooms, questioning their practice. Jan's presence in their classrooms increased the level of anxiety, even though her focus was on the teacher leader's practice. For teachers who felt threatened, building trust was extremely hard and proved impossible in a few cases. Other personality issues emerged when groups met for consensus-building or problem-solving.

Time Constraints

From the first day of school of Year 2, it became evident that we teacher leaders did not have enough release time for the amount of responsibility connected with our job. Juggling time was a recurring theme in every one of our lives. We were trying to handle working with teachers, teaching our own classes, continuing our own learning, presenting at many meetings, and defending The Learning Network and ourselves. Many times we felt physically and mentally exhausted from the pace of our days. We had clearly taken on too much, given the structure of our job assignments.

Professional Limbo

Teacher leaders found themselves in a new position, not administrators and no longer on equal footing with other teachers. At the onset of this training, we were not aware of the power or controversy that was inherent in our new role. Usually new positions are negotiated between the teachers' union and the administration, but the development of this new role for teachers had evolved without a formal process. We were now privy to confidential information from administrators, teachers, and each other. At times it proved uncomfortable to harbor such information, creating gaps between teachers and teacher leaders. When the teachers from other schools actually requested that teacher leaders be excluded from the forum held by teachers of our system, they were publicly acknowledging that we were no longer considered neutral. Teacher leaders became highly visible and with the attention they received from both principals and central office administrators, it began to appear that they were receiving preferential treatment. During an initiation meeting at a new school site, one veteran teacher publicly stated that this entire issue about whether to bring in two teacher leaders was about power.

Ironically, we felt power*less* many times. Early in the process, when attempting to schedule our dialogue sessions, other priorities from administrators took precedence. Third-year plans involved changing schools for two teacher leaders and new classroom configurations for the other two teacher leaders. There were times when we were unsure of the support from the central office administration. Finally, continued implementation became a publicly debated item, with finances central to the discussion. At times we felt battered by both administrators and colleagues.

Expectations

Everyone involved seemed to have their own set of expectations and this created some vagaries. Teacher leaders were unclear about what our new position actually entailed. In the beginning we had the expectation that we would have complete support from the administration and that this training model would become a top priority throughout the district. Later that message changed as the new superintendent declared that involvement was to be voluntary.

The new associate superintendent proved invaluable in defending the program and in arranging for continued funding. Our building principal, once invested, defended the process and became a spokesperson; his power, however, was often limited and defined by union contracts.

The teachers working with teacher leaders all had their individual ideas about what professional development entailed, and it became a challenge to clarify expectations from a teacher leader standpoint since there was no precedent.

The program coordinator and The Learning Network expected us to open the process to other teachers and to allow visitors to share our observation and instructional dialogue processes. When we complied some of our colleagues began to feel like goldfish in bowls.

Finally, since this model of literacy teaching and learning would be affecting their children, there were expectations from the school parent community to become informed. It seemed as if we were being observed through many different lenses.

Resources

Currently our school system is facing difficult budgetary decisions. There is much debate over whether to continue involvement in The Learning Network, whether to continue to support Reading Recovery®, and whether to fund full-day kindergarten classes. This is a challenging situation since all three initiatives promote exemplary learning opportunities for students. It seems unfortunate that the discussion leads to pitting one good program against another.

Two textbooks, *Dancing with the Pen* (Ministry of Education 1992) and *Reading in Junior Classes* (Ministry of Education 1985), were recommended for each teacher working with a teacher leader. However, we did not have enough copies to go around, so it was difficult to use them to their full potential and to suggest further reading.

IMPLEMENTATION IN YEAR 3: THE 1995–1996 SCHOOL YEAR

In an attempt to offer all teachers in the district the opportunity to apply for the position of teacher leader, our associate superintendent negotiated another two-year contract with The Learning Network. Debate continues to ensue around extra salaries for release faculty and the other expenses, including the summer institute fees for the participants and contracted services for the program coordinator. One of the other teacher leaders and I agreed to go to a neighboring school for Year 3 of implementation. At the original school where all four of us had been housed, two teacher leaders stayed to support teachers who had chosen to continue in the process. At the new site, my teacher leader colleague and I shared one third-grade classroom and worked with a total of sixteen teachers in three different schools. We received a mixed reception from the teachers in the building. The principal and a vocal group of parents were very welcoming.

The third year proved to be a tremendous improvement over the previous year. There were five major differences: 1) we were working with teachers who had *requested* this form of professional development; 2) our meetings were more informal, with the teachers supplying the agendas; 3) when we left our classroom duties, the teacher who was in charge of the class was someone who had common beliefs and understandings about teaching and learning; 4) we had a more favorable work load. A new job called a mentor release position was created, which enabled teacher leaders to be released from classrooms for fifty percent of the day to work with teachers. During Year 2 our district filled one full-time mentor release position and during Year 3, two full-time mentor release positions; and 5) Jan was no longer observing alongside the teacher leaders, which reduced the anxiety level for those teachers who were working with teacher leaders.

RECOMMENDATIONS

There were several things that have kept the four of us teacher leaders moving forward: 1) our belief in the theory behind the model. We really believe that meeting the needs of all learners should be the foremost priority in our classrooms; 2) the abundance of current research articles which support our new understandings; 3) our strong feelings and high professional regard of our fellow teacher leaders; and 4) student learning outcomes. We are seeing evidence that students are becoming more invested in their own learning process through our new teaching practices. Our system now finds itself deeply involved in systemic change. We believe this model has been instrumental in opening conversations about change. There are eight recommendations that we teacher leaders propose to schools implementing The Learning Network:

1. Administrators should make a clear visionary statement regarding the implementation, including a time line and a commitment to the theories supported by this model. This must be communicated to the entire faculty, the teachers' union, the parents of the students involved, and to the general community.
2. Implementation should include a thorough investigation into the topic of educational change, including professional reading, attendance at conferences, and discussions with other educators in the same position.
3. Scheduling mandatory monthly meetings for the teachers working with teacher leaders should take precedence over all other training. These are in addition to the teacher leader focus meetings.
4. Requirements of the teacher leader position should be clearly described and agreed upon by the teachers' union, administration, and teachers.

5. Teacher leaders should be allotted enough release time from regular classroom responsibilities to fulfill the requirements of the job.
6. The expectations of the teachers involved with the teacher leaders should be clearly defined at the outset of the program.
7. Program coordinator observations of the teacher leader working with teachers should be prearranged.
8. All of the teachers working with teacher leaders should have easy access to copies of the texts *Dancing with the Pen* and *Reading in Junior Classes* and any other recommended resources for professional reading.

The vision of teacher leaders reflects our confidence that a common theory can be attained as we continue to read, dialogue, and reflect. We now realize that building a professional culture is a monumental task. Robert Evans suggests that this process "operates at a level that is very far below the surface, as a glacial movement that is very slow and meaningful" (1995). This process cannot be rushed. In Northampton, everyone involved in The Learning Network will continue to discuss and reflect upon our work on fragile relationships, refining and refocusing whenever necessary.

KATHY ITTERLY *is a second-grade teacher in Leeds School, a Learning Network site in Northampton, Massachusetts. She has been a teacher leader with The Learning Network since 1993. Kathy has written extensively about her experiences with change and collegial mentoring in Northampton School District with Nancy Allen, Betsy Conz, and Nancy Harrington. When she was first introduced to the Literacy Learning model she was teaching sixth grade.*

CHAPTER 4

The Critical Triangle

Deborah Backus

"Never doubt that a small group of committed people can change the world; indeed it is the only thing that ever has."

Margaret Mead

RECOGNIZING THE NEED

In 1988 I began what was to be the most exciting and satisfying period of my career. I had been selected to lead one of Aurora, Colorado's most challenging schools—a school facing the problems of urban demographics in a time of great public speculation about the effectiveness of public schooling itself. In my preparation for becoming principal of Montview Elementary, a kindergarten to fifth-grade school in Aurora, I began a very thoughtful and diligent process of getting to know my school (Stewart, Prebble, and Duncan 1997, 105), asking: "What strengths did we have? What are our next steps?"

As I explored the educational practices and outcomes of Montview, I began to understand that there was an undeniable connection between what each teacher knew and how well their students learned. My goal became to improve the outcome of that learning school wide. My next question to myself was: "How do we as a faculty increase learning?" The answer seemed simple: focus on developing effective instruction. However, I knew that there would be no miraculous cure; no trendy set of materials; no quick fix. The question then became: "How can I as principal lead my teachers toward self-improvement?" Therein lay the challenge that has fueled a passion for my professional life. That passion has now, nine years later, created a school with achievement data for literacy that exceeds that of most other schools in our district and quite possibly exceeds most across the nation.

CHANGE FROM THE OUTSIDE IN

Educators cannot continue to do things as we always have. Our profession carries as much responsibility to cure the ills of the intellect as the medical profession carries in its pursuit of treating physiological ailments. Would anyone consider using the services of a doctor who had not upgraded his or her skills or questioned his or her practice in the last several years? That question led the faculty at Montview to valuing professional development as paramount in our daily job performance.

In 1993, after five years of a professional development model focused on inservice days, faculty meetings, and attachments to weekly bulletins, which resulted in small increments of improved student achievement, we joined The Learning Network. We had come to realize that we needed a more comprehensive, job-embedded approach–an approach that focused on the individual teacher's needs and also addressed the needs of the school at large. It was then that I came to understand the power of the critical triangle: a team composed of the school's teacher leaders, the principal, and the program coordinator from The Learning Network.

ORIGIN OF THE CRITICAL TRIANGLE

The concept of the critical triangle (Figure 4.1) created by a school's principal, select members of the teaching staff, and an outside change agent originated in New Zealand. In 1990 the Ministry of Education of that country contracted Colleges of Education in Wellington, Christchurch, and Dunedin to implement and evaluate "Achieving Charter Curriculum Objectives," one of several teacher development programs, in 54 primary and eleven secondary schools. Data in the

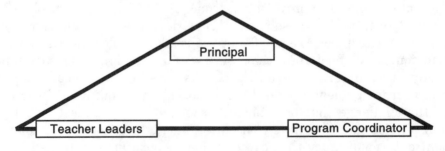

Figure 4.1. The critical triangle.

form of questionnaires, visits to schools, interviews with personnel, and an in-depth study of some of the Wellington schools were collected. In October of 1992 the project was summarized for the Ministry by J.K. Millar (1992).

The Role of the Principal

The evaluation of the data revealed many consistencies among all the schools involved in the initial implementation. The most telling were the findings relating to the working relationships of key personnel.

The findings of the evaluation indicate that the most important role in the ACCO project was played by the principal. The achievement of aims of the project was dependent on the principal's ability as a leader to involve all staff members, and provide ongoing practical support for the project (Millar 1992, 4).

In a Learning Network school, the principal is at the apex of the critical triangle. He or she needs to have a clear vision of the goals of the school and of the means to achieving those goals. The principal's responsibilities go beyond those of the traditional figurehead or administrative leader. The principal becomes an educational leader, actively involved in the teaching and learning that occurs in the school.

In a Learning Network school, the principal is expected to take an active role in the practices that are occurring in classrooms. He or she accompanies the program coordinator on every campus visit and participates in the cycle of observation and instructional dialogue that occurs between the program coordinator and each teacher leader, and also between the teacher leaders and the teachers. The principal provides opportunity for and engages in professional growth in the form of reading, attending institutes, and arranging for appropriate resources and support. He or she engages in conversations pertaining to educational theory and practice as a fellow educator, not as an evaluator.

The Role of the Outside Change Agent

The principal does not lead the school alone.

The findings [of ACCO] also suggest that the objectives of the programme were more readily achieved where the principal had collegial support both within and outside the school. The

College of Education coordinator, and a contact teacher se-
lected from the school staff, provided ... support regarded by
most of the principals as being of vital importance .... A com-
mon factor among schools which succeeded in achieving their
objectives was the strong professional relationship and mu-
tual respect which existed between these three key people (Mil-
lar 1992, 4).

A Learning Network program coordinator comes to a school expecting that change in the attitudes, understandings, and behaviors of
the administration, faculty, and students will occur. In Year 1 the program coordinator focuses on increasing the understandings and reflective practice of literacy teaching and learning of the teacher leaders
and of the principal. In Year 2 the focus shifts to leading the teacher
leaders to effective practice in working with other teachers.

I have learned that the involvement of an outside change agent, in
the case of The Learning Network a program coordinator who possesses deep knowledge of effective educational theory and practices in
literacy learning, is critical in empowering real change. It is the key to
the rigor necessary in stretching each professional to an expert instructional level and, without a doubt, it is that kind of precision teaching that leads us away from excuses and toward measurable achievement for all kinds of learners.

The Role of the Contact Teacher

The ACCO study reported that:

the contact teacher was the staff member in each school nomi-
nated to assume responsibility for the project, provide support
to staff members and operate as a first point of contact in rela-
tion to the project. The findings of the study suggest that ap-
propriate training should be given to those appointed to the
role of contact teacher (Millar 1992, 5).

In a Learning Network school, this key contact position is embod-
ied in the role of the teacher leader. Teacher leaders are selected by the
principal and faculty for their willingness to learn, their experience in
the classroom, and their ability to work with other teachers. To ensure
that teacher leaders will be able to support colleagues in examining

and changing their understandings and classroom practice, they receive intense contact from the outside change agent during the two years of formal involvement of The Learning Network. In most schools there are two teacher leaders who can support one another during and beyond the active involvement of the program coordinator. They are also part of a teacher leader class made up of other area teacher leaders that meets at least twice a month to further their professional dialogue, to offer one another support, and to continue their growth.

THE ROLE OF THE CRITICAL TRIANGLE

The research into the ACCO study suggested that the roles of the principal, the outside change agent, and the contact teachers are "interdependent, and the manner in which they interact determines the effectiveness of the project in that school" (Millar 1992, 69). In Montview, the critical triangle has become a support to solve our greatest challenges. The school has become, in Roland Barth's words, "collegial," rather than simply "congenial" (Barth 1990). Congenial faculties can be described as those who happily eat lunch together. Our faculty is one that together chews on the research for our professional nutrition and fulfillment, hence a deeper relationship, called "collegial." Key to this situation is the interaction of the elements of the triangle.

The Principal and the Program Coordinator

The relationship between the principal and the program coordinator is key to the success of The Learning Network. It needs to be at the same time respectful and friendly. The program coordinator has to understand that the principal may need to restructure responsibilities throughout the school to allow time for classroom visits. The principal has to understand the need for this restructuring and be willing to give up some of the "administrivia" that has traditionally fallen on his or her desk. In schools that have had "closed-door" policies both the program coordinator and the principal may be viewed as intruders into classrooms. They both need to make it clear that they are observing teachers, not to evaluate them, but to treat them as professionals with the capacity to improve their practice. The principal and the program coordinator may also need to join forces when communicating the goals of The Learning Network to the faculty, the school board, the parents, and the wider community. They may work together to create a new mission statement for a school or to arrange for a presentation about The Network. In all of their efforts, the principal and program coordinator must be communicating with one another so they can present a clear picture of where the school is going.

The Program Coordinator and the Teacher Leaders

As we look at the program coordinator/teacher leader side of the critical triangle the emergence of the leadership team becomes evident. The selection of teacher leaders, who will develop the skills of the rest of the faculty, determines the composition of the leadership team. On-going weekly meetings of this team determine the direction of the building, assess the effectiveness of both teacher and student learning, and measure the results in achievement data. The teacher leaders model a level of professionalism desired in all faculty. They serve as models of instructional expertise and passion for the profession as they develop the knowledge of the faculty.

It is within this part of the critical triangle that the plan for "self-windedness" emerges. After the formal involvement of The Learning Network and the regular visits from the program coordinator end, how will the faculty continue to grow in expertise; to develop understandings? It is the interaction between the program coordinator and each teacher leader that leads the teachers to deep understandings not only of theory and practice pertaining to teaching, but of the process of reflection itself. An effective program coordinator instills in teacher leaders the ability to both internalize questions about their understandings pertaining to teaching and learning and to ask these questions of others.

The Principal and the Teacher Leaders

The principal/teacher leader side of the critical triangle is, as I see it, the heart of the organizational conversation. The research of Linda Darling-Hammond (1993) and Ann Lieberman (1995) refers to this concept of ongoing conversation as the basis for any lasting reform in education. It must be building-based and embedded in teachers' own meaningful practice. The critical triangle creates and maintains this conversation as the core of the organization of the school. It requires a shift from thinking of the principal as "boss" and the teacher as "employee" to both thinking of each other as educational professionals charged with the responsibility of bringing the other teachers in the school to the same level of in-depth reflection and professional practice. This level of trust is developed through regular conversations in many forms. When conversation occurs regularly and leadership responsibility is shared, ownership is the result. This builds a climate based on shared purpose within a community of learners.

At Montview, administrators and teacher leaders meet with one another weekly. In Year 1 and 2 the program coordinator attended these meetings monthly to assess the effectiveness, depth, and focus on important issues and long-term building direction. Now the movement is self-directed.

RESEARCH INTO PRACTICE

As I reflect on my past four years in The Learning Network, I believe the most important feature of the organization is the critical triangle. It is the basis upon which rigor is thrust upon the school. It provides the environment of challenge that forces the school toward systemic change that stays. It creates and models a new culture of shared responsibility and ownership. In the years preceding our participation in The Learning Network we made small changes, but we had not developed the culture to support change. We had not developed a core leadership team nor committed to the level of rigor that an outside change agent working over time within a school provokes.

Ted Sizer, founder of the Coalition of Essential Schools, and Richard Elmore, co-director of the Consortium for Polity Research in Education and professor at Harvard, state in their interview, "Changing the Conversation" (1996):

> *The real question is how do you get teachers engaged in long term improvement of pedagogical practice? The best way to learn is by teaching in an increasingly reflective way and by being engaged with peers around problems of practice. If we created workplaces where people could thrive, we would see a dramatic change in the makeup of the teaching force and in the performance of students. Reading a book and having no one to talk with about it or teaching a class that no one else sees is a recipe for mediocrity.*

Elmore goes on to state "we are where we are because of an absence of faculty development, administrative structures and school organization that are designed to maintain this conversation over a career."

In the history of education, the late twentieth century is a time of great emphasis on shared decision making and site-based management. The principal/teacher leader arm of the critical triangle is a natural beginning. Through the consultation of the program coordinator in taking this team to a rigorous level of skill, the school is left with a leadership team that demonstrates a standard of expertise, professionalism, and best practice.

THE FEEL OF THE CRITICAL TRIANGLE

The program coordinator at Montview was Jan Duncan. Each visit from Jan would leave me in a state of disrepair, although perhaps a better term might be *repair* because, after the initial shock was over, I would take a deep, objective look at what we as a faculty knew and needed to know, where we had come from, and where we needed to go next. The feeling was both invigorating and intimidating. I grew to greatly respect our program coordinator, but in that feeling always lurked my fear of disappointing her. I would observe her questioning the teacher leaders–probing the understandings that lay beneath their instructional decisions. Furiously I recorded these interchanges, marveling at the depth of introspection and the excitement of the "aha" moment, when new learning occurred. At that moment I could see the relaxation and sheer delight in the teacher's face, as if she had come through some kind of metamorphosis. A renewed energy and sense of competence welled up from within; a drive to jump back into instruction with personal and professional renewal.

And then it would be my turn. Jan and I would walk through classrooms examining practices, she asking me to determine the understandings that drove them. Together we would observe the energy and activity in the media center. Was it the literary heartbeat of the school? How did I assess that? We would analyze the print that dripped from the walls in the corridors. What did I see there and within it? What understandings did it reflect in the faculty and in the students? She never told anyone, including me, any answers; she only asked and asked and asked those hard questions. I remember especially in the beginning wanting to answer those questions correctly–to say what Jan wanted to hear. Then, over time, I began to understand that there were no right answers. Jan wasn't asking those questions to hear a specific response. She was asking them to get to the understandings in my head. She recognized that my developing understandings were on a continuum and that it was her job to continue them.

Jan Duncan brought me to a new vision of my role as principal. She set a new standard for me as an instructional leader. She would intimidate me and question me and challenge me and exhaust me and help me to reach professional heights that I never knew existed. I have come to understand the depths of knowledge I am responsible for leading this team of professionals toward and I have discovered the fact that "there is no there, there" because there is always more to know. I emerged from this two-year experience a different teacher and a different leader.

BUILDING THE LEADERSHIP TEAM

As my understandings and the understandings of the teacher leaders began to develop together we found great energy at our meetings. An air of friendly challenge would frequently exist as we discussed our shared and personal reading and explore new ideas together. As our confidence in our own learning grew, we began to expand our circle. We were ready to bring other teachers into the process. Our conversations often urged us to present an article to the faculty or a question or issue to a team of educators for dialogue, and other faculty members began to come to the group with their own "I wonder" questions.

One such conversation occurred regarding "play" in kindergarten. Our kindergarten classrooms look much the same as any other classroom in the school. We had long since eliminated play houses and had students moving along the reading and writing continuums during their half-day programs. One kindergarten teacher suggested from some reading that she had done that we really should reconsider our practices. Was our program supporting the developmental needs of our five-year-olds? Rather than the leadership team simply making a decision, we brought this issue to all of our primary faculty for full dialogue. We believed all were stakeholders in the decision. We had shared reading which included a variety of authors, such as Lev Vygotsky and Marie Clay, to come to a deeper understanding of the definition for and the importance of play in the school day. Our learning did not stop with a simple decision about whether or not to have play houses in kindergarten classrooms. We also came to greater clarity in knowing what is developmentally appropriate and what is individually appropriate. We came to focus on the learner.

What differed from conversations about classroom practice that might have gone on before Montview's involvement in The Learning Network was both the atmosphere in which it took place and the actual outcome. The members of the critical triangle had been modeling the possibilities for in-depth examination of current classroom practice in a setting that was supportive rather than invasive. Teachers were coming to see challenges to their practice as opportunities to improve professionally. We and they were also learning to question educational practices. Instead of simply jumping on a new bandwagon and restoring play houses to kindergarten rooms or ignoring the issue and continuing our practice as before, as we might have done in the past, we examined the issue with the needs of the learners in mind. We asked ourselves difficult "why" questions. We wondered together about our expected outcomes for kindergarten students.

The faculty involved emerged from this month-long discussion with new understandings both about the specific topic and about their role in their own professional development. The collegial climate established by the existence of the critical triangle was intact. We all knew the importance of fact–that this development had occurred in a research-and-discussion setting. It had helped us all to focus on the issue, not on the people involved. It reminded us to always use research, rather than opinion, as the basis for our decisions about practice, and to always open questions to dialogue.

What now characterizes the faculty at Montview is collective dialogue. Teachers' work is now anchored in the environment in which they practice: the classroom. Work can be defined as that learning which we encourage students to do, and that which we expect of ourselves as a natural responsibility to our profession and to ourselves as models of life-long learning. A culture of professional questioning had developed, an indicator of our self-windedness, the core of which has been established with the critical triangle. Through the support of the critical triangle the members of the faculty can now describe those children experiencing difficulty learning to read and write as temporarily tangled, not handicapped. Teachers are familiar with the teaching and learning cycle and see its value. Still, the learning is not over. The teacher leaders and I continue to challenge the faculty to bring us all to higher knowledge and greater expertise, just as Jan as our program coordinator once did.

Much of what occurs in schools today is based on what individual educators–teachers *and* administrators–believe. Unfortunately, it has been my experience that practice is based too often on "What I think I understood" or "What works best for me" rather than sound theory. That is unacceptable. Students' needs are paramount. If we are to significantly impact student achievement and rise to the challenge of educating all children to high levels of competence, we can no longer allow ourselves the luxury of being driven by what is most comfortable for us. We must look deeply at the child–what the learner knows, what comes next, and how to best get the learner there. I now know that the labels educators have used to define the needs of children (poverty, ESL, SPED, single parent, minority) had stalled our efforts and distracted us from meeting the real challenges that lie beyond the labels. They became a barrage of excuses and defenses for our lack of sound instructional knowledge, energy, and commitment as a profession of educators.

Great truths do exist in education. There are more effective ways than others to teach reading and writing. And like all professions, ours is one in which new knowledge is constantly discovered. The teacher as practitioner, like the doctor, must take his or her responsibility to act competently to assist the child toward greater knowledge each day. It can be done and has been done.

As I reflect on my journey I can say that it has been the most profound professional experience I have ever undertaken. I have exceeded my own expectations of myself because I was fortunate and brave enough to open myself to one of the greatest teachers of all time. And perhaps the most profound understanding that I developed was to realize that she simply knew instruction in a deep and significant way. She has instilled in me a standard for all teaching, one that every child has a right to, one I was not even aware of.

The critical triangle was for me then, and today four years later remains, a resource that continues to develop my leadership skills. As The Network has grown so has its services. It now includes a leadership seminar inspired and developed by Peter Duncan, who has become a mentor as he challenges me to reflect upon my leadership practices. I now ask myself the important questions: "Why I am doing what I am doing?" "What structures are in place to accomplish my mission?" "How effective are they?" Without the critical triangle–without that interaction of me as instructional leader, the teacher leaders as effective instructional practitioners, and Jan as the program coordinator leading us to new understandings–I believe I would still be living a role as a building manager charged with the responsibility of putting out fires. Now I spend my time lighting them and there is an incredible difference!

I often wonder if the "whole language" movement would have been so miserably misunderstood and so poorly practiced had those of us in the field used a critical triangle concept to develop understandings of pedagogy, rather than simply attempting to replicate practices without understandings to guide us. Now we can. It is not our time to waste. The time belongs to our children.

DEBORAH BACKUS *has been the principal of Montview Elementary School, a Learning Network site in Aurora, Colorado, for nine years. She has also served as an administrative trainer for The Learning Network. Prior to coming to Colorado she was a teacher and educational diagnostician in Massachusetts and Illinois.*

CHAPTER 5

The Role of the Principal

Ben Carson

*"I never realized how important the apex of the critical
triangle really is. You have to be very strong and you have to
believe this will make a difference in kids' lives."*

Claudette Gronski
Principal, Phoenix, Arizona

The role of the principal in a Learning Network school cannot be described in detail in a single chapter, only in general terms and by way of actions. The role is one of communication and of facilitating, but mostly it is one of setting up conditions for learning (Cambourne 1988). The principal's role is distinctive, for it encompasses far more than traditional expectations. The principal must become a learner, an observer, a listener, a teacher, and a keeper of the vision that all children can and will become readers and writers.

When schools join The Learning Network, the principal signs a Declaration of Support (see Figure 5.1). I know from past experience how challenging it can be to adhere to the Declaration. Principals fill many roles and often find it difficult to define their behavior so specifically. In the last few years I have learned the importance of the Declaration.

I am currently a principal at Hutto Elementary School, a Learning Network site in Hutto, Texas. I was first introduced to The Learning Network and the Literacy Learning model when I was principal at Flatonia Elementary School in Flatonia, Texas. Both schools were involved in teacher leader training in The Learning Network from 1993 through 1995.

PRINCIPAL'S DECLARATION OF SUPPORT

I understand that as the principal of _____, a Learning Network site, I will:

1. Actively support The Learning Network as the focus for teacher development.

2. Devote professional faculty meetings to the content of The Learning Network.

3. Attend focus meetings and make myself available for classroom observations and instructional dialogue with the program coordinator on each monthly visit or when the program coordinator is on campus.

4. Attend the Literacy Learning in the Classroom summer institute with the teacher leaders prior to implementation of The Learning Network.

5. Send teacher leaders to the summer institute.

6. Send all teachers who will be working with teacher leaders to the summer institute.

7. Attend and send teacher leaders to The Learning Network conference starting in Year 2.

8. Meet with teacher leaders on a weekly basis and be available for classroom observation as needed.

9. Maintain the guidelines for determining the number of teachers who can be supported by each teacher leader by providing appropriate release time.

10. Actively support teacher leaders in the commitments specified in the teacher leader declaration.

11. Incorporate my evolving understanding of the Literacy Learning model into my interactions with the program coordinator, faculty, students, and learning community.

12. Work toward a personal goal of becoming a life-long learner and a school goal of developing a community of learners.

_____   _____
signature   date

Figure 5.1. Principal's Declaration of Support, © 1997 by Richard C. Owen Publishers, Inc.

IN THE BEGINNING

As an elementary principal and an elementary classroom teacher, I have seen countless literacy programs, all promising (if not guaranteeing) student success. Most came packaged with complete instructions which, as the directions implied, would make my life as an educator much easier. The most troublesome "package" was the basal reader. It outlined everything that I was supposed to do. Solutions were readily available in the teacher's manual for all the problems one might encounter. The problem was that the teacher's manual did all of the thinking. I just followed directions. I failed to recognize my worth as a teacher and the value of my professional judgment. I was not encouraged to learn or to question. The basal was "teacher proof" (Goodman et al. 1988).

As a teacher, I used the basal every way I knew, but the "high" kids stayed "high" and the "low" kids stayed "low," and of course I bought into the assumption that if a child did not make progress, there was something "wrong" with the child. He or she needed a special program to bolster achievement. After all, I had done my job, hadn't I? Deep down, though, I knew that there had to be a better way. Many of my students were learning to make sense of text, but it wasn't because of what I was doing in the classroom. I needed to know how to help *all* of my students. What was missing?

That question remained in my head as I moved into the principal's position at Flatonia Elementary School. Here I observed the same problems with literacy instruction that I had experienced, only on a much broader scale. The solutions remained static: identify the problem and prescribe a program to "fix" the child. We tried phonics, recorded books, thematic units, special education classes, and so on. What I needed was an opportunity to break this "fix the child" pattern.

In the spring of 1992 it came: a flyer about a "Whole Language in the Classroom" workshop, presented from a New Zealand perspective. As a leader of a Texas Partnership School Initiative (PSI) school, I felt it was my duty to explore every opportunity for my faculty to learn, but I was hesitant. I wanted some assurance that what we would be looking at had some proof of success. I didn't relish the thought of experimenting with students, including my own children. However, the workshop these teachers were interested in attending proclaimed a connection to New Zealand. The words New Zealand were the key. New Zealand teachers had been successful; rated as offering the best literacy instruction in the world (Burns 1991). Finally, I decided that it was worth a try and signed up two teachers. They could come back and let me know if it was worth it, and if it was, I would have them teach the other teachers "how to do it."

Then Joe Parks intervened. Joe was Executive Director of the Regional Education Service Center in Austin and well-known throughout Texas as an innovative leader. As executive director, Joe had taken personal control of Partnership Schools. In his wisdom, he recognized the importance of hands-on administrative involvement in education. He offered PSI administrators an opportunity to attend any training anywhere in the U.S. My decision was easy. I did what I instinctively knew I needed to do: be involved with what I asked of my faculty. Thus began a journey that continues today and into tomorrow as I consider each element of the Declaration of Support as it relates to my practice.

My First Institute

> 4. Attend the Literacy Learning in the Classroom summer institute with the teacher leaders prior to implementation of The Learning Network.

In the summer of 1992 I attended the first of what now totals six summer institutes. One of the most important lessons I have learned about being a leader is the necessity of having a knowledge base; of absorbing everything that I can; of understanding so that I can model for my learners; and of reflecting on where I have been and where I might venture next. The institute provided me with an added shot in the arm.

It was on Day 2 of my first institute that my attention suddenly focused. A statement from Margaret Hayes, a facilitator from New Zealand, in response to a question about special education programs changed my whole demeanor. The question concerned alternate placements for children who were not successful with the "New Zealand" approach. What caused the commotion was Margaret's matter-of-fact response: "Our teachers take the responsibility for a child being successful. It's our job to find out what's right for the child, not the child's responsibility to adapt to us. The answers lie in careful assessment and planning." I began to realize that New Zealand's approach to literacy development was nothing like "whole language" as described by educators in the United States. I had to know more.

I asked questions at every opportunity. How was this model organized? What did a day in the classroom look like? What materials did you use? How did you evaluate children and teachers? Looking back, I realize that I was convinced it was the *how* that made the difference. I did not yet recognize the significance of knowing *why* things were done.

On the third day the discussion got around to the resources used in reading instruction. We talked about supports and challenges and a topic I was certainly not used to considering: a child's strengths. Could these resources really be that effective or even that different from what we already had in our classrooms? A teacher who had visited New Zealand must have read the doubt in my eyes. With a little background knowledge from me, she selected several short books and gave me some simple directions to try with my daughter, who would be entering first grade, when I went home that evening. "You'll see," she said. That night, I sat down with Alisa and began with the statement, "I want you to read these books with me." Alisa trusted her daddy or she wouldn't have tried. We began. I introduced the book and we read it together. Then I said, "Now you read it to me." She looked at me with a weak smile and began. She worked through the brief text slowly and hesitantly at first. I gave her some encouraging remarks and reminders of how she could create meaning. I heard myself ask for the first time "Does that make sense?" "Does it sound right?" She finished the first book. "Let's try the next book," I said. Eagerly she jumped in and almost flawlessly went through the book. At the end she stopped and looked up at me, and her smile said volumes. "Go read to Grandma," I said, and she was a reader.

When it's your child, something like this hits home. It grabs your attention like nothing else. Of course I knew that it was not always this easy, but my background told me that this approach made sense, it was logical, and most importantly it was a proven process. What would my two first-grade teachers think?

A Journey's Beginning: Fall 1992

The fall of 1992 brought a refresher course and an opportunity to hear another New Zealander talk about literacy, and talk she did, with a strength and clarity of purpose that made understanding seem easy. She spoke that day about asking ourselves as educators *why* we did things a certain way. She could articulate why and she challenged us to do the same. Jan Duncan would forever change my understanding of teaching. I left that meeting full of energy, but with one nagging observation. There were hundreds of educators present, but I was one of only a handful of administrators. How would principals know what their teachers were about? How would they support this magnitude of change?

My introduction to The Learning Network was through the summer institute. Because I have experienced for myself the power of the institute and the questions it raises, I strongly support teacher leaders, teachers, and administrators attending not just once, but as many times as possible. Each time I attend, I hear things in a different way based on my past year's learning. I am renewed and eager to start the school year.

In the spring of 1993 came the much-needed guidance from the same people who had created the powerful institute. Flatonia joined The Learning Network, which was in its infancy. Support consisted of monthly visits from a program coordinator. Donna Byrum was a refreshing voice. She dialogued with teachers all day and sometimes later. She listened, she suggested, and often she challenged. She became my confidant in developing my role as an instructional leader. We spent hours dialoguing. I also spent a lot of time with the faculty. My responsibility was to ensure that "administrivia" such as procedural issues and paperwork were handled in the most efficient manner possible, such as through memos, so that the faculty and I could use most of our time together to concentrate on instructional issues. We talked, we speculated, and we disagreed, but mostly we just kept trying to figure out the *how*. We tried, but we never knew if we were headed in the right direction or were entirely off base. Something was missing.

RECOGNIZING A POWERFUL MODEL OF TEACHER DEVELOPMENT

Concerns about effective training had become a real issue. My observations of the faculty showed me that little or no change was occurring. So I reflected, first back to my days as a teacher. I thought about the training that I had received. What was the result of that training? Did it stay with me? Did it cause a change in my teaching? The answer to these questions was no. What was wrong? We attended top-rated training. Still, we could not affect long-term change.

The Learning Network recognized that something was missing too. At this time Jan Duncan was working in Easthampton, Massachusetts, Aurora, Colorado, and Phoenix, Arizona, refining understandings and practices. New ideas were being formulated about The Learning Network. At a meeting with Richard Owen, Jan, and Donna, I learned about the plans for setting up a structure for formal, long-term teacher development—development that would result in the Literacy Learning model being implemented throughout my school. The meeting was lively, serious, and in the end very productive. I remember that Jan and Richard had a structure very much in mind, but I also had some critical concerns to address. As was her nature, Jan would ask why and I would respond. She and Richard would make their point and I mine.

I knew that professionally I could be going out on a limb with this venture. Although the process they described made sense, I knew that change doesn't happen very easily in education in the U.S. and logic doesn't often play a key role. What I believe finally brought us together was and is an unbending belief in doing what is best for children. I agreed that the new system of the program coordinator working intensively with two teacher leaders would begin in the fall.

IMPLEMENTING THE LEARNING NETWORK

> 6. Send all teachers who will be working with teacher leaders to the summer institute.

In the summer of 1993 the whole staff attended the institute. This provided an opportunity to prepare both the staff and myself, and it gave us an introduction to the theory. As principal, I understand that allowing my faculty to concentrate on slowly increasing their understandings and ability to reflect on their practice rather than jumping from inservice to inservice and practice to practice is the most effective way to implement lasting change.

That fall there were three Texas schools involved in the training. Each school had to select teacher leaders–those teachers who would learn about this model in their own classrooms and eventually be responsible for bringing the rest of the faculty along in their understandings. Based on my own experience, I supported the criteria for the selection of teacher leaders established by The Network: 1) they needed to have significant classroom experience; 2) they needed to be respected by and have credibility with the staff; 3) they needed to be committed to the district for the long term; 4) they needed to fully understand the time and commitment that would be required for the initial two years and beyond; and, perhaps most importantly, 5) they had to be willing to change, to make significant paradigm shifts (Richard C. Owen Publishers 1995a). A close working relationship with the principal would also be essential.

> 3. Attend focus meetings and make myself available for classroom observations and instructional dialogue with the program coordinator on each monthly visit or when the program coordinator is on campus.

My relationship with the program coordinator would also have to be strong, for it is here that the critical triangle would take shape. My whole schedule would need to adjust, especially when the program coordinator was on campus. This is the opportunity for the principal to gain deep understandings of both the Literacy Learning model and the process of facilitating change in teachers' classroom practice. I would need to shadow the program coordinator everywhere she went; to observe, to question, to listen, and to learn why. She would be my guide for coming to understandings of this process. Then I would be able to approximate my understandings with the faculty and come back to dialogue with the program coordinator to check my understandings.

> 11. Incorporate my evolving understanding of the Literacy Learning model into my interactions with the program coordinator, faculty, students, and learning community.

The critical triangle of principal, teacher leaders, and program coordinator is an essential element of implementation of The Learning Network. My role in the triangle is to grow in my own understandings of effective classroom practice so that I can support the teacher leaders and teachers. To do so I need to be involved in discussions pertaining to instruction, both in and out of the classroom, and to observe the program coordinator bringing teacher leaders to new understandings through reflection.

Working alongside the program coordinator has enabled me to see my school from a different point of view. The program coordinator is in my school once a month. I clear my calendar to work alongside her as she observes in the teacher leaders' classrooms. I watch her interactions with the teacher leaders as they observe the teachers they work alongside and conduct instructional dialogue. I internalize what I can as I observe the tiered dialogue between the teacher leader and the program coordinator that follows. I value the honesty of the program coordinator as she shares what she sees as our strengths as a faculty and is open about the direction we must take next. She continually asks me to reflect about what I see for this school in the future. She helps me, as the principal, articulate my vision for what can be and provides me with suggestions and strategies to make the vision a reality.

I share my enthusiasm of this vision with the faculty, who through their skillfulness as teachers are key to making this change happen. The sharing does not stop here. There is tremendous pride from the parents and community regarding the successes this school has experienced. We have had three hundred visitors come through our school this year, and the tour guides are parents. In order to share our successes and our vision, parents have to have a strong understanding of the process. We spend much time communicating this understanding through parent meetings, visits to the classrooms, and parent/teacher conferences.

My personal professional growth also took a significant step forward. I had always read professionally, but never with as much focus. My reading took on new meaning. It became a direct connection to what was happening in the classrooms in my school. As the year progressed, I would read, observe, and reread a text, each time coming to a new understanding. I became more and more connected to the literacy process. My success provided the impetus to start professional reading with the faculty. If this is not already a habit with teachers, it can be difficult to get started because it may be seen as simply another duty with no direct benefit to the teacher's daily needs. I bought every resource they requested and more.

---

8. Meet with the teacher leaders on a weekly basis and be available for classroom observation as needed.

The teacher leaders and I meet weekly to see where we are. I may act as a sounding board for concerns or a springboard for new learning. More importantly, we're together to plan the clear direction of what we need to do next as a school. We plan staff development based on the assessment samples we have evaluated. Regular interactions allow us to develop a common language and a level of comfort in working with one another.

The most important proficiencies I acquired as an instructional leader were observing and dialoguing. Observation for the purpose of teacher development is not the traditional summative evaluation I had done as a principal in the past. In Learning Network schools, observation goes beyond noting what the teacher says and does to watching the teacher's students. The behavior I see in students reflects the understandings of the teacher. If the students know why they are doing what they are doing, I know that the teacher can also articulate his or her understandings. From there I can identify new learning steps that I want to address with the teacher. I came to value this instructional dialogue as a vehicle for guiding teachers to new understandings–to know what drives their practice; to be able to articulate why they do what they do. In addition, when a principal exhibits these behaviors and understandings for the teacher, teachers will see the principal as the model of the learner that they are expected to be.

Not every aspect of administering The Learning Network proved to be as fulfilling or positive. Funding became an issue. Anticipated sources fell short. The district superintendent suddenly resigned. It tested my resolve. I had to be sure that money was available for The Network, attendance at the summer institute, and for the purchase of a wide array of literature for children. Through some creative restructuring of Title I funds and other prioritizing, funds were temporarily secured, although they would continue to be a problem over the next few years.

One challenge for the teacher leaders was that they couldn't see where we were going or just what the process looked like. Could someone really be successful at this? What does a classroom look like? How did the children behave? As learners, teachers need to see demonstrations, frequently and from knowledgeable sources (Cambourne 1988). It helps them make sense of their world, which at this point is turning upside down. It was an issue that could not be solved then, but certainly has a solution now. Site visits to Network schools allow teachers and administrators see the process in place and observe skillful teachers in their classrooms.

> 7. Attend and send teacher leaders to The Learning Network conference starting in Year 2.

The Learning Network conference is a powerful opportunity to share experiences with other educators who have been through the good and the bad times of this model. It gives participants the chance to further their own learning about both instructional and procedural issues in The Network. Attendance at The Learning Network conference gives teachers and teacher leaders a chance to attend sessions offered by educators from other Learning Network schools. Accessing Learning Network communication vehicles on the Internet also provides opportunities for all educators to continue the discussions throughout the year.

> 9. Maintain the guidelines for determining the number of teachers who can be supported by each teacher leader by providing appropriate release time.

The teacher leaders were also concerned initially with being out of their classrooms so much. It's a legitimate concern, but answered when they realize that the increased expertise the teachers take back to the classroom far outweighs the lost instructional time. They also had questions about evaluation. The teacher leaders must feel free to explore and approximate and not feel as though they are being held to a level of perfection or judged on what they don't know. Most importantly, the principal must understand the teachers' feelings when they are letting go of the known and venturing into the unknown. It can be a frightening thing.

I know that the teaching and learning cycle is as valid for adult learning as it is for student learning. I need to assess and evaluate my learners before I plan and teach, or I run the risk of challenging them too much or not challenging them enough. To keep the process moving forward I need to ensure that teachers, students, administrators, parents, the school board, and the wider community are all communicating with one another, and I do so by knowing them all as my learners.

Perhaps the most important revelation for me during that year was an understanding of the frustrating, teeth-grinding question "Why?" Jan says it best: "For American teachers, it's a threatening question. They think it means they're doing something wrong. But that's not it at all. The purpose is to get them to articulate the theory that is driving their practice." It was a major step for me. At last I was able to see that the focus on *why* is so much more important than the search for answers to *what* and *how*.

Fall 1995

By the fall of 1995 we had completed the two years of formal involvement in The Network. I had become principal at Hutto, one of the original Learning Network schools in Texas. We had two teacher leaders eagerly continuing their own professional development and attempting to support colleagues. One roadblock to expanding The Learning Network at Hutto was lack of adequate time for the teacher leaders to spend in the classrooms working with teachers. Without daily planned time to work with teachers, progress was at a snail's pace and many teachers were left frustrated.

My experience in Hutto proved to me that this intense a model of teacher development is simply not possible when limited to lunch, planning periods, and after school. Observation and instructional dialogue during the teaching day is crucial in furthering teachers' growth. As principal, I have to take the responsibility for guaranteeing sufficient release time to ensure that each teacher receives the in-depth attention required from the teacher leader to become reflective. This may mean reallocating funds or support staff or finding new resources through grants.

Progress also brings about new needs. In Hutto the teachers' growing understandings about materials with charm, magic, impact, and appeal created needs far beyond the capabilities of our original resource room. We needed a highly organized instructional resource room that would be well-supplied with materials for shared, guided, and independent reading with a range of emergent, early, and fluent readers. In 1996 we moved the resource room to an ample space adjacent to the library. We set up the structure of the resource room to reflect our understandings of approaches and levels (see Chapter 15) and we took inventory. One useful outcome of the new organization was the information we gathered about coverage. We discovered gaps where we had few appropriate resources. Identifying the gaps has helped us to shape our buying policy. Now we know how to determine our needs for particular resources and how to go about improving the resource room for all teachers.

I make it a point to reflect on our progress. Teachers in Hutto have gained a great deal of professional expertise and pride. They are making instructional decisions based on their assessments and evaluations of their learners. They, not a teacher's manual or a scope-and-sequence chart, determine each student's next learning step. They know what a child-centered curriculum is and how to put it into practice. Teachers are learners, dialoguing with one another about what they have learned and want to learn.

> 12. Work toward a personal goal of becoming a life-long learner and a school goal of developing a community of learners.

I see myself as a learner. I attend Literacy Learning institutes, The Learning Network conferences, and instructional dialogue sessions expecting to be challenged, and I value those challenges as the means to further my reflection and growth. I read and reread professional resources to discover meaning that was not available to me before. I want the students in my school to be life-long learners who know that reading is the creation of meaning, writing is about communication, and that they will succeed as readers and writers. I want our students to internalize their own ability to determine why they are doing what they are doing, to identify what they do well and what they are ready to learn next, and to know how to find the resources they need to take that step.

> 1. Actively support The Learning Network as the focus for teacher development.
> 2. Devote professional faculty meetings to the content of The Learning Network.

At Hutto the focus of our professional development this year has been through the development of a policy statement on spelling. During faculty meetings, we have come to grips with a collective vision of what we want our students to look like as spellers when they leave this school. We have defined our beliefs about spelling, read the research, and re-defined our beliefs. We have determined how the spelling practices in our school will look and how we must monitor the growth of our students over time. This process has taken time and effort, but it has been given priority as we strengthen our commitment and solidify our theory of learning.

> 5. I will send teacher leaders to the summer institute.

I am always surprised by the enthusiasm with which the teacher leaders and I return to the institute each year. That enthusiasm is contagious. Taped to the office counter at Hutto is a list of twenty-one names of teachers who have once again chosen to attend the Literacy

Learning in the Classroom summer institute; many for the third time. We make every effort at this school to find the funds for teachers to attend the institute. The more teachers who attend, the more we bring back to the staff.

CONTINUING THE COMMITMENT

My job now is to maintain the environment where this growth can take place and to provide the support and encouragement to see that it continues. One document I return to again and again is the "Principal's Declaration of Support." I know now what it means to actively support and commit to this teacher development initiative. Each point this document makes has been borne out by my experiences in Flatonia and Hutto.

These experiences will bring new learning to the staff at Hutto. In some cases, we will simply tweak our understandings, and in other cases we will be learning something new for the first time. I have learned the lesson that I heard for the first time from Jan Duncan: "When you're green, you grow. When you're ripe, you rot." Stay green and growing.

Ben Carson is the principal at Hutto Elementary, a Learning Network site in Hutto, Texas. He has been involved with The Learning Network for five years. He has been a principal for nine years and was a classroom teacher in second, third, and fifth grades for ten years.

CHAPTER 6

The Role of the Teacher Leader

Peggy Iannella Grubel

"Just when you think you're there, there's no there, there."

Gertrude Stein

I am presently in the second year as a teacher leader and my seventh year as a teacher at Madison Park School, a third- through eighth-grade multicultural school in Phoenix, Arizona. Half of my day is spent working with teachers. I observe them in their classrooms and dialogue with them, helping them to move toward greater understandings of the reading and writing processes. The other half of the day I spend with my multi-age third- and fourth-grade class, increasing my own learning as their language arts teacher.

LEARNING TO JUGGLE

At some point during my first year as a teacher leader I saw a similarity between the development of my new understandings and learning to juggle as a child. I remember when my older brother tried to teach me the art of juggling one summer afternoon. He brought out a bucket of oranges and demonstrated how to flip just one up in the air, rotating from hand to hand. Then he threw an orange to me. After a few tries I began to get the hang of it. We moved up to two oranges. This was tricky. Timing seemed to be everything. If I went too slowly my hand was not there to pass the orange on. If I tried to rush the process, the oranges met in a sticky midair collision. Yet there were moments when my timing, rhythm, and immature understanding of juggling all came together. Suddenly the oranges seemed to propel themselves effortlessly through the air. At other times keeping up the pace of passing the fruit through my hands overwhelmed me. Over and over again I dropped an orange or two, slowed the rhythm down, and started again. By the end of the afternoon I could easily juggle two and tentatively juggle three oranges at a time.

That day marked the beginning and end of my juggling career, yet the image seems to be the perfect metaphor for my evolution as a teacher leader. There were times when the new learning meshed easily with my other practices. Frequently, though, my new understandings did not come so easily. Many sticky midair collisions occurred along the way, when everything was dropped momentarily. At those times I've remembered to take a deep breath, regroup, and slowly juggle the new learning into my daily practice.

NEW UNDERSTANDINGS

When I first heard about The Learning Network I had no idea what it was or what teacher leaders did. I had been teaching for about seventeen years. My reading of Donald Graves (1983), Nancie Atwell (1987), and Lucy Calkins (1986) had influenced the way I approached the teaching of writing; and I had been using the writing workshop model in my own classroom, first as a seventh- and eighth-grade language arts teacher, and then as a third-grade teacher, for the past six years. I had no idea what the "Literacy Learning model" was; nor did I have any familiarity with New Zealand educators, other than seeing their names cited in the American books on writing that I had been studying. At one of our district's language arts task force meetings, our assistant superintendent, Kay Coleman, invited Marilyn Herzog to speak. Marilyn was then a half-time multi-age first- and second-grade teacher and a teacher leader for The Learning Network at Las Brisas Elementary School. As Marilyn spoke about teaching that was student driven rather than curriculum driven; about accurately knowing where the learners were in terms of their reading and writing, and then taking them to their next learning steps; about gathering and pooling resources for students so that teachers could have a variety of materials from which to choose for each learning step; I began to get excited. I recognized the pieces that were missing in my own teaching. I couldn't contain my enthusiasm. I went back and talked to my grade-level teammates. We all seemed to have that hunger to tighten up our teaching practice–to really know our learners–but we didn't know how to get there.

Both our principal and assistant principal, after observing several staff and literacy development programs, had come back to our school's site-based management committee to recommend The Learning Network as the optimal school-wide model for development. The committee decided to adopt it and I was delighted to be selected, along with three others from our school, to be trained as teacher leaders for the 1995-1996 school year.

I remember the fear and excitement I felt as I tried to put together what I was hearing and seeing with my personal experience in the classroom while attending the Literacy Learning in the Classroom summer institute for the first time in 1995. After each general session, groups of teachers would huddle together, talking about how we could put some of the ideas into practice. By the fourth day my head ached from the effort of trying to assimilate so much new information. I was disturbed as well by the discomfort of disequilibrium–a pain that was to become familiar.

I wanted to become a more effective teacher, but did that mean I had to let go of some of my previous ideas about good teaching? My colleagues were asking the same question. Each of us had our own Achilles heel–that aspect of our teaching to which we were holding tight. For me, it was the idea of requiring students to always begin their writing with a plan. For one of my colleagues it was changing her spelling program. This was the beginning of the difficult, even painful, process of letting go of old habits. There were always justifications for continuing as I had always taught. Yet there were also the questions "Why am I doing what I am doing?" and "Is this the best teaching practice?" I clenched my teeth and wrote my first action plan: Set up draft book standards with two other teachers in my grade level. One of those standards stated that all students would begin a new piece of writing with a plan.

During the weeks before school started I got together with my grade level teammates, Dori Pollack and Sandy James. We collaborated on draft book standards, on the setup of our monitoring notebook, and on rubrics for revision and editing conferences. We discussed how we wanted our lesson plans for language arts to look. When school began I felt confident.

When the program coordinator, Marilyn Herzog, came to observe me the first time, I remember thinking, "She won't have much to teach me in the writing area." After all, I had been using a writing workshop model for several years. My ego was gently deflated during our instructional dialogue when Marilyn asked me why I was doing editing conferences in small groups. I sputtered. I justified. I paused. What was I accomplishing? It dawned on me that it wasn't the most effective way. Meeting with each student individually for an editing conference, helping each one to his or her next learning step, and going on to someone else certainly made much more sense in terms of management and effective teaching.

My feelings about Marilyn's visits changed as the year went on. I went from inflated confidence to fearing what she would find wrong to interest in how she would steer me back on course. While I was on this emotional seesaw Marilyn remained the same. She came in. She sat with my students and questioned them about what they were doing. She observed me in terms of the objective on my most recent action plan. In our instructional dialogues she asked me questions. What was my understanding of revision, of proofreading, of spelling, of shared reading? Her questions prodded me. They sometimes caused me to say, "I don't know." They almost always stretched me to a new level of understanding.

I began to look forward to her visits. As in my juggling days I could sense when the rhythm in my classroom was faltering. I needed her second pair of eyes to help me see what was out of kilter. An amazing thing was taking place. While I was helping my students to become writers who had the shadow of a reader on their shoulders, I was becoming a teacher who had the shadow of a supportive observer on my shoulder. I began to anticipate the questions that Marilyn might ask about my teaching. And slowly, very slowly, I began to answer my own questions.

WE ARE ALL LEARNERS

The more deeply I dug into the Literacy Learning model of teaching and experienced the supportive structure of The Learning Network, the more in awe I was of the parallels between my own learning and that of my students. Just as I was assessing my students' level of writing and reading development and helping them to move on to their next learning steps, so I was being nudged to my next level of understanding about the reading and writing process by Marilyn.

This continuum of developing understandings was most apparent to me when I was involved in a tiered dialogue session after an observation in my classroom. Twice during the school year Jan Duncan, a trainer of program coordinators and the person we all considered the "expert," accompanied Marilyn to our school site. We had heard rumors that when Jan observed something less than ideal in a classroom, she was apt to mutter "rubbish." I prayed that nothing she observed me do-ing would cause that word to be said. As it happened, both her obser-vation of and dialogue with Marilyn accelerated my own learning.

In a tiered dialogue, Marilyn would first ask me questions based on what she observed in my classroom. Then Marilyn would assume the role of the learner and Jan would ask her questions about our dia-logue. As Jan questioned Marilyn I understood what a keen eye she had. In a matter of minutes she had assessed the group of students I was working with, as well as my own understandings. Hearing their dialogue I could see how Marilyn was continuing to develop her own understandings by being stretched to her next learning step by Jan. Not only did I see how the development and refinement of understand-ings about the reading and writing processes never stopped, but also how my own learning was enhanced by hearing their discussion. I wondered, though, who or what stretched Jan.

The monthly observations by the program coordinator also added a new dimension to my relationship with my principal, Scott Meyers. In previous years his observations in my classroom had centered mainly on my evaluation. Many teachers and administrators refer to these observations, linked to teacher evaluation, as "dog and pony shows." Yet when our school became involved in The Learning Net-work, Scott made the commitment to be in my classroom for every one of Marilyn's visits. As I went on with my teaching I noticed that Scott was also talking to students, asking them questions and looking at their draft books. I often heard Marilyn explaining to Scott some as-pect of the Literacy Learning model as it pertained to the class. After-ward, Scott sat in on the instructional dialogue sessions. As the year went on I began to see my principal and myself as fellow learners. In-stead of constantly feeling I had to prove I was a competent teacher to him, we began to talk about what we were noticing with some of my students. We were fitting our pieces together to look at the whole child. Often his insights were things I had missed. I moved from that sense of accountability to a feeling of collaboration and co-responsibility to the students.

A SAFE ENVIRONMENT FOR LEARNING

There were other supports throughout the year. Once a month we had a half-day teacher leader focus meeting led by Marilyn. Teacher leaders from all the district's Learning Network schools took turns bringing videotapes of themselves involved in the various parts of the

Literacy Learning model, such as reading to students, modeling writing, working on spelling, guided reading and writing, shared reading and writing, revision and editing conferences, taking running records, and focusing on handwriting. We all observed the videos together, the teacher leader being viewed nervously waiting to discover what was "wrong." Afterward, Marilyn dialogued with the teacher, again helping to deepen both that teacher's and our own understandings.

Another valuable aspect of these teacher leader focus meetings was that all district administrators involved in The Learning Network–the superintendent, assistant superintendent, and all participating principals–were there once a month. Throughout the year a sense of camaraderie and support developed from these meetings. We were all talking about common goals for our students. Our administrators were learning how to put the Literacy Learning model into place in their district and school. They were also there to find out how to support us in our new role as teacher leaders. It was comforting and enlightening to discover that our administrators had many of the same questions that we had.

In addition to these meetings with the program coordinator and the administrators, we had monthly half-day meetings in which just the class of teacher leaders came together. During these sessions we often brought assessment samples of our students, such as running records and draft books. These meetings were more relaxed. We spent the first part of each meeting voicing our frustrations and setbacks. We always seemed to ask "How can we do it all?" It was therapeutic to know that I wasn't the only one having a problem juggling the oranges. Still, the meetings never deteriorated into complaint sessions. We discussed and worked through many "tangles" in our classroom practices. Often one of us offered an idea that benefited the others. Throughout the year we shared what worked and what didn't. As our own learning deepened, we changed and modified our thinking and our practices.

By the second month we were setting our own agendas for those meetings. We never had a problem coming up with a topic we wanted to examine or question. In the spring we decided that we wanted to take on Benchmarks and Indicators for Teachers, the written understandings of knowing the learner, the approaches, and the resources (Richard C. Owen Publishers 1995b). Page by page we talked through them–arguing, clarifying, closing the holes in our own knowledge–until we could all agree on how to state what we knew. It was tedious. Some meetings we would go back and cross out what we had written the month before because our classroom practices were snagged. In time we understood that our learning was a vital, ongoing process, not a static force which allowed us to say "I'm there."

JUGGLING THE ORANGES

Having Marilyn on campus each month, our monthly teacher leader focus meetings with Marilyn and administrators, and the monthly meetings of the teacher leaders by themselves all served as strong supports for me that first year. There were plenty of challenges as well. The first semester of the school year I had a wonderfully energetic student teacher. She embraced the Literacy Learning model immediately, wanting to learn as much about it as possible. Yet I was a novice myself. Many of her questions about writing sent me searching through *Dancing with the Pen* (Ministry of Education 1992) for the answers, and when it came to reading, many of her questions remained unanswered. At that point I was in the beginning stages of learning how to take a running record; she was much more proficient in that task than I. Many times that semester I wished that I was further along in my own understandings so that I could be of more help to her.

Often my juggling act of putting just one more piece of the reading and writing processes into place caused everything to come crashing down around me. Sometimes, especially early in the year, I took on too much too quickly, as can be seen in many of my first action plans (Figure 6.1). Sometimes the new bit of learning would graphically point out the precariousness of my prior learning. For instance, when I added small group revision conferences to my language arts block it became apparent that there were some major snags in classroom management. I couldn't go two minutes working with the small group without being interrupted by a barrage of students coming to ask a question. If I wasn't interrupted by students working "independently," I ended up interrupting the revision conference myself. It seemed that I couldn't help but notice students who were supposedly working independently were actually fooling around or talking too loudly. I knew something was out of place, but again, it was Marilyn who skillfully guided me in the right direction. I had to step back, drop the ball of revision, and set up guidelines for students working independently. When I went back to having revision conferences I made sure that I first made clear to students my expectation of not being interrupted. I then had to follow through with that action by ignoring any and all interruptions. The students got the message and they learned to solve many of their problems without my intervention. I also learned to selectively screen out the distraction of students not engaged in their work (although this skill seems to ebb and flow with me). I knew that instead of yelling to them from across the room to get to work, I could more effectively steer them back on task by roving around the room after the revision conference.

The Learning Network | ACTION PLAN

Name *Peggy Grubel*   School *Park*
Grade *3/4*   Date *9-19-95*

What am I going to do?

  Take running records

How am I going to develop my understandings?
1. Read appropriate sections of *Reading in Jr. Classes*.
2. Read Summer Institute notes on running records.
3. Ask Kim to copy section on running records in Marie Clay's *Observation + Survey* (not sure of that title)
4. Work with Dori, Sandy, + R.J. — take 2-3 running records daily. Discuss information collected and where to go.
5. Read conference notes from last year on running records.

How will I know when I'm there?
1. I'm able to explain to someone else the value of RR
2. I'm comfortable using the conventions.
3. I know how to analyze the information.
4. I know how to use the analysis to choose appropriate materials.

Figure 6.1. An early action plan—too much, too soon.

In November of that first year I decided to take on the challenge of guided reading. I thought I was well-prepared because my running records were in place as assessments. I wrote up guided reading as my next action plan. I read up on it. I was ready. Then I tried it several times, but it didn't seem like I truly understood it. Marilyn observed me and dialogued with me. Jan Duncan was even there to observe a guided reading session. I struggled to integrate the idea. No, I wasn't ready. In my perpetual juggling act I had to drop the ball. I revisited it again. And dropped it. I tried again. Again I dropped it. I couldn't seem to conduct a guided reading session successfully. Instead of guiding I was pushing students by doing all the talking and analyzing. Jan had pointed that out to me, but knowing and doing it were not quite the same. Yet each time I tried it I came a little closer. It became a little less fuzzy. I was getting the rhythm. This process of focusing on particular aspects of my practice became easier. By spring my action plans reflected my increased understandings of my own learning process (Figure 6.2). Although by May I still didn't feel like I was where I

The Learning Network | **ACTION PLAN**

Name _Peggy Grubel_   School _Park_
Grade _3/4_   Date _4/1/96_

What am I going to do?
    Increase my understandings and expectations of student revising.

How am I going to develop my understandings?
1. Read pages 55-56 in _Dancing with the Pen_ (& p.60)
2. Read pages 123, 118 in _Dancing with the Pen_.
3. Model the revision techniques listed on page 60 (D.w/the P.) in my Write-tos.
4. Postpone teacher edits (return draft books) until student incorporates some of the suggestions from revision conference.
5. Require that students do some revising before they participate in a revision conference.

How will I know when I'm there?
1. When I can state the purpose of revising — both to teachers & students.
2. When I can demonstrate in my own writing, the different revision techniques.

Figure 6.2. A much more focused action plan.

wanted to be with guided reading, I knew I was getting increasingly closer.

Sometimes, even when I had the knowledge of a specific aspect of reading or writing that I wanted to add, I just couldn't keep up the pace of juggling. When I added spelling to the day I had to drop revision conferences temporarily. When I tried guided and shared reading I often had to let revision conferences slide for awhile. When my student teacher left I realized that perhaps a more realistic goal for me was to take only one running record a day. These setbacks were difficult for me to accept, but I had to honor my own capacity to learn and realize that I couldn't do it all. Perhaps I would never be able to close the gap between my unfolding understandings and my actual teaching practices. That was and is the challenge. The other teacher leaders and I had a running joke: "Where were the 'wee steps' of learning that we had first heard about?" Marilyn later revised the idea of "wee steps" by saying that teachers could take wee steps. Teacher leaders took giant strides.

A TRUE COMMUNITY OF LEARNERS

One aspect of this experience that progressed throughout the year was the creation of a common language. In previous years if someone were to walk into a faculty meeting they would have seen teachers sitting at tables divided by grade level. Kindergarten teachers sat with other kindergarten teachers, eighth-grade teachers with their grade-level peers. For the most part, discussions among teachers followed the same pattern. We tended to share or discuss our teaching practices with those who shared the same teaching philosophy or grade level.

Discussions among teachers between grade levels were usually limited to the grade directly above or below our own. We might ask teachers in the grade level below for insights about students with whom we were not making progress. There was also a conversation we always dreaded. A teacher from the grade above would come to us and ask, "Aren't you teaching _____? None of the students coming to us seem to have this skill." Of course, this did not help to open up dialogue between grade levels because we felt defensive.

Slowly, through the year, this began to change. I noticed it first with the teacher leaders. As we began to use similar methods of assessment and teaching in language arts we also began to develop a common language. We weren't just echoing empty jargon. The more we delved into the reading and writing processes the closer we came to the same meaning for words such as assessment, evaluation, running record, and a student's next learning step. We teacher leaders began to compare notes and to ask for input from each other. It did not matter whether our students were kindergartners or eighth graders. We were observing the same learning processes occurring in our classrooms.

This common language was not limited to teacher leaders. Many of the teachers at our school had attended the summer institute but were not receiving additional training during that first year. They were eager to try out some of the new concepts they had learned. Some of these conversations were started during weekly book study sessions that our assistant principal, Karolee Hess, set up. These sessions were open to anyone interested in examining more closely the two books, *Dancing with the Pen* (Ministry of Education 1992) and *Reading in Junior Classes* (Ministry of Education 1985). Conversations among the entire faculty began to occur. It was not unusual to see a seventh-grade teacher discussing the evaluation of running records with a kindergarten teacher, or a first-grade teacher and a fourth-grade teacher brainstorming together on how to model revision in writing, or a special education teacher and a classroom teacher discussing what the teaching point in a guided reading session would be.

The tone of our teacher and administrative conversations began to change as well. For those people digging into knowing their learners, getting together with a colleague became an opportunity to celebrate new learning rather than a time to sit and complain. These conversations were occurring everywhere—in the faculty lunch room, in the teachers' lounge, even on the sidewalk. The climate of our school began to change subtly.

May rolled around—the end of the school year. I would like to say that as my first year as a teacher leader ended, I was able to look back at all I had learned and accomplished. The truth was that I was too exhausted and too immersed in the process to notice what progress had been made. My brain was weary from all the new learning I had taken on (and attempted to take on). I needed the summer.

KNOWING THE RESOURCES

Along with knowing the learner and knowing the approaches, one of the legs of the Literacy Learning model is knowing the resources. That first month after school was out we took this understanding on in earnest. The ten teacher leaders from our district took turns working in each of our schools' instructional resource rooms. Our tasks varied. Sometimes we worked on leveling the books, based on the supports and challenges in the texts for emergent, early, and fluent readers. For older readers we categorized books based on their content area and attempted to match that with an appropriate age level.

We also determined how the books could be used, either for shared or guided reading sessions or for independent book boxes. As books were leveled we labeled them with stickers and set up boxes to hold them. Throughout this work we were talking. We discussed the books in terms of their supports and challenges. We talked about their value to readers. We found that some of the older sets of books we had been using didn't measure up in terms of use for teaching points in guided or shared reading groups. We began to have new criteria for looking at books.

Surprisingly, those eight-hour days seemed to speed by. Other than backaches and stiff necks, we were all enjoying ourselves. I also noticed that the reading process lost some of its murkiness in my mind. A faint shape to the process began to emerge.

All of our talk did not center on books. Working together was a great opportunity for us to reflect on what we had learned during the year. We laughed over some of the things we had said and done in our classrooms. It was comforting to know that I wasn't the only one who had done all of the talking in a guided reading session. One feeling we all had in common was the belief that we were not ready to take teachers to new understandings. I didn't see how that could change in the next two months.

ORANGES FALLING INTO PLACE

At the end of June I attended the summer institute for the second time, along with administrators, teachers, and instructional aides from our school. I remember sitting in the first general session. I couldn't believe how much new information I was hearing. I turned to my friend, Sandy James, who had also attended the previous year's institute, and wrote in her notebook, "I can't believe all the new information I'm hearing." Sandy smiled and wrote back, "It's not new. We heard it last year." It was only then that I realized how far I had come in one year. At the previous summer's institute so much of the information had been new that it had not even penetrated. It had passed right over me. Now, with my newly established foundation of learning, I was able to tie the information to my past experiences and understandings.

Throughout those four days Sandy and I had a standing joke on how much we "hadn't heard" the year before. Nor did I grasp everything I heard during that second summer. I found that even with my increased understanding I was not ready to incorporate it all into my classroom, but I was able to tuck it away, and knew that eventually it would be reflected in my practice. As I witnessed the disequilibrium of the teachers going through the institute for the first time I could appreciate how my own comfort level had been stretched. I wondered about the next institute I would attend and what "new" information would surprise me.

Two days after the institute ended I attended the Second Annual Learning Network Conference in Tempe, Arizona. There was a different atmosphere to this gathering. Nationally and internationally known educators came together with administrators, teacher leaders, program coordinators, and teachers all sharing the knowledge they had acquired. I saw how The Learning Network valued all its learners, no matter what level they were at. No one acted as an "expert." The session leaders were not there just to dole out their knowledge, but also to question their colleagues' and their own understandings. I watched in awe as Margaret Mooney, in her keynote address, questioned the color leveling practice that she and others had been doing on children's instructional reading books for years. She wondered aloud if adding the dimension of supports and challenges to that leveling process might better help teachers in their selection of materials. I was reminded of Marilyn quoting Gertrude Stein: "Just when you think you're there, there's no there, there." We were *all* on that continuum of learning. Once we arrived at a new level of knowledge there would always be a next step, and a next.

For me, the high point of the conference was the two-hour teacher leader session led by Jan Duncan and Marilyn Herzog. When I walked into the room where we were all gathering a shiver went up my spine. I had not realized how many teacher leaders there were; how many schools across the country were touched by The Learning Network. Jan began the session by asking us to watch a video of a teacher engaged in a guided reading session. We were to look at it in terms of the teacher's stated action plan. As we watched we were to take notes that would guide us if we were to have an instructional dialogue session with that teacher. I watched. My mind was blank. I watched more intently. My notebook remained blank. I looked around and noticed blank looks on the faces of most of the teacher leaders from our district. I looked out at the sea of teacher leaders from all around the country and was relieved to see that many pens were poised in midair.

Jan called us back together. She suggested that when we received a teacher's action plan we could draw out a web of what we knew about that subject. If there were missing areas in our own knowledge we could read up in that area or talk to other teacher leaders. We could then use that web as a road map for our classroom observation. The point at which we had a question or saw a hole would be the point where we would begin the questioning in the instructional dialogue.

I thought back to the video. What had I noticed? My brain felt stretched to its limit. Still only blankness. I looked around again. Everyone at my table was leaning forward, straining to come up with something, mumbling questions under their breath. Then a question about something I had heard the teacher say at the very beginning of her guided reading session formed itself in my mind. I tentatively asked the question aloud to the other teacher leaders at our table. At the same time all of the teacher leaders began to put forth their questions. We had broken through that barrier. All over the room lights were coming on. At that moment I was certain I would be able to dig deep for those questions that would help teachers move to their next level of learning.

Jan asked Marilyn to model an instructional dialogue session with the teacher who had been videotaped. I was thrilled when I heard Marilyn ask my question. Of course Marilyn's questions had more breadth and depth than mine. Nevertheless, I was convinced I could handle instructional dialogue.

I wished I could start working with teachers immediately, while my newly earned confidence was still fresh in my mind. Instead, I went home and updated my indicators with the new information I had learned at the conference.

JUGGLING SHOT-PUTS

The first two weeks of the new school year began relatively easily. In terms of juggling, I was flipping only one orange into the air—my classroom practice. I hadn't yet begun working with teachers. The week that I began observing and dialoguing with teachers marked a period of intense disequilibrium for me. My lone orange suddenly changed into two oversized shot-puts, neither of which I could keep in the air. One ball entailed adjusting myself to teaching my class of third and fourth graders for only half a day and sharing my classroom and my students with a teacher I had met only two weeks before. It was further weighed down by trying to get the reading and writing momentum that had been there the previous May going again. The teacher leader ball included developing a relationship with teachers with whom I had not previously worked, adjusting to the new constraints that being a teacher leader put upon old friendships, *and* trying to find the appropriate questions to ask during our dialogue sessions. If I concentrated on the teacher leader part of my job, my classroom practice suffered. If I focused on my students, I fumbled in my dialogue sessions with teachers.

About the fourth week into the school year I looked around and wondered what had happened. Paradoxically, I seemed further behind in my classroom than I had been the year before, when I was a novice. I seemed to have totally forgotten how to incorporate classroom management into my language arts block. None of the students (including the ones I had had the year before) seemed to be able to work independently. I had also managed to offend one of the teachers I had begun working with, tactlessly bringing up something she was not ready to hear.

I was plagued with self-doubt. Some of the teachers I was observing and dialoguing with were at the same point if not further along in their own learning about literacy. How could I lead them on to new learning? Who was I to presume to make suggestions when my own classroom was falling apart? I struggled on, feeling vastly inadequate for both jobs.

I was not the only teacher leader struggling. "Disequilibrium" described the atmosphere of the entire campus. Teachers who had readily agreed the previous spring to having a teacher leader come into their classrooms were having second thoughts. How could they be expected to take on all these action plans and observations while dealing with a new math curriculum and a social studies pilot? They felt it wasn't fair to have their peers evaluating them. Snarling was occurring everywhere. Even our principal admitted to losing sleep over the negativity that was sweeping over our campus.

We teacher leaders felt like we were in no man's land. We would walk into the teachers' lounge and all conversation would stop. No matter how many times we reassured certain teachers that we were not there to evaluate, they still felt that we were. I began to question not only whether I should be a teacher leader but whether I was even cut out to be a teacher. It was a difficult time. Looking back I credit Marilyn and yoga with helping me get through it.

I felt somewhat better after our first teacher leader meeting of the year. Teacher leaders at the other schools in the district were also struggling with the adjustment to their new roles. Marilyn assured us that this state of disequilibrium with the teachers at our school was to be expected. It would pass. She urged us to go slowly and work at developing a rapport with the teachers with whom we were working.

As the day approached when Marilyn was to observe at our school I pondered what to write for my action plan. We teacher leaders were to write an action plan based on our work with teachers as well as one for our own classroom practice. It was the one for my classroom practice that had me gritting my teeth. Although I knew it was necessary, it was embarrassing to admit that I needed help in classroom management.

Marilyn came. We observed my friend Sandy's class together. Marilyn then listened to my instructional dialogue with Sandy. At the end of our dialogue Sandy and I switched places and Marilyn began to question me. Afterward Sandy told me how valuable it had been for her to sit in that tiered dialogue session.

That afternoon Marilyn observed me in my classroom as I modeled writing. She stayed briefly to watch as students began their independent work. I was apprehensive as I walked into our dialogue session. That session marked another important step in learning for me. Marilyn didn't add to my self-doubts about my teaching ability. Neither did she shy away from telling me what I needed to hear. She smiled and, in a matter-of-fact tone of voice, said that I was just having trouble finding my footing in teaching half- rather than full-time in my classroom. She reminded me of things that I had forgotten—how I should step back and rove for awhile to get students back to working independently. She also gave me some suggestions that I hadn't thought about—like setting up with my students their responsibilities and my responsibilities for every part of the language arts block. She said, "You'll have this turned around in a couple of weeks, Peggy." Because she hadn't lost faith in me, I regained faith in myself. I left our dialogue session already forming in my mind how I would begin setting up classroom responsibilities.

That session also pointed out to me a part of my role as teacher leader that I hadn't considered. In addition to being the second pair of eyes in a teacher's classroom and helping them stretch to new understandings, I was also there as a support. Regardless of the level a teacher was at, or any setbacks that might befall them, I was the constant who encouraged them forward. I was the person who never lost faith in the fact that they would move on, even if they temporarily lost faith in themselves.

REGAINING THE RHYTHM

My classroom management problems did improve within two weeks. Gradually I found it less difficult to add the pieces I had dropped back into my juggling routine. I took a step back in my work with teachers. I used my action plans to help me become more skillful at leading other teachers to their next learning steps (Figure 6.3). For those with whom our relationship had begun on a strained note, I took time to know them as teachers and as learners, exactly as I did with my students. I sat down with the teacher I had offended a few weeks earlier. I began by saying, "I can't believe all the new learning going on in your classroom. Your write to's are moving along. Your students are

The Learning Network — ACTION PLAN

Name *Peggy Grubel*   School *Park*

Grade *Teacher leader*   Date *10-24-96*

What am I going to do?
Take more focused notes during my teacher observations (to help in my questioning)

How am I going to develop my understandings?
① Look at Marilyn's notes. Notice what she puts down & how that leads to a question.
② Listen to and observe the teacher more carefully.
③ Listen to and observe the students more carefully.
④ At the top of my page write major headings to focus my observation & notes.
⑤ Attach my observations to questions – What do I wonder?

How will I know when I'm there?
– When I see a more direct correlation/connection between my notes and the questions I formulate.
– When my questions during dialogue are based more on my observations than on pre-planned questions.

Figure 6.3. An action plan focused on working with teachers.

eagerly diving into their draft books. You've created a wonderful atmosphere in which students can learn." She looked surprised and then smiled, saying, "At first I wasn't sure I was going to like this. I was really uncomfortable having you come into my room. But I am liking it now. I enjoy what I'm seeing in my classroom and I appreciate the value it has for my students." I realized how far we both had come in a short time.

In doing these things I have noticed subtle changes. I now go into teachers' classrooms with a sense of wonder at the growth I am seeing. My view has broadened to encompass both where these teachers started the year and where they are headed in the long run. I find myself looking more carefully at the people who are experiencing this incredible learning and wonder how I can help to enhance this experience for them.

As I observe in teachers' classrooms and talk with them about what I see, I find that I am learning at least as much as they are. Much of what I see I can take back into my own classroom. It causes me to examine my own teaching practices, look to fill in the gaps, and forever ask myself Jan Duncan's favorite question, "Why am I doing what I'm doing?"

For now my oversized shot-puts have disappeared. In their place are most of the old oranges I managed to juggle last year. On good days, when those oranges seem to be flying effortlessly through the air, I find that it's difficult for me to tell where one sphere of learning ends and the next one begins. Being a teacher and a teacher leader blend together as I continue on my own journey as a learner.

PEGGY IANNELLA GRUBEL has taught third, seventh, and eighth graders, as well as autistic children and adolescents, for over nineteen years. She is currently a teacher leader and a multi-age third- and fourth-grade teacher at Madison Park School, a Learning Network site in Phoenix, Arizona.

CHAPTER 7

The Role of the Program Coordinator

Katie Moeller

"In some Learning Network schools, students' draft writing books are black and white marble composition books. When I was in a teacher leader's classroom in Phoenix, I began writing observation notes in my plain spiral notebook. A kindergarten student, age five, came to me where I was sitting and asked, 'What is that?' (pointing to my spiral notebook). I replied, 'That's my draft book.' She looked at me, leaned closely, and whispered in my ear, 'You can get the real ones at Walmart.'"

Marilyn Herzog
Program Coordinator

MY INTRODUCTION TO THE LITERACY LEARNING MODEL

I am a multi-age primary classroom teacher and a program coordinator for The Learning Network in Tallahassee, Florida, but my current role had an inauspicious beginning. In the early 1990s a friend and fellow teacher, Dale Woodruff, called to ask me if I would join her in attending a Richard C. Owen Publishers, Inc. Whole Language in the Classroom workshop (now the Literacy Learning in the Classroom summer institute) in Atlanta. At the time I was pretty smug in the evaluation of my teaching practice and replied, "do you think we will learn anything?" In 1992, I had not encountered anyone who questioned my practices or asked me why I did what I did. Had someone asked me hard questions I would have glibly given answers without a great deal of thought about their meaning. I was a queen of "whole language" and thought very highly of my teaching. In reality, I was basing my practice on hope and faith. My beliefs could be summarized as:

◆ purchase as many trade books as you can; immerse the children in books;
◆ use paperback novels and chapter books to allow children free choice as to which book they would like to read in a literature group;
◆ free writing or journal writing;
◆ thematic units are the most important thing to be taught;
◆ thematic units should be chosen by the teacher.

You might notice that my belief system was based upon teaching practices rather than theoretical understandings of how children become readers or writers. Teaching practices were my background knowledge; I had not spent much time asking myself *why* I embraced those practices. I was an expert in telling others *what* I did, or *how* I did it, but I gave little thought as to the *why*. Someone might have asked me questions such as:

◆ With thousands of books in your classroom, what is your understanding of the leveling of text? Should children be left to flounder in text?
◆ What was the learning outcome for the six weeks a group spent reading *The Sign of the Beaver*? Was there only one learning outcome, and if so, why?
◆ Where is the evidence in your students' journals of documented growth across time? Or are your students simply doing bedtime to bedtime writing with no evidence of the development of the writer?
◆ Do you, as a life-long reader, keep literature logs? When you read John Grisham's *The Chamber*, did you write in a log after each chapter? What is the value of literature logs?
◆ Because you believe it is your right to select themes, where is the consistency and continuity in your school's curriculum? Do you know how many of your students have already studied dinosaurs three times before?

Those would have been difficult questions for me to answer that summer I went to the workshop with Dale. Prior to attending the workshop, I had forgotten the most important lesson every teacher should engrave upon his or her heart: "Who dares to teach must never cease to learn" (John Cotton Dana 1912).

The Whole Language in the Classroom workshop was a wake-up call for me. What I was hearing was logical, made sense, but stood very much in the way of some of my assumptions. I began to sweat bullets. By the third day Dale and I were in so much disequilibrium that we decided we would skip the fourth day because our brains just could not handle any more. We had our money's worth—we were leaving! I remember going back to the hotel at night and agonizing with Dale about the fact that as the "whole language leaders" in our school district we had helped many teachers throw out much of the structure of a lockstep basal program without offering any real guidance in how to replace it. I was scared!

Despite misgivings about our own abilities, after our experience in Atlanta Dale and I worked to bring the Literacy Learning in the Classroom institute to the Tallahassee area, and that started me on a long, hard, but satisfying journey to becoming a successful program coordinator.

BECOMING A PROGRAM COORDINATOR

My journey to becoming a program coordinator began with the sometimes painful experience of being willing to question my assumptions about the nature of teaching and learning. Dale and I became facilitators for the summer institutes. When I was hired to become a facilitator I was excited. It was an opportunity to continue growing in my understandings about literacy. For a while, there was my nine-month teacher life and my three-month on-the-road facilitator life. For some odd reason, in my mind they were two separate roles.

When I came to realize that there was no real defining line between my teaching job and my facilitating job, I really began to grow. Why did this make a difference? It was all too easy to tell teachers about theories and give them suggestions without having worked hard putting all those theories and practices in place in my own classroom. I knew I had many gaps in my understandings about the Literacy Learning model. In fact, I once described myself to Jan Duncan as being a giant piece of Swiss cheese—full of holes. In fairness, I know now what I was lacking. During the summer the facilitators themselves experience intensive professional development after spending each day working with participants at each institute site. I was receiving a great deal of theory through my ears. I took copious notes–I felt that I could somehow capture the understanding I was lacking if I could just get it down on paper. What I truly needed was a more knowledgeable "other" to come into my classroom and guide me through the process of attaching *meaning* to the theory I so diligently wrote down in the context of my own classroom practice. That was the only way I would come to a deep understanding of the classroom practices that are supported by the theory. This is what the Learning Network is all about–an experience I was yet to have.

In 1995 Richard Owen asked me to begin training as a program coordinator for The Learning Network. This was the opportunity that I needed. At long last I was involved in the process of developing my theory alongside my classroom practice. There could be no "faking" it. My summer life and my teaching life melded as a trainer of program coordinators, Jan Duncan, began to come regularly to visit my classroom and question my understandings. Along with my training as a program coordinator, we began the process of preparing some schools in the area to join The Network. Finally, in the fall of 1995, my dream was realized when The Learning Network began in four schools in Tallahassee.

When Richard Owen invited me to become a program coordinator I thought he had taken leave of his senses. I still believed in "experts" and I knew I was no expert in the area of literacy learning. Now I understand that when Richard seeks individuals to become program coordinators it has little to do with what they already know and being an expert; and a great deal to do with their willingness to learn and their ability to take the risk of critically examining their practices and theory. The question becomes: "Are you willing to change to become an agent of change?"

The first evening of program coordinator training terrified me. Six program coordinators in training sat around a conference table and Peter Duncan, a developer of The Learning Network, described the initiative to us. As Peter laid out the big picture in his eloquent manner I sat there stunned, ready to offer to pay for my airplane ticket back home because I knew it was all a mistake. Peter began by talking with us about long-lasting change and what the characteristics of successful change across time were. I really began to panic as he went on to say we program coordinators had to become so articulate and sure of our theory that, if need be, we could speak to superintendents and commissioners of education. I was in awe of the ideas Peter was describing, but fearful that I did not have the capabilities for this massive undertaking.

Since that time, Peter and Jan Duncan have taught me valuable lessons about leadership. First, they both taught me to question everything. Never be so complacent as to accept what is—have the vision to see what can be. That vision must not be just for educational institutions, but for individuals as well. I have come to have much higher expectations of myself and others.

Second, question all of your own assumptions. I was being conceited when I asked Dale, "Do you think we will learn anything?" Now I not only question my teaching practice and theory in the light of new evidence, and I expect to be doing so for the rest of my life, but I can now say that we educators in The Network are not simply giving teachers simple recipes for practices. We have developed teachers with the ability to ask themselves those very hard questions.

Third, be willing to explore your assumptions and experience these changes in public. Part of our training involved going with Jan Duncan, the trainer of program coordinators, into schools and observing The Learning Network in action. In Massachusetts, I was amazed by the authenticity of what I was observing. We observed Jan work inside classrooms, with principals, in faculty meetings, and with parent groups. I watched as Jan never backed away from asking the really tough questions—even of administrators. It was obvious that the teacher leaders expected her to be intellectually demanding; they seemed to thrive on it.

Another part of the training included Jan coming to observe me in my classroom. Those visits were exhilarating and challenging and that was when some very real changes began to occur. Jan would question me about all aspects of what she observed and I began to be able to make the links between the theory and what I was practicing. Humorous things occurred along with those visits. The other teachers in the school and I were beginning to organize our instructional resource room and, naturally, we wanted to impress Jan with our efforts. Because the resource room is a physical embodiment of the theory, every visit brought suggestions from Jan, which would refine both the physical arrangement of the resources and our understandings. I remember showing her the first independent book boxes we developed, which had 25 copies of one book. Jan looked at me quizzically and gently asked how we intended one book to be appropriate for a group of children at different levels of reading ability to read independently.

Visits from Jan continued as I began my work as a program coordinator. Those visits always included tiered dialogue, in which both Jan and I visited a teacher leader's classroom and made an observation based on his or her action plan. I engaged the teacher leader in instructional dialogue about his or her understandings with the goal of bringing him or her to new understandings. Then the teacher leader watched as Jan questioned me about the instructional dialogue that had just occurred. Every tiered dialogue was a powerful experience. In the early stages, I sometimes had difficulty remembering that the theory was the same for adults and students–through assessment and evaluation of the learner's strengths, the teacher has to identify one teaching point. Sometimes I was overwhelming the teacher leaders with too much too soon; I learned about the power of building one new understanding upon another until the learner has taken a giant stride across time. Under Jan's guidance, and with a great deal of reflection on my part, I was developing my skillfulness in instructional dialogue.

VISIONARY CHANGE AGENT

Franklin D. Roosevelt once said, "Where there is no vision, the people perish." The same can be said for our schools: "Where there is no vision, the children perish." I have observed teachers with a vision and with high expectations for their students. They have students who not only meet, but exceed, those expectations. Sometimes just down the hallway is another teacher, without vision and with low expectations, and his or her students are performing poorly. That teacher is always willing to share with me that the students are "AHAD," "economically disadvantaged," "learning disabled," or have "a low IQ." I often wonder why that teacher is content to blame the students and about what would happen if he or she raised her vision.

Developing Vision

As a program coordinator, I help to build within schools a climate that no longer allows teachers to feel comfortable labeling or blaming the learner. Instead, through instructional dialogue, I get teacher leaders to examine their classroom practice and to ask themselves "Do I believe that every child can learn?" If they say that they believe every child can learn, I push their self-reflection further. How do they act upon that belief? What can they cite as evidence of this belief from their classroom practice? Are the conditions for learning in place in their classrooms, and in the school?

Common Language Facilitates Communication

Every profession has a distinctive language system, which serves to assist practitioners in communicating about common ideas. In the field of education, unfortunately, all too often our words have a multiplicity of meanings and therefore we do not truly communicate what we intended. During facilitator meetings at the Literacy Learning summer institutes, we have been asked to define the terms that we use. For instance, we considered the questions "What does the word *journal* mean? Does it mean the same thing in your classroom as it does in mine?" To some facilitators, journals were literature logs and their audience was the teacher. Others felt that journals were used to write about a variety of topics and almost all pieces were published. Some people considered journals as a way to keep students busy during morning routines such as taking attendance and lunch count. Through discussion, it became clear that everyone present had different concepts for the terminology we used in the institutes and in our classroom practice. With so many different meanings for the word *journal*, how could we be clearly communicating thoughts about theory and practice to the institute participants? This is true in any school, as well.

Part of the program coordinator training was coming to grips with terminology so that we overlap common meaning for the terms that we use and we use terms that have common meaning, not just for all the program coordinators, but for all the teacher leaders, the administrators, and eventually for all educators involved in The Learning Network. Why is this important? If we want students to experience continuity across time, then it is essential that we have basic understandings of the concepts about which we speak. Two teachers with dramatically differing definitions of writing cannot easily communicate about student progress.

CHALLENGES THAT PROGRAM COORDINATORS FACE

While having a clear vision, common language, a trainer of program coordinators and the other program coordinators available for discussion, and the renewal I get from my facilitation of the summer institutes are supports for being a program coordinator, when I first walk into a school in my new role I find myself faced with many challenges that all program coordinators share.

The Outsider Syndrome

Visiting a variety of schools made me aware that each school represents a distinct community. That community has its own way of doing things and its own personality. Sometimes in the first few months

I am viewed as an outsider. Across time, however, a strong bond develops between the teacher leaders, the principal, and the program coordinator. The critical triangle becomes a team for the improvement of the school. We are able to put aside false pretense and be honest about what is happening and what needs to happen.

Developing the Structure to Support Lasting Change

Across time, the teacher leaders, principals, and program coordinator become very close as a result of working so hard together for the same goals. As successes begin to come, the principals come to respect and admire the teacher leaders. In turn the teacher leaders know that continued progress is dependent upon administrative support. Each person in the critical triangle begins to understand how this massive change process comes about successfully only with each piece of the triangle in place. This relationship between the teacher leaders and the principal will become even more important when the formal involvement of The Network is over, so it is the program coordinator's responsibility to ensure that the change process is firmly established throughout the entire school, and not just within the triangle.

Last year a Reading Recovery® teacher and facilitator for the summer institutes came to Tallahassee to observe The Learning Network in action. She told me later that she was amazed at the level of questions that I posed to the principal and the teacher leaders. She asked me how I could have the courage to ask those hard questions. I responded that I am responsible to use everything I know to bring about positive change and growth for the school. I have come to understand that although we all like to be praised, it is not from praise that we grow. It is continual reflection upon why we are doing what we are doing and coming to grips with new theory that brings about change, and I need to model that process so the principal and teacher leaders can continue once I leave. The principal at this school commented that at first she was afraid the situation might be disturbing to the faculty; they would not be comfortable being challenged. Now she has been amazed at how it has brought the faculty closer together. She attributes this to developing a sense of community and at the same time developing independence. As program coordinator I must build independence in the faculty while helping supportive relationships to evolve.

Dealing with Conflict

When conflict arises, it must be managed. I would be less than honest if I implied that engaging in The Learning Network is conflict-free. Some guiding principles taught to me by Peter and Jan have helped me manage conflict:

♦ It is a rare occasion when an immediate response is needed. I have learned not to react immediately to problems and conflicts. I give myself time to think about the situation.
♦ Strive to keep the critical triangle intact. Sometimes the critical triangle begins to come apart and it is my job to knit it back together. This means maintaining open lines of communication among the teacher leaders, administrators, and myself.

Once at our monthly focus meeting, after the administrators left, a teacher leader began to fuss a little about her principal's lack of empathy for her. Her complaint was that she thought he expected her to put the charges for attending The Learning Network conference on her credit card. It so happened that this principal had left his notebook in the room and came back in for it just as the teacher leader finished stating her case. I asked the principal if he would mind joining us for just a few more minutes. I told him that his teacher leader had a concern he needed to know about. I turned to the teacher and asked her to explain her problem, which she did. It turned out that the principal had not expected her to use her credit card.

With the lines of communication now more open, the teacher leader and principal went on to discuss another perhaps more sensitive issue while the rest of us watched in awe. The teacher leader was concerned because at a faculty meeting about the school's involvement in The Learning Network for the following year, a teacher had asked the principal if they would have to write action plans and he had replied no. The teacher leader did not want to contradict him in a faculty meeting but was concerned because she knew that observations are always based upon an action plan. We were witnessing a teacher leader with the courage to state her convictions and a principal with such high regard for the teacher leader that he was able to listen carefully and therefore to understand the problem. The two of them came to the conclusion that from then on, when answering questions about The Network in discussions with the faculty, they would check their answers with each other.

The other teacher leaders and I talked about the incident. The teacher leaders had been holding their breath as the principal walked back into the room. We talked about how problems are not resolved unless we can sit and discuss them together. We talked about the fact that our focus meetings are not gripe sessions and that one purpose of meeting with the administrators once a month is to have the opportunity to work out any problems. I think the teacher leaders learned a valuable lesson that day—that each of us, as professional educators, must have the courage to face conflicts and trust other individuals to help us work through them.

Developing Relationships

Bringing about positive relationships is part of the journey of becoming an effective, self-winding school. Positive relationships and developing a community of learners are the fruits of hard labor. That hard labor involves being open and honest with each other, trusting each other, and not being afraid to face the realities with which we deal. It comes from being professional in all of our interactions. As program coordinators and teacher leaders work through problems and issues, we become a team. We look back and we are proud of our accomplishments. I think all of us know that those accomplishments would not have occurred if we simply went around patting ourselves on the back. We have to be willing to open ourselves up to peeling away all contradictions between what we say and what we do and taking a long, hard, honest look at ourselves.

There are occasions when teachers are resistant to the process; this is usually at the beginning because it is all so new to them. Program coordinators are taught that no scheduled observation can ever be ignored—or a learning opportunity missed. Time spent on teacher development is too precious. Therefore, I must be prepared to move quickly to help teachers and teacher leaders move beyond any resistance or defensiveness.

One day when I arrived at a school the teacher leader told me that she had no action plan for our visit to a teacher's classroom and that she didn't really think that the teacher wanted us there that day. However, we were scheduled for the visit, so I told her that we were going in anyway. We were there to support that teacher in her growth and we couldn't miss an opportunity to do that. When we arrived at the teacher's classroom with the principal and assistant principal in tow, the entire class was doing some writing. I roved around the room observing the writing samples. I saw that there were some students who needed guidance on accurate finger, voice, and print/text matching. The teacher leader had told me prior to the visit that the classroom teacher had not yet used any of the books for students available in the school's resource room. I asked her to get me a set of books that would be appropriate for shared reading with these emergent readers and writers. While I was doing all of this, the classroom teacher would wander away from me. I would go right to her and ask her to come back to me. The principal's and assistant principal's mouths were wide open. I had high expectations for this teacher and I knew that none of us could just let her off the hook.

Soon the teacher leader returned with copies of *Pigs Peek* (Cox 1996). I asked the teacher if I could clear off a round table, bring a group of children over, and try some shared reading. I explained to her that I would start the shared reading and model for her, but then I would move away and expect her to finish the lesson. We brought the children I had identified over to the table and I began to read the book with them, showing them with my finger how the words on the page matched what I said. By the third page, I did stand up and step away and watched in awe as the teacher did a beautiful job of continuing the shared reading with the group.

The learning was not over then. The teacher, teacher leader, principal, assistant principal, and I got together for instructional dialogue. The classroom teacher knew that we were all very proud of her. I asked the teacher leader what I had done. She replied, "You never gave up on her. You kept following her when she walked away and bringing her back to what it was you wanted to teach her. She was able to use your modeling to try some shared reading for herself and she felt successful with what she taught the children. You were like a bulldog with her; you never let her get away."

I have learned not to be afraid to push teachers, because when they do succeed at new learning, when they do come to a new understanding, they are proud of themselves. As a program coordinator I have learned to have very high expectations and not to waver, even when the teachers want to waffle around. Administrators want to waffle around too, sometimes, and I have to be willing and able to lay it on the line with them as well.

POLICY STATEMENTS

Professional educators want to put the students on a continuum of learning. The consistent application of theoretical principles in a school ensures that students thrive in an environment that is supportive of their learning from classroom to classroom and from grade level to grade level (Richard C. Owen Publishers 1996b, 4). By planning for experiences and curriculum across time it is possible to deliver consistent, continuous, and high-quality instruction. This does not occur by allowing a faculty to organize the curriculum based upon the whim of the teachers. How does a faculty develop such consistency? It comes from developing policy statements. We will not all teach alike or in the same manner. However, across time, as we develop understandings about how reading and writing develops we begin to value consistent approaches, which provide for continuous student development. No teacher in September should have to spend six weeks getting to know the students. If there is a consistent theory and practice, then each year builds upon the one that came before.

Policy statements cannot be taken from a book or borrowed from another school district. While examples such as the one shown in Figure 7.1 are helpful, it is vital that the faculty think and discuss its way

---

Reading Policy Statement

Reading Vision: Children will become life-long readers.

Value Statements

We value readers who:
Understand that reading is the creation of meaning.

Objective(s):

Read for enjoyment and information.

Objective(s):

Read a diverse selection of material.

Objective(s):

Use multiple strategies for handling challenges in text.

Objective(s):

Share their enthusiasm for favorite books or stories.

Objective(s):

Know how and where to select reading material for independent reading.

Objective(s):

(Objectives to be completed by faculties at the school and grade level.)

Figure 7.1. Sample policy statement on reading.

through any statement itself. It is through the process of writing a policy statement, among others, that a faculty can become a life-long community of learners. For example, when focusing on literacy, they might start the experience by asking themselves what it is they value in a reader and a writer. They spend time talking together about what they mean when they say that reading is the creation of meaning. They wonder if they would value learners who know how to select a topic and how they should act upon that value. Writing policy statements develops common understandings about the teachers' craft–the act of teaching and learning.

How does a program coordinator help? I have started discussions by asking a faculty what it is they value in a reader and a writer, and how can they can act upon those beliefs. With my guidance, this experience allows the teachers and the principal to articulate what it is they know and what they think they need to know. This continual refining and reflecting about teaching and learning is a natural outgrowth of the instructional dialogue. I encourage faculties to write down a goal statement for a subject area such as spelling, reading, or writing. I work on developing their articulation of their values and beliefs, and from those values and beliefs, objectives are developed for each subject. We then write a school action plan for this area.

Continual Revision as We Come to Learn More

Skillful teachers are life-long learners who are willing to reflect on their understanding and practice when faced with new information. Similarly, policy statements are always considered to be in a state of revision. As new research develops we should be prepared to revise our policy statements to reflect new evidence.

THE CHANGE PROCESS

Schools vary and change at different rates. As a program coordinator, I work with a group of three to five schools with two teacher leaders per school. This makes a class of six to ten teacher leaders, all within about a one-hour commute maximum from one another. When I work in different schools and with different faculties, I have to recognize the distinctiveness of each school. Schools change at varying rates and in differing ways. I have to bear the uniqueness of each school in mind while always pressing forward with that vision of where the school must be going.

I maintain the consistency and quality of my work through my theoretical understandings about teaching and learning and with the procedures to which I adhere. Procedures and understandings that keep me focused include:

- ◆ my monitoring notes, whether of a teacher leader's classroom practice or a meeting with a principal, must be current, complete, and meaningful;
- ◆ my observations are based upon each teacher leader's action plans;
- ◆ I need to talk to the students to determine their understandings as well as focus on the teacher leader's behavior;
- ◆ I expect the principal to be part of the observation and instructional dialogue;
- ◆ my goal for instructional dialogue is to lead the teacher leader to his or her next learning step and action plan;
- ◆ when engaged in tiered dialogue I focus on increasing the teacher leader's capacity for teacher development;
- ◆ I do not do demonstration lessons because I do not know another teacher's learners;
- ◆ I expect the teacher leaders to have a schedule for each of my visits so that we maximize the use of our time;
- ◆ I expect each teacher leader to keep a monitoring notebook housing notes and action plans for the teachers with whom they are working.

These guidelines come together as expectations of how The Learning Network is generally "done" in any school. However, just as each school will differ in the way it approaches change, so too will my day-to-day activities in different schools look different, and my actions as a program coordinator will differ from those of other program coordinators.

As a program coordinator, I have to remember that all change can be subject to erosion; just as wave action can wash away a beach, without proper leadership, support, and vision, the changes brought about by The Learning Network can suffer from erosion. What appears to sustain long-lasting change?

Resistance to Fads

Teachers are far less vulnerable to fads and whims when their practices are based upon strong theory. In other words, when teachers know why they do what they do, and see the results in their students' achievement, there is a much greater chance of sustaining the long-range changes. Teachers are susceptible to *programs* when their theory resides in a teacher's edition. When teachers understand the conditions for learning and how we become readers and writers, their theory is in their head and they become highly critical of slickly packaged new programs offered almost annually by a variety of educational interests.

Managing Change

Change can be stressful. It has been compared to the grief process. Figure 7.2 (Richard C. Owen Publishers 1997c, B-6) illustrates the various aspects of change.

This model includes the factors that must be accounted for. In The Learning Network we design the process to address the need for peer support, for resources, and for administrative support. We human beings seek stability in our lives. So why do teacher leaders and administrators actively seek out this often radical change?

Change has become part of being in education. However, we believe the process can be managed; when managed well the stress is lowered and the changes brought about become successful and long lasting.

How do we go about managing change? First, we take it in small steps. Each action plan is based upon one focused part of the theory; rather than trying to learn everything at once, we are only asking a teacher to choose and take control of one small step at a time. However, across several months, each small step taken cumulatively be-

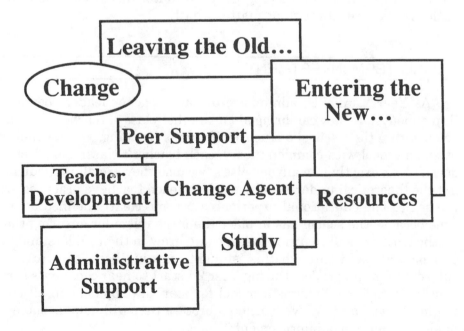

Figure 7.2. The change process.

comes one giant stride and represents significant change. The Learning Network offers teachers a high level of support from teacher leaders, visits by the program coordinator, the creation of resource rooms, the writing of action plans, and involving the administrators in every step of the process. Teachers are not left to feel alone in their struggle to make meaning of new theory. We know that teachers need all of the key supports to make these changes and it becomes vital that the program coordinator leads and monitors so that these supports are in place.

The Effective Change Agent

Sometimes, "when the going gets tough, the tough get going." There are times when things do break down, when communication of problems must be dealt with, or when standards have to be set, articulated, and met for the good of all. In The Learning Network this has occasionally been referred to as "the steel girdle." When things get uncomfortable I sometimes do have to take the heat, but I do so knowing that the theory and structure I am bringing to my schools are sound and will lead to the best possible outcomes for their faculty and children. The little bumps along the way become just that–little bumps. As a program coordinator I try not to allow anything to lead me away from my ultimate duty of bringing about that independent, self-winding school with a vision for every child. Perhaps a better word for the steel girdle is determination; the program coordinator has a steely determination to see it all through no matter what!

A LONG-TERM INVESTMENT

As Year 2 unfolds, administrators and teacher leaders begin to think about how they can bring along another class of teachers and develop within their school a true continuum of learning. When children attend a school with common theory, each teacher's classroom practice doesn't look exactly like anyone else's because they are all individuals, but the theoretical understandings driving each teacher's practices are the same. The educational experiences become clearly defined across time because the school has in place the mechanism for ensuring that all the teachers will continue to learn and grow in their understanding and practice, and through this, student learning benefits across all subject areas and grades. During Year 2 I start to hear comments from principals such as: "This is a model for staff development in all curriculum areas" and "We've learned a process that will help us succeed in all areas of school improvement."

Coming to the close of Year 2, as I prepare to end my formal involvement with a school, I look back and find two highly trained teacher leaders, classes of teachers taking on new understandings, and faculties able to articulate their policies for curriculum areas in ways that place a high value on acting upon their beliefs. In other words, by the end of Year 2, entire faculties are learning how to "walk the walk, not just talk the talk." School reform is on everyone's mind and agenda.

As a program coordinator, I am not prepared to walk away. Through The Learning Network I have learned how to bring about authentic change at all levels of the educational environment. I know that even a self-winding school will need continued support. I plan to be available to that faculty for questions that arise in the future. I know that I or another representative of The Network will make periodic visits to each school to ensure that the vision is still moving forward. I look forward to seeing familiar faces at The Learning Network conference each summer and discussing new understandings, both my own and those of the principals, teacher leaders, and teachers.

In each Learning Network school, the principal, the teacher leaders, and I have been able as a team to engage in authentic, powerful learning which has changed us as professionals and has impacted on:

- individual teachers;
- administrators;
- parents and the wider community;
- the school's capacity to meet the needs of all its students and teachers;
- how money is spent;
- the articulation of curriculum and student outcomes;
- district-level decision making.

We are only at the beginning, but it is such an exciting place to be!

KATIE MOELLER has been a teacher in a kindergarten/first grade classroom and a program coordinator for The Learning Network in Tallahassee, Florida for the past two years. She has been a primary and intermediate multi-age teacher, and an assistant principal in Florida. She wrote Gecko's Story *for the Books for Young Learners collection. During the summer Katie works as a facilitator for the Literacy Learning in the Classroom institutes.*

PART II

Inside Learning Network Classrooms

CHAPTER 8

Focus on Young Writers

Debbie Shelton with Mike Shelton

"A mother of a six-year-old reported that her daughter was smitten with writing—so smitten that she insisted that she not only have a draft book at school, but one at home as well. One afternoon, she heard her daughter calling from the bathroom, 'Mom, you'd better bring me my draft book. I'm going to be in here a long time.'"

as reported to Judie Gustafson
Assistant Superintendent of Curriculum and Instruction, Manor, Texas

All students who come to us are writers. They vary only in their stage of development as a writer. Some come to us using a variety of marks or scribbles to represent letters (precommunicative spellers). Others use random letters of the alphabet (precommunicative spellers, random letter writers). Still others represent some of the sounds in words they write (semiphonetic spellers) or most of the sounds in words they write (phonetic spellers). When asked to "read" their writing they will do so willingly, reading a message that has meaning and syntactic consistency. Some may come with a visual memory—a picture of how some words look—and are already experimenting with some of the spelling conventions of our language, such as silent *e*, vowel combinations, digraphs, and so on, with evidence of syllables represented (transitional spellers) (Gentry 1982).

A number of individuals have researched these developmental stages of writing and spelling, such as Charles Temple, Ruth Nathan, Nancy Burris, and Frances Temple in *The Beginnings of Writing* (1988) and J. Richard Gentry in "An Analysis of Developmental

Spelling in *GNYS AT WRK*" (1982). We believe in these stages and in children's natural ability and desire to write.

Mike and I are currently practicing this belief and our theories about reading and writing at Las Brisas Elementary, a Learning Network school in Glendale, Arizona. I have twenty-five first graders. I have been teaching young children for twenty years, but my understandings of children as writers began developing only about fourteen years ago. Mike's route was a bit different, having spent ten years in the field of special education. We actually began practicing our theories about writing development simultaneously with my first graders and his intermediate resource students, working together in a "writer's workshop" on a daily basis. A few years later Mike taught a first-grade class of his own, then worked as a Reading Recovery® teacher and Teacher Leader. He became a facilitator for the Literacy Learning in the Classroom summer institutes in 1995. Prior to becoming a teacher leader and then a program coordinator for The Learning Network he was dividing his day between Reading Recovery® students and a half-day class of kindergartners.

We have known about The Learning Network since 1993, when we had the opportunity to meet Richard Owen at the IRA conference in San Antonio, Texas. I also attended my first Literacy Learning in the Classroom summer institute in 1993, where I found many of my theories in reading and writing supported and strengthened and others challenged. I have spent the years since reconsidering and revising some of my earlier theories with the help of The Learning Network as it became a part of our school, my thinking, and my practice as a teacher leader.

Mike joined the Las Brisas team the next year, after being challenged by Jan Duncan to try out some of his newly forming theories about emergent and early writers with a class of kindergartners. As a teacher leader, Mike was visited regularly by Learning Network program coordinators–first by Jan, and then by Marilyn Herzog. The observations and instructional dialogues allowed Mike to reflect on his theories and refine his classroom practice. This powerful cycle led Mike to become a program coordinator and a trainer of program coordinators so he could continue The Network's work of acting as a catalyst to bring about true change in classroom practices.

CHANGE

Recently we had the opportunity to observe caterpillars munching away on leaves until that certain moment in their lives when they felt the unquestionable urge to hang upside down, slowly wiggle out of their skins, and before our very eyes turn into a strangely shaped pupa called a chrysalis. This is utterly amazing in itself, and as we continued to observe these silent teachers, we also witnessed another miracle of change: the emergence of totally different creatures–beautiful butterflies ready to take on the world. As teachers we have felt this complex mystery of metamorphosis within ourselves, and have seen this change process within those young writers we have the opportunity to work beside in our classrooms. As our theories about reading and writing evolve, so do our interactions with these emerging butterflies.

LEARNING FROM OUR OWN CHILDREN

When our sixteen-year-old son Jeremy was just emerging as a writer, I was still pretty much in the dark about how writers develop. I had been using a phonics-based reading program in teaching reading for many years and was taking a class through Arizona State University on language acquisition that was allowing a bit of light into the darkness in the area of writing. However, I had not yet made the connection between levels of reading and levels of writing. We have very little evidence of Jeremy's early writing. Knowing that some children entered first grade reading, I wanted my child to have that edge also, so I did the only thing I knew at the time: I bought him a phonetic reader. We slowly and deliberately sounded out each word together in *Jog Frog Jog* and I was sure that Jeremy was well on his way to becoming a reader. I was unaware that our reading to him each day since his conception had a far greater impact on his ability to pick up the reading process than our frustrating sessions with that phonetic reader. His writing was not consciously encouraged or instructed for many years either by me or his teachers, except to copy from the board.

Fortunately for our fourteen-year-old daughter, Casey, by the time she was five years old I had already read *Beginnings of Writing* (Temple et al. 1988), so my understandings were beginning to grow in the area of writing. The summer before she entered kindergarten, I bought her a notebook and asked her to write a story. "How?" she asked. "Just listen to the sounds and write down what you hear," I told her. Reading her first draft of *Those Three Girls* (Figure 8.1), I discovered that she was an early graphophonic speller. I assessed her writing by observing her and I responded to her questions. I supported and encouraged some early steps for her writing. The lessons within this first piece of writing were: the sound of *th*; lining out what she no longer wanted; and when she got tired she could stop and finish writing when she

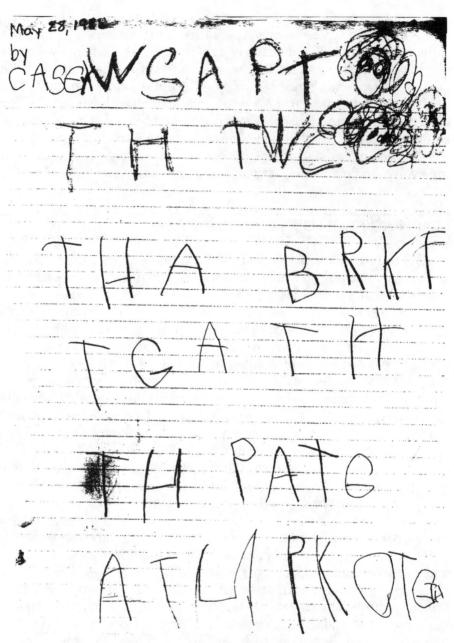

Figure 8.1. Casey's first draft of *Those Three Girls*.

woke up in the morning, which is just what she did. I published her story that day, and it is a book we treasure to this day.

OUR METAMORPHOSIS

Now, looking back at that time, I can see I did do some of the things we continue to practice to this day with the emerging writers in our classrooms. Although I did not have the understandings and practices I have now, I acted on what I felt was best for Casey as a writer based on my newly forming theories at the time. I continued developing my theories by reading Lucy Calkins' book *The Art of Teaching Writing* (1986) and Donald Graves' book *Writing: Teachers and Children at Work* (1989) and by engaging in dialogue with my partner, Mike, and with my friend and colleague, Marilyn Herzog. At about that same time Mike and I experienced the writing process first hand in a writing class taught by Donald Murray, author of *Write to Learn* (1984).

Our theories continue to evolve through our roles as teacher leader and program coordinator in The Learning Network. We read and refer to *Dancing with the Pen* (Ministry of Education 1992) and engage in developing action plans, observation, and instructional dialogue with a trainer of program coordinators, Jan Duncan, our program coordinator, Marilyn Herzog, and our other teacher leader, Bonnie Rhodes. We have also attended the annual Learning Network conferences and the past few years' summer institutes. Most importantly, dialogue with our colleagues within our school and across the nation, sharing, teaching, challenging, and questioning has deepened our understandings of *why* we do what we do.

One of the latest young writers in our lives is Kami, our "just turned" five-year-old daughter. Recently, she read the title of a book she wanted me to read to her in the evening and said, "You know why I keep reading so much? So I can be a better writer!" She made the connection! Like her older siblings, she has been immersed in books and read to since she was an infant, growing up in a home where the conditions for learning are more important than the conditions for a clean kitchen counter. Kami has always seen herself as a writer as well as a reader (Figure 8.2).

Long before she was actually putting pen to paper, she composed a poem. As we were driving in the car one day, she said, "Mommy, I love you higher than a tree!" I responded, as I would to any of my students, "That sounds like a poem," so when we got home, I published her first poem.

Figure 8.2. Kami at two years old signing a birthday card.

When she began writing her name, the slanted lines of the *K* did not meet where she intended and the vertical lines of the lower-case *a* and the lower-case *m* were also out in space. At the age of about four and a half, she developed the small muscle control and eye/hand coordination necessary to direct her pencil, and since then her letter formation has steadily improved. She now carries a notebook wherever she goes to do her work alongside of Mommy and Daddy while we study our students' draft books.

Kami writes on a daily basis, for a variety of reasons: letters to us or friends, shopping lists for pretend shopping trips, and last weekend she made a birthday card for the party she was attending. She said she knew how to spell *birthday* and *love*. She actually had the conventional spelling for *love*, and her approximation for *birthday* was only missing the *irt*. Her spelling usually consists of combinations of letters found in her name and *mom* and *dad* (the words she knows), so she is somewhere in the early graphophonic stage of spelling.

However, because Kami likes to do things right, we have already faced the challenge with her that many primary teachers face: "But how do you spell it?" "Is this right?" She would rather have us do the work, even in pronouncing the words for her to hear the sounds, than to take the risk herself. Recently I said to her, "Just write what you hear. That's how my first graders do it. You won't learn how until you try it yourself." She finally took the risk of writing alone. She wrote, *T E A m F* (Teddy is my friend) (Figure 8.3). She started in the middle of her paper and wrote one letter on top of the other as she mouthed the words. I knew what my teaching point was. I simply pointed to where to begin her next thought, moved my finger once across the page, and said, "I write it across the page, just like when I read a book to you." She continued with *I LOVE T E AMF* (I love Teddy). She knew to look

Figure 8.3. Kami's writing.

at her first spelling of *Teddy*, which is why she followed it with *AMF*, but when she went back and read what she had written she quickly lined this part out, a technique I must have previously modeled for her.

CLASSROOM PRACTICE

It is easy to see Kami is an active constructor of meaning, as Marie Clay would say (1991, 61). The same can be said for children in our classes. Although their set for literacy may vary, they all come to school with oral language and with experience of the world around them. These attitudes, understandings, and behaviors form the basis for our instruction in reading and writing.

Most of these children have found that language is the most efficient way to communicate with others. The need for meaning is reinforced time and again as they work to make themselves understood. Each child's oral language provides the syntactic structure for his or her writing. Once the child realizes that what is spoken can be written down and what is written down can be read, the value of writing becomes apparent.

Every time children experience something, they add to their background knowledge. Every experience with the world provides them with valuable information that they can bring to their reading and writing. Some of the information tells them that much of what happens around them is predictable and makes sense. The understandings of these patterns become a stable part of most children's lives, such as: the light switch is usually up for on and down for off; the sun is out during the day; the moon is out at night. Other information about the world around them will be highly personalized and specific to them. Many of their life experiences form the foundation for the personal narrative stories they will be writing.

Prior to the beginning of school we administer the Observation Survey (Clay 1993a) to assess and evaluate our incoming students. This battery of six assessments includes Running Records, Letter Identification, Concepts About Print, Word Tests, Writing (Samples and Vocabulary), and Hearing and Recording Sounds in Words (Dictation Task) and takes about thirty minutes per student to complete. This gives us a picture of our students as readers and writers. The nature of the assessments also provides us with the first opportunity to convince our students that they are readers and writers. It makes the first day of school far less stressful for the children, for the parents, and for us because we have already established a relationship of trust and support.

From the very first time our students meet us, there must be no doubt in their minds that we consider them readers and writers. To ensure this we try to have the conditions for learning that Brian Cambourne (1988) has defined (immersion, demonstration, expectation, responsibility, use, approximation, and response, accompanied by engagement) in place in our classrooms. Discovering what our students understand about reading and writing prior to the start of school makes establishing the conditions for learning for each student easier.

In the Beginning

It is our job to take our students from where they are when they come to us to their next level of understanding. We do this by supporting and encouraging their "wee steps" along the way by scaffolding learning experiences within their daily writing. The writing process for these young learners just spreading their wings is truly the delight of our lives. As we begin the year and establish the community of learners in our classrooms, we share stories from our own childhoods or from our lives that are within the conceptual understanding of our students, modeling the oral telling of personal narratives. Then we have the students form small groups and give everyone the opportunity to tell a personal story. When they write, these stories become some of their first topic choices.

Starting on the first day of school we invite the children to gather around our teacher draft books (chart tablets) and we model the writing process for them daily, just as comfortably as we model the reading process by reading to them many times a day. We model the telling of stories, topic selection, planning our writing, dating our writing, and drafting each day (Figure 8.4).

Modeling Writing

Our chart tablets rest on an easel in the most visible and roomy area of our classrooms. We model planning, drafting, revising, proofreading, editing, and the entire recursive writing process while sharing bits and pieces of our lives that gradually become personal narratives, poems, and communications. Planning can take the form of sketches, webs, or lists, depending on the abilities of the writers. We quickly sketch and talk to the students about the process of planning as we sketch. We write our story, thinking about our focused learning outcome and the needs of our young writers. The stories at this point may be only one or two sentences long.

Figure 8.4. Modeling writing in a chart tablet draft book.

Sometimes modeling takes the form of shared writing, with the teacher acting as scribe for shared class experiences or reports based on the class's interests and "I wonders." The "I wonders" are questions that we would like to answer based on our interests, and they become the basis for research. The shared writing demonstrates what can be talked about can be written and what can be written can be read.

Of course, we do not do all of this in one sitting. We engage them with our stories and our writing for as long as their interest is there. At the beginning of the year, based on assessment samples that we have evaluated and our knowledge of each child's development, modeled writing is usually kept very short. As the year progresses and as our writers' needs change our modeling also changes. We show them that we can stop writing before a piece is complete. The following day, when we pick up our markers to continue, we model re-reading the piece to continue the flow, the meaning, and the structure of our writing. We refer back to our sketch or other plan and may model revising it.

Some teachers may find writing in front of their students difficult, but they need to believe that they, too, are writers. This modeling of the entire process needs to start on the first day of school and follow its natural recursive process throughout the year. These emergent and early writers need to see a writer at work and see the writing process

Figure 8.5. Draft writing books.

in action. When this happens, they become motivated and excited about sharing their own stories in their draft books.

Later in the morning on the very first day of school, we place in our students' hands a small composition book, their first draft book (see Figure 8.5). We want to keep a record of their growth from Day 1. The writing in their draft books may initially look much different from ours. However, because we model writing for our children daily, they work very hard at using the same conventions they see in our models. Their draft books are the black and white composition books you can buy in any stationery store, but any bound notebook would do. The object is to keep all drafts in one place, so papers do not get shuffled, disorganized, or lost. One critical element necessary to document growth over time is dating all drafts, including where the writer continues the following day. This, of course, is modeled while writing to our students and closely monitored until it becomes habitual for even the most emergent writers. Another challenge for some is the ability to turn to the following page to continue or start their next piece. This concept may be one of the initial learning steps for some, depending on their knowledge of how books work.

We continue with oral story telling for several weeks as they establish the connections among oral language, writing, and reading. After these first few weeks, the story telling is usually within a revision conference concerning the content of what they have already written, to clarify meaning and to add to their story.

Conditions for Learning

The following samples (Figures 8.6 to 8.9) are from beginning-of-

Figure 8.6. Trent, Day 1: I went on the Black Widow ride.

Figure 8.7. Nick, Day 1: Waterslide.

the-year draft books from our kindergarten and first-grade classes. Later in the chapter are comparative samples from these same writers approximately fifty to sixty days into the school year.

Much of our learners' growth is the direct result of the immersion of reading and writing of all kinds of texts in our classrooms, the daily modeling of writing, and when we comment on how texts are constructed and used as we read to our children several times a day.

We also have the expectation from that very first appointment with each student prior to school starting that each one of them is a writer. From Day 1, students are responsible for their own topic

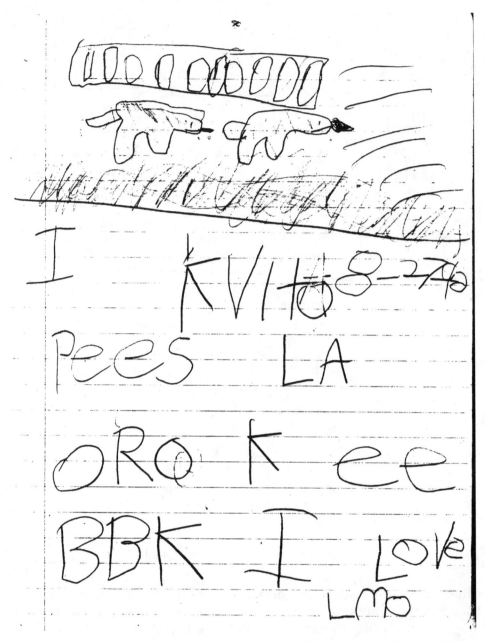

Figure 8.8. Amber, Day 1: I have two puppies. They are cute because I love them.

Figure 8.9. Andrea, Day 1: I swung on a rope into a river.

choices, writing daily, where they will sit to do their writing, and how they will convey their meaning with an audience in mind. They write for a variety of purposes, from sharing stories with the class or their parents to writing a letter to last year's teacher to ask if they can read to her class.

A large block of time is set aside for these writing and reading choices to take place. Our young learners feel free to approximate to get their meaning across, because the environment we have established is truly risk free. Their approximations in all of the aspects of writing are celebrated because that is how we know learning is taking place. Their wings are being tested. At the same time, these approximations provide us with the student's next learning step.

Writing Conferences

A critical condition for learning to take place is the way we respond to these writers (feedback). We confer with these writers on a daily basis. Revision conferences focus on clarifying and extending the meaning of the written piece. Teachers "need to demonstrate ways in which information can be reordered, reoriented, changed, deleted. They should show how honestly that, although writing is fun, it involves hard work—writing a quality piece takes time" (Ministry of Education 1992, 58). We have many revision conferences such as:

Teacher: You wrote, *I wat to my fad haemes* (I went to my friend's house). What did you do at your friend's house?
Student: We jumped on his bed and played Nintendo.
Teacher: I don't see that you have written that yet. Go on. I'll check on you in a little while to find what game you played when I read your story.

Later revision conferences can be done in small groups with the children asking each other genuine meaning-based questions. It is our opinion that revision is sometimes not given enough time to truly develop, and meaningful pieces are not written. Asking your children authentic questions to clarify meaning is how they hear their own oral responses, so they can either add that picture to their plan and/or simply write down what they just said. They are still solidifying the concept of what they say can be written down and what is written down can be read.

Tina's draft from September 13th in Figure 8.10 shows evidence of a brief revision conference. She first wrote *MBERiT RiT Di* (My bunny rabbit died). In a revision conference I responded to this by saying,

Figure 8.10. Tina's draft 9-13-96: My bunny rabbit died. I am sad. He is the best bunny rabbit in the whole world.

"Oh, I'm sorry. How do you feel about that?" She added *i M SAT H .SH MB BERIT RIT VTLT YT LT* (I am sad. He is the best bunny rabbit in the whole world).

As we rove through our classrooms of emergent and early writers during our language arts block, we also have the opportunity to do many brief editing and spelling conferences. We do this by checking our monitoring notebook in which we have documented our observations and plans for each child. We quickly choose a next learning step based on their latest approximations, show them how close they were, and model the correct way to do it. This can be as simple as spelling a word or teaching an editing convention.

Teacher: You wrote, *i y t v ml* (I went to the mall). You know the word *I*, but did you know that it always needs to be a capital *I*, like this? (Demonstrate.) What did you do at the mall?

Student: I ate an ice cream cone.

Teacher: Okay, now write that using a capital *I*, like this one.

This is an example of teaching at the point of need!

Figures 8.11 to 8.15 are samples of the same writers fifty to sixty days into the school year.

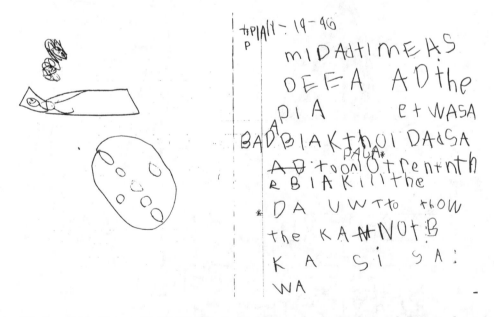

Figure 8.11. Trent, 11-19-96: My dad told me a story at the pool. It was about a black hole. Dad said to Paige, "Do you want to throw Trent in the black hole?" She could not because I swam away.

Figure 8.12. Nick, 11-14-96: Yesterday Steve came over. We had fun. My mom was with me. We went to Castles and Coasters. We went on the green roller coaster.

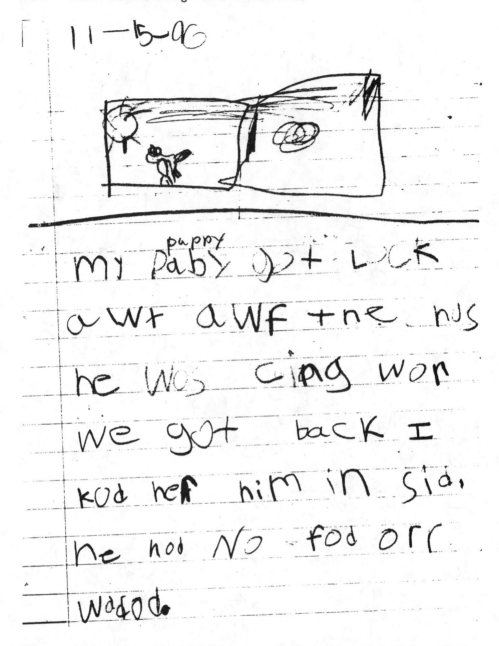

Figure 8.13. Amber, 11-15-96: My puppy got locked out of the house. He was crying. When we got back, I carried him inside. He had no food or water.

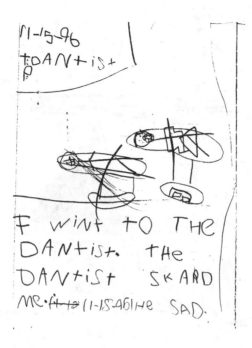

Figure 8.14. Andrea, 11-15-96: I went to the dentist. The dentist scared me. 11-18-96. She said.

Publishing

As soon as these stories are drafted, the teachers become the editors and publishers. For young writers, we publish every day. We simply get a small booklet made up of a few of sheets of paper stapled together and publish each child's story while sitting with them. By writing their words using standard conventions, we again model for them sentences beginning with capital letters, spaces between words, correct spelling, ending punctuation, and so on, but it is on their stories, in their own words, from their personal draft books. They can read the books they have written and we have published far more easily than they can those from a textbook company or from the library. The structure of the language and the content of the story are familiar to them, allowing them to attend to the visual aspects of the print. They read their stories, learning one-to-one finger/voice/print matching. As they read, they draw illustrations to match the text on the page so that they can read it tomorrow and the next day, as Andrea has done in Figure 8.16.

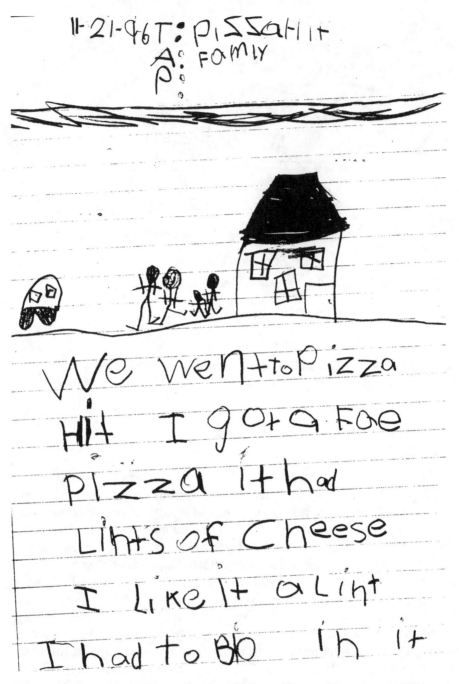

Figure 8.15. Tina, 11-21-96: T: Pizza Hut. A: Family. We went to Pizza Hut. I got a free pizza. It has lots of cheese. I liked it a lot. I had to blow on it.

Figure 8.16. Part of Andrea's published piece.

The Recursive Process

We repeat these processes and build upon the learning of each child every day in our classrooms. We write their next learning steps on a back page of their draft book and move their "I am learning to" steps onto another page or a second column entitled "I can" when their understandings show up as part of their independent writing, or as one of our students so aptly put it, "Oh, I see ... you write it there when we get the hang of it." At the emergent and early stages of writing development the "I am learning to/I can" page serves primarily to show the student how much he or she is learning about writing and acts as a reference for the teacher. Later, as the child becomes more proficient as a reader and writer, this page will serve as a personal reference during the proofreading stage of writing.

What we have shared in this chapter deals with students at the emergent and early stages of writing. This is not determined by a grade level, but rather by where each child is assessed in his or her writing development. Some of our students come to us further along on this continuum and are considered early writers, as Tina and Trent are soon to become. Early writers are capable of individual responsibility for more of the writing process, so our interactions are a bit different than those with our emergent writers. We simply meet our children wherever they are and support their next steps. Some of these next steps may include mastering the idea that a revision conference can be with a teacher, another student, or a group of students and focuses on clarifying meaning. They learn that proofreading means checking their own work with a red pen for previously learned spelling words, capital letters, and other conventions that they know they are responsible for because these skills appear on their "I can" lists. They come to understand that in an editing conference the teacher will teach them a specific new convention based on what they can do nearly right (Figure 8.17). They become aware of different genres and new ways of planning and researching. They learn how to help their fellow students by asking questions pertaining to meaning in revision conferences. Early writers are developing the confidence and ability to move on to fluent independent writing.

MOVING ON

Emergent writers are also usually emergent readers, so at this stage it is important that we edit and publish alongside the child. Because these published materials will become one of the child's primary reading resources we must be sure of the child's awareness and use of natural language and book language, and the child must see the piece develop. In addition, working alongside the child gives us an opportunity to assess the piece's effectiveness by watching the child's initial response to the finished piece. As early writers also become early readers, it is easier to read their pieces without them beside us and it is also easier for them to read their own published work without us beside them.

Teaching, like writing, is a process of growth. As our understandings about writing and teaching evolve, our skills as teachers grow. The Learning Network has provided a scaffold for our small steps in the teaching process, just as we support the small steps our students take as they try out their wings as writers. At the end of our students' year with us, we know they will be like those butterflies we had to set free–beautiful writers ready to take on the world.

Figure 8.17. Editing by the teacher and proofreading by the student.

Debbie Wepfer Shelton *is a first-grade teacher and a teacher leader at Las Brisas Elementary School, a Learning Network site in Glendale, Arizona. She has been teaching young children for twenty-one years, the past eleven in the Deer Valley School District.*

Mike Shelton *is a teacher leader and a kindergarten teacher at Las Brisas Elementary School, a Learning Network site in Glendale, Arizona, and is learning to be a trainer of program coordinators. He has taught special education and first grade and has been a Reading Recovery® Teacher Leader. Mike works as a facilitator for the Literacy Learning in the Classroom institutes during the summer.*

CHAPTER 9

Focus on Writing Conferences

Lisa Toner

"Why don't you ever really tell us what to write about? What I mean is, why do other teachers think they always have to tell you what to write?"

Amanda, Age 9
Phoenix, Arizona Learning Network Student

My journey with The Learning Network began in 1993 when I attended the Literacy Learning in the Classroom summer institute. I had no idea at the time what an impact The Learning Network would have on my career as an educator. Four years later, I continue to be challenged in my understandings of teaching literacy, especially writing instruction. It is this challenge that drives me to question my instructional practices in order to be the most effective teacher that I can be.

When I first began to implement what I had learned in the institute, I taught third grade. Since then, I have taught kindergarten as well as worked with teachers in kindergarten through fifth grade as a teacher leader. I have learned that the process of writing is not limited to certain grades. It is accessible to all writers, beginning as early as kindergarten.

My experiences in my own classroom and in the classrooms of others have shaped my understandings of the writing process. These understandings are constantly being reconstructed as I grow and reflect upon new learning.

COMING TO KNOW THE WRITING PROCESS

The summer after my first year of teaching I was offered the opportunity to attend the Literacy Learning in the Classroom summer institute sponsored by Richard C. Owen Publishers. I had no background knowledge about the institute before I attended. What I did know is that I consider myself a learner and that I probably could benefit from the workshop. Little did I know how much I would benefit.

I was introduced to many new ideas during those intense four days: the recursive model of writing; the importance of modeling the writing process; and the interrelatedness of reading and writing, to name just a few. However, by far, the most powerful piece of learning I took away from those four days was learning to question my current practice.

As I thought toward the 1993-1994 school year I wanted to implement as much of what I was learning as I could. We were cautioned in the institute to take "wee steps" and only implement a little at a time. I had grand hopes of taking giant steps because I felt that I had so far to go. My new class was composed of 27 Title I third graders. The thinking at that time within my school was that if all the children identified as at-risk were put in one classroom they could be given intensified instruction to accelerate their learning. It was a successful approach for us at the time even though now it is a practice we would not repeat.

Those children would certainly be a challenge for me. They had not yet discovered the power of writing. They were very reluctant to put their ideas down on paper. Many of them saw writing as drudgery and a source of failure. These children had somehow fallen through the cracks and I had the challenge of developing them as life-long writers.

At the start of the 1993-1994 school year, Montview made the commitment to join The Learning Network. During this school year a program coordinator would visit our school to support and build the literacy understandings of two teacher leaders. One teacher leader worked in my classroom and helped me to question my current practice and build new understandings.

I began the year by having my students write every day in spiral notebooks we call draft books. At the summer institute, we had been introduced to the writing process as described in *Dancing with the Pen* (Ministry of Education 1992). There were several steps within this process that I had not previously considered. I decided to use this model as a focus when teaching my children to write. Within this model, writing is seen as recursive. The process is circular rather than

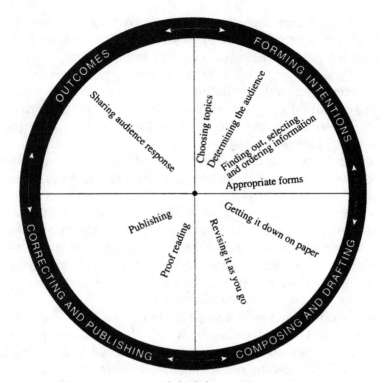

Figure 9.1. A model of the writing process.

linear. Students move in and out of the stages of writing just as writers do, crafting and refining their piece of writing (see Figure 9.1). In the model of writing that I had previously used, the movement from prewriting to publishing was almost always a forward, linear progression. As writers passed through each step they were not encouraged to revisit any of the previous stages of writing. Doing so was often seen as regressive. The recursive model of writing consists of four stages: forming intentions, composing and drafting, correcting and publishing, and outcomes. The book *Dancing with the Pen* became a valuable source of information in helping to build my understandings about these stages of the writing process.

USING THE WRITING PROCESS

My first goal was to bolster my students' attitudes toward writing. I wanted them to understand that writing is the creation of meaning. I also wanted to create a safe environment where students could approximate in their writing without fear of reprisal.

To measure growth of our student's writing each teacher at our school collects a beginning-of-the-year writing sample, which is then evaluated for content, conventions, and organization. This task is repeated at the end of the school year with another writing sample. When I attempted to get my students to write this first sample I was not prepared for what occurred. When I first explained to them what I expected I got many comments such as "What if I can't write?" and "I can't do that." I responded by telling them to do the best they could and assured them that whatever they wrote would be just fine. Some went to work, some cried, and one frustrated little girl just crumpled her paper and threw it on the floor.

We survived this controlled writing experience and what it gave me was valuable information about my students' attitudes toward writing. Their writing samples were assessments, which I could evaluate to plan for their first teaching points. In spite of this negative writing experience, I found my learners to be eager for new information when it was presented in a non-threatening way.

I made sure that I read and wrote to my students every day. When I read to them I picked pieces in which the language was alive. We talked together about things we especially liked in the language the authors used. We also talked about the reasons people write and who an author's audience might be. I referred back to these discussions later as I was modeling writing in front of them to help them make the connection between reading and writing.

I modeled all stages of the writing process—not in one day, but over time. As I modeled, I talked aloud, sharing the thinking that was going on in my head as I created my piece of writing.

Slowly, my students' attitudes about writing began to change. Of course, it was different for every student, but it seemed that once they completed and shared their first piece of writing, their outlook became more positive. They were feeling successful at writing and success breeds success. My students also turned out to be remarkable role models and sources of support for each other.

I let go of my previously held belief that all students needed to be at the same stage of the writing process at the same time. They worked at different speeds. Since my editing load was now more evenly spread out, I was able to work individually with students more often. As a teacher, I no longer dreaded editing conferences. Instead, I found it exciting to see the progress my students were making.

One day near the end of our writing time I looked at the clock to see that it was almost time for recess. I asked my students to put their things away and get ready to go outside. I was surprised to hear several groans of disappointment. Seeing the puzzled look on my face, one student, Shamica, asked me, "Can't we stay and finish our writing?" Needless to say, I was pleasantly shocked. I let them stay to finish their work and from then on recess became an option. Many students frequently chose to stay in the classroom to work on their writing. What a change in attitude from the beginning of the year!

It was about this time that I began to notice certain trends in my students' writing. Up until this point I had been meeting with students only to give them feedback when they had reached the editing stage of writing. They needed more frequent and varied feedback than they were getting. I needed to once again question my practice and thus began to strengthen my understandings of writing conferences.

THE ROLE OF WRITING CONFERENCES

In order to help my students to reach their writing potential I came to understand the importance of writing conferences and the feedback given to students during these conferences. An article by Gordon Wells (1990) challenged me to examine whether I was encouraging literate thinking in my classroom. He wrote that literacy acquisition is a collaborative effort. He makes the point that "children learn most effectively through participation in meaningful joint activities in which their performance is assisted and guided by a more competent member of the culture." I saw writing conferences as the venue in which I could guide and assist students in writing.

The conferences I would hold with students needed to occur at all stages of the writing process. It was a crucial piece, which I had never before implemented. I came to realize that the better I got to know my learners as writers and the more I learned about the writing process, the more specific and meaningful my feedback and teaching could be within a writing conference.

My discoveries about these conferences did not occur in any logical sequence. As any learner, I took on bits and pieces of learning as I was ready for them. Each new piece of learning caused me to reflect on my current understandings and practice and then to reconstruct my thinking and possibly my practice to accommodate this new information. Although this learning was random, it was constant and ongoing. What I learned is that conferences look different and serve different purposes at each stage of the writing process.

WRITING CONFERENCES IN THE FORMING INTENTIONS STAGE

In the forming intentions stage students lay the foundations for their writing. They think about what they want to write, who this piece of writing is for, and what form it will take. With these things in mind, they make an appropriate plan for their writing.

Writers must first choose a topic they want to write about. As often as possible students should be able to self-select their topics for writing. I found that students need support when given the responsibility of choosing their own topics. I think most clearly of Sharee. Sharee wrote about what was most safe and comfortable to her—her family. Sharee wrote many stories about her family even though I encouraged her and others to write about many different topics. It wasn't until I modeled the use of an ongoing topic list that Sharee began to broaden her horizon of topics. Sharee and other students began to keep topic lists, which they added to frequently. Ideas for topics came from a variety of sources, including life experiences, the asking and answering of questions, and sometimes through the suggestions of others. Occasionally I would introduce a phrase such as "Places I Have Been To" to spark new ideas. Brittany used this phrase to brainstorm many writing ideas (Figure 9.2).

I brought together students like Sharee, who had difficulty selecting new or different topics, for a small group conference. In these conferences I talked with my students about their topic lists and their possible ideas for writing. The outcome of these conferences was not only for each child to have something to write about at that particular time, but also to develop skills to help them generate future topics on their own. Another outcome was for these students to hear from each other what kinds of topics their peers might be interested in reading.

During these conferences we also talked about potential audiences for their published work. In the past the audience for my students' writing was always me, the teacher. But, as they chose their own topics they also began to develop an awareness of who they were writing for. Students who struggled with the concept of audience usually had not had much of their writing actually reach an audience. Once students began publishing and their publishing began to reach the intended audience, they began to understand this abstract concept.

Just as the building of a house requires an architect's well-conceived plans, a writer must also plan for his piece of writing. My students used sketches, webs, lists, and other graphic organizers to plan for their writing and to help organize their thoughts. The type of plan a

Places I have been to

in the tree	Zoo
South Cara lina	at home
air Port	Class meeting
fishins	farm
the Park	library
Mountains	The mall
back Yard	at Heather house
MY room	at Recess
School	Friday funday

Figure 9.2. A topic list to help students generate writing ideas.

student uses depends on their developmental level as well as the type of writing they are working on. Jonathon used a web to organize his thoughts for his story about the shack (Figure 9.3). I held one-on-one and small-group conferences about how to develop a plan. The students and I talked about what they wanted to write about and what would be a logical sequence for this information. The tendency of my students

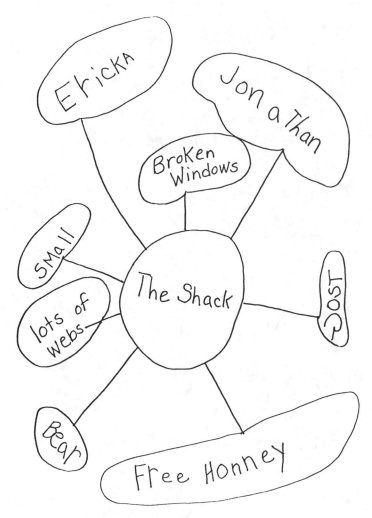

Figure 9.3. Web of "The Shack."

was to rush into the composing and drafting stage without enough information to support their writing. I found that good plans led to
clearer writing and taught students how to create a plan for their writing. These planning conferences sometimes occurred even after students had begun their drafts. This happened when students realized
that they didn't have enough to write about. I have also had students
go back to add to and revise a plan if their writing was rambling or going nowhere. Sometimes the comments of peers in these conferences
helped to get writers back on track.

I always tried to take notes about my learners during writing conferences. These notes helped me to know my learners and to plan for future learning. I also tried to have a specific outcome for the conferences I facilitated. When my teaching was focused and my outcome was clear I felt my students were able to take away valuable information from the conference. If I was too general in my teaching or not prepared, the conferences never seemed to be quite as successful.

WRITING CONFERENCES IN THE COMPOSING AND DRAFTING STAGE

Moving on to the composing and drafting stage, students begin to get their writing down on paper. As they write, they refer to their plan to make sure all of their original ideas are included in their writing. Also as they write, they continually read and reread what they have written to make sure that it makes sense.

When writers want to confirm that the intended meaning of their writing is apparent to their audience, they choose to have a revision conference. The purpose of a revision conference is to clarify the meaning of their text to ensure that the reader will understand what is written. My students' need to revise their writing for meaning caused me to form revision conference groups. These groups would consist of three or four students who were ready for feedback on a complete draft of their piece. The students would take turns reading their writing while the others would listen. The members of the group would then pose questions to the author about parts they found confusing or lacking in information. This process of questioning can be difficult for students, but with practice and guidance the revision conference becomes an effective place for students to receive valuable feedback. When I introduced this process I was present to model questions focused on meaning, but as the year progressed, students began to have revision conferences in small groups without me. One student in the group would record the questions the other students asked. It was then the responsibility of the author to determine which questions he would answer to clarify meaning within his piece of writing.

In the following excerpt from a revision conference Alex shares his story about bears with Dustin and Pete.

Alex: "Bears have claws to attack their prey. Bears eat meat because they don't like dirt. Bears are strong to face their prey."
Dustin: What kind of prey do bears attack?
Alex: Other animals.

Pete: What kind of animals?

Alex: I'm not sure.

Teacher: Where could you find out that information?

Alex: I could look in a book I have about bears.

Pete: Why are bears strong?

Alex: Because they have big muscles.

Dustin: I think that too, because they do have muscles and strong legs. I know because I saw a movie about bears on television.

After this conference, Alex revised his piece to include more information about his topic. His final story was more complete and interesting than his draft. When students have revised their draft and feel that the intention of the piece has been conveyed, they move into the correcting and publishing stage of writing.

WRITING CONFERENCES IN THE CORRECTING AND PUBLISHING STAGE

Correcting

In the correcting and publishing stage of the writing process, emphasis is put on ensuring that the piece of writing is syntactically correct and print conventions are accurate. For this to happen, a partnership is formed between the student writers and their teacher. The students' role in this partnership is to take responsibility to make all corrections of which they are capable. This is called proofreading. For example, if a student has learned the appropriate use and placement of quotation marks, they are expected to check their writing for this convention.

I use "I am learning to/I can" pages to keep track of what individual students have been taught, and what writing conventions they are expected to control and demonstrate. Each student has a blank sheet in the back of his or her draft book. When a student shows he or she is ready to use a particular convention in his or her writing, such as question marks at the ends of questions, I teach that convention in an editing conference within the context of the written piece. Then I record the convention on the "I am learning to" side of the sheet and date it. When I see evidence of the student using the new skill independently, I put the date of this observation on the "I can" side of the sheet (Figure 9.4).

Editing conferences are individual conferences with students. Before an editing conference takes place I check that the student has proofread his or her piece of writing, and that they have taken respon-

date	I am learning to.......	I can........
8-2	* proofread using my I am learning to/I can sheet	8-18
8-10	* Capitalize names of cities and states ex: Denver, Colorado	8-12
8-18	* use dictionary as a resource to spell words	9-6
8-25	* use an apostrophe s to show ownership ex: Mary's cat	8·27
9-2	* take notes during a revision conference	9-6
9-9	* use "our" and "hour" correctly	9-11
9-17	* use speechmarks when someone is talking	9·29
9-23	* add more details to my web when I plan	10-1
9-30	* Capitalize words in the title	10·7
10-7	* Add 's' to the end of words when there is more than one person	

Figure 9.4. Example of an "I am learning to/I can" page.

sibility for the conventions on which they have demonstrated success. Then it becomes my responsibility to make all other changes in grammar, spelling, and punctuation that are needed. I make these corrections using whatever writing utensil the child used. As I make these corrections, I look for one aspect of writing that the student has nearly correct. That is the next learning point, which I will teach to the student. When I find this teaching point, I do not correct it. I save this point to be corrected during the editing conference. At this time I also look for approximations in spelling and handwriting and make note of them in my monitoring notebook.

After these observations are noted, I sit down with the student for an editing conference. This conference is meant to be quick and to the point. My objective is to give the student feedback on evidence of his or her application of previous learning and to teach the student one new piece of learning. All of this is done within the context of the student's written piece.

The following is an editing conference between Heather and me. Heather has written a short essay on her desire to be a police officer (Figure 9.5).

Teacher: Heather, do you remember what we talked about at our last editing conference?

Heather: Yes. I learned that the words in the title of a story need capital letters.

Teacher: Can you show me where you used this in your police officer story?

(Heather points to the title.)

Teacher: Great! Is there anytime you wouldn't use capital letters in a title?

Heather: Yes, if there are little words in the title.

Teacher: What do you mean by little words?

Heather: Um, like *a* or *the* or *an*. They don't need to be capitals unless they are the first word of a title.

At this point, I dated Heather's "I am learning to/I can" sheet to note that she understood and was using something I had previously taught her. She was now ready for a new piece of learning.

Teacher: Heather, can you read to me the first sentence of your story?

Heather: "I want to be a police officers... (goes back and rereads) a police officer when I grow up because I want to fight lots of crime."

Teacher: Why did you go back and change *police officers* to *police officer* when you read your story?

Heather: Because it didn't sound right.

Teacher: That was a good strategy to use, rereading something that doesn't sound right. What did you decide sounded better?

Heather: *Police officer.*

Teacher: What would you need to change in your writing?

Heather: I need to cross out the *s*.

(Heather takes her pencil and crosses out the *s* at the end of the word *officers*.)

Teacher: Is there anywhere else in your writing where you may need to cross something out? (Heather reads through her draft and finds the same error in two more places. She corrects her error.)

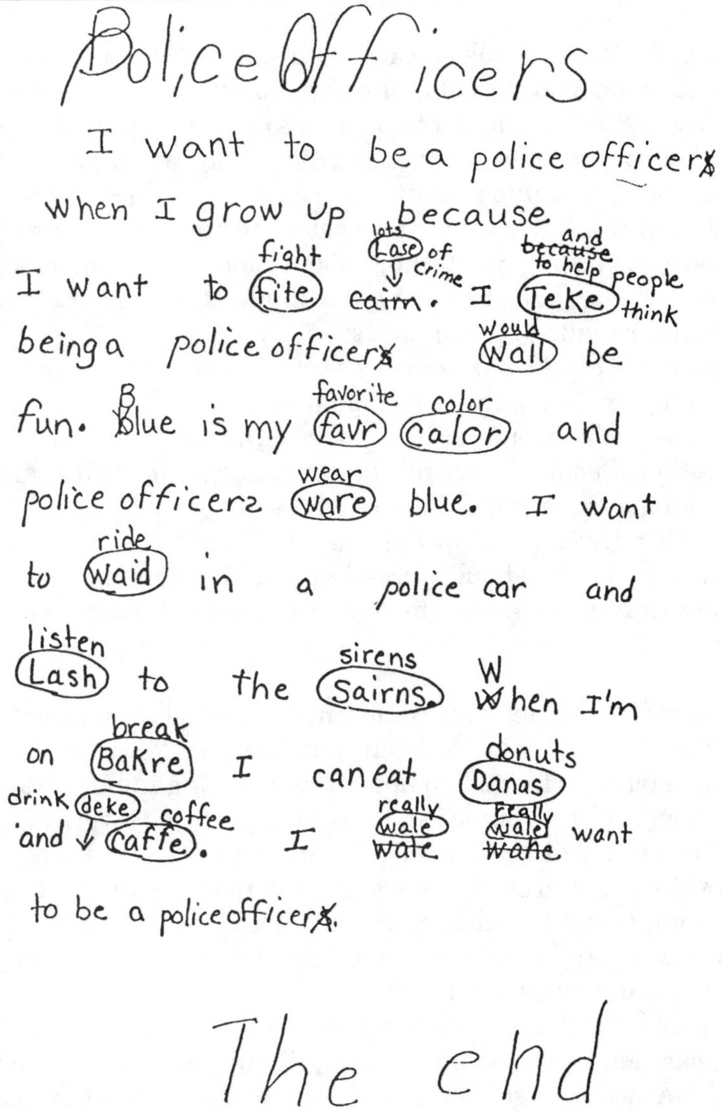

Police Officers

I want to be a police officers
when I grow up because
                          lots and
                   fight (ase) of because
I want to (fite) eaim. I (TeKe) to help people
                         crime   think
being a police officers (Nall) be
                                would
       B   favorite color
fun. Blue is my (favr) (calor) and
                    wear
police officers (ware) blue. I want
        ride
to (Waid) in a police car and
listen   sirens W
(Lash) to the (Sairns) When I'm
       break   donuts
on (BaKre) I can eat (Danas)
drink (deke) coffee   really really
'and ✓ (Caffe). I (wale) (wale) want
                    wate wate

to be a police officers.

The end

Figure 9.5. Heather's draft of "Police Officers" with changes from an editing conference.

Teacher: Heather, do you know why *police officers* didn't sound right in that sentence?

Heather: No.

Teacher: Listen to this sentence that you wrote: "Blue is my favorite color and police officers wear blue." Does *police officers* sound right in that sentence?

Heather: Yes.

Teacher: When I look at those two sentences, I see that when you were writing about yourself and what you wanted, it sounded better to say *police officer*, without the *s*. You are one person. But when you wrote about more than one police officer, like when you talked about their uniform, it sounded better to say *police officers*, with an *s*. So, when do you think it would sound better to add the *s* to a word?

Heather: When I was talking about more than one person.

Teacher: Can you show me an example of this in your story?

(Heather reads over her essay.)

Heather: Here, I put *police officer* with no *s* at the end because it says "I really, really want to be a police officer."

Teacher: Why wouldn't it be *police officers*?

Heather: Because it sounds better to say *police officer* and because I am talking about myself. I am one person.

Teacher: Heather, what did you just learn?

Heather: That I should reread my writing to make sure it sounds right and that an *s* goes at the end of a word if I mean more than one person.

Before Heather left this conference, I wrote her new piece of learning on her "I am learning to/I can" page on the "I am learning to" side. I would watch for Heather to apply this learning in her future writing.

Although I had planned to focus on a surface feature of writing, in this case the use of the plural *s*, Heather took away from our conference a valuable writing strategy about rereading her writing to make sure it sounds right. Teaching points should not be limited to conventions, but also can include any point about the writing process in which the student may need support.

Implementing "I am learning to/I can" sheets appeared simple at first. I soon learned that maintaining them was much more of a challenge. I learned that to be effective, the teaching point I chose needed to be within each student's zone of proximal development. The concept of the zone of proximal development comes from the Russian psychologist Lev Vygotsky. In *Tools of the Mind* by Elena Bedrova and Deborah Leong it is described as:

Those behaviors that are on the edge of emergence. It is defined by two levels. The lowest level is what the child can do independently and the highest level is what the child can do with maximum assistance (Bedrova and Leong 1996, 162).

Finding a teaching point within a student's zone of proximal development starts with knowing what the students can do independently and then looking for evidence of what a student is attempting to do. I found that the more experience I had evaluating students' writing for approximations, the better I became at selecting appropriate teaching points. I also learned that as my understandings of the writing process deepened, the teaching points I chose became more specific and effective.

When I taught students something new that was in their zone of proximal development, they were much more able to take the information and use it in their writing. If I choose a piece of new learning that was above their zone, it was much more difficult for the students to use the information and the teaching episode was usually full of confusion for the learners.

Publishing

After the editing stage is completed and all corrections have been made, students are ready to publish their writing. With younger writers, publishing is done daily. As children produce longer and more complex pieces, publishing is done less frequently. The form a published piece will take is limited only by the imagination of the writer. When selecting an appropriate form, the writer must take into consideration who the audience is and what the purpose of this piece of writing is. Students may need guidance in selecting an appropriate form for their published piece.

The students in my third-grade class had a very narrow view of publishing. They thought that publishing was putting a story into a book format and then illustrating the book. This format was indeed appropriate for some of their writing, but it was limiting. Robert and James wanted to write to a local professional football player. They planned, drafted, proofread, and edited their letter and were ready to publish. They had some experience with writing letters but needed support in determining the correct form a letter would need and how to address an envelope. We met in a conference and ended up consulting actual letters and addressed envelopes for models of appropriate forms.

Sometimes conferences at this stage focus on the illustrations or artwork, which enhances the message of the student's writing. Input from peers helps students to make decisions about what to include and how the finished piece will look. Publishing conferences help students get their message to their intended audience.

WRITING CONFERENCES IN THE OUTCOMES STAGE

Getting writing to an audience is the ultimate goal of writers. Occasionally this is not true, as in the case of a personal journal or diary, but for the majority of writing genres, the purpose for writing something is for it to be read by someone other than the author. In the outcomes stage of the writing process, students not only get their writing to an audience, but also reflect upon the responses they receive from the audience.

Response to writing is an often overlooked but very important aspect of the writing process. If a student receives a positive response it may be the spark that causes him or her to move on to a new piece of writing. With my original group of reluctant third-grade writers, I saw this phenomena occur over and over. These students were experiencing success at something they had previously only associated with frustration. Their excitement grew with every piece of writing they got to an authentic audience.

Conferences at this stage can be very exciting because they show the learner how to take feedback and use it to expand on learning. For example, Josh wrote a story about sharks, which he shared with the whole class. When he finished his story it was clear that his audience had many questions that he had not answered. Shalenia had the same experience with a story she wrote about New Mexico. These students were pulled together in a conference to discuss how they felt about the feedback they had received and what they planned to do about it. The result of the conference was that both students decided to begin new stories on the same topic to provide more information.

Response from an audience is not always positive. Although we have no control over audiences outside of our classroom, we have the responsibility to ensure that within our classrooms students have a safe learning environment. Therefore, it is important for students to learn how to appropriately respond to each other. I used to get frustrated with the shallow responses I would hear from my students when they listened to each other's writing. I would hear "That was good" or "I liked that." I came to realize that students didn't always realize how powerful critical, genuine response can be to a writer. The more they reflected on how they valued genuine response, the more valuable responses I began to hear. Questions emerged such as: "What made you decide to have the setting of your story in the forest?" or "How did you find out that information about Mars?" and comments such as: "I thought the part of your story where they were eating breakfast at night was funny! You used funny words like *squished* and *splat*."

Before looking at this model of writing I had always considered sharing as an ending point of writing. Now I see that in the writing process there are really no ending points. Instead, there are many new beginning points.

THE TEACHING AND LEARNING CYCLE

During this time, as I was developing my understandings of the writing process, my teacher leaders were helping me to understand the teaching and learning cycle. They helped me to see that as I observe a need that a student has in his or her writing, I am actually using the student's writing sample as an assessment tool. I then evaluate the sample to determine what new learning the student is ready for. Concurrently, I listen to students during writing conferences and evaluate them for their understandings of the writing process. Any verbal response from a student, such as a question, an answer to a question, a comment, or a direct response might also reveal a misunderstanding of the writing process.

After evaluating writing samples and student responses, I can plan for teaching. I may look for students with the same needs and group them together for a conference. I also choose resources that I may need to help me make a teaching point.

The teaching occurs during the editing conferences, in which I would endeavor to teach each student at his or her point of need. The cycle begins again with assessments I gathered during and after the writing conferences. With the knowledge of the writing process, I am able to use the teaching and learning cycle as a guide to teach my students what they need to know about writing.

THE JOURNEY CONTINUES

I began my journey four years ago and it still continues. I am constantly being challenged to ask myself why I am doing what I am doing. Although some of the challenge comes from my peers or professional reading, now I mostly challenge myself. My involvement with Montview Elementary and The Learning Network has caused me to grow and change professionally in ways that I doubt I would have come to on my own.

Within the past four years I have witnessed the power of empowering teachers with knowledge of reading and writing processes and the teaching and learning cycle. I have also witnessed my students grow immensely as readers and writers. At the end of each school year I have felt enormous pride as I see how my learners have grown and moved along the learning continuum. The Learning Network and the support that it provides allows schools to be able to support teachers where they need it most: in the classroom and working with children. The Learning Network helps teachers to reach all of their learners, not just those who would learn in spite of the teaching. This type of support should be available to all teachers.

LISA TONER is a kindergarten teacher and a teacher leader at Montview Elementary School, a Learning Network site in Aurora, Colorado. She is in training to be a program coordinator. She has worked with learners from many backgrounds, including new learners of English and special education. During the summer Lisa works as a facilitator for the Literacy Learning in the Classroom institutes.

CHAPTER 10

Focus on Reading

Elizabeth Reilly Welsome

"I never planned for individual needs before and didn't actually group for instruction. This is an amazing thing. I never thought I could do it, and now that I see it's possible, it's a revelation for me."

Florence Temple
Teacher Leader, Brooklyn, New York

MY PERSONAL JOURNEY

In the spring of 1993, I was finishing my second year of teaching at P.S. 191 in New York City. In my first two years as a teacher, I taught a fourth- and fifth-grade bridge class as well as a second-grade class. During those two years, I spent a great deal of time researching and planning lessons. I searched for curriculum guides, studied city and state mandates, and tried my best to integrate everything into some kind of thematic approach so that learning wasn't segmented. I also spent a great deal of time trying to find ways to make my classroom a place that students felt was their own. I always wanted a room where students could move around, use materials, and get to work as if in a workplace, where everyone knows what to do and why they are doing it. Most attempts at this resulted in chaos, behavior problems, and headaches, but I kept trying. During this time, I was doing a great deal of work, and although I was going through the motions, I did not feel that I was getting the results I wanted.

P.S. 191 is located in Community School District 3 in Manhattan.

District 3 is a place where staff development is alive and well. Each year, the district offers a range of workshops and seminars free to its teachers. Soon after being hired by the district, I began to soak up all that was being offered. I went to monthly study groups, after-school workshops, and took whatever help I could get. I knew that somewhere out there, I was going to find the support that I needed to get my classroom functioning as I saw it in my head. P.S. 191 was lucky enough to have an on-site staff developer. Jacquie Morison was the first person to get me thinking about the children in my classroom as individuals, not just as second graders. I listened to everything she had to say and I changed my practice a little at a time. At the end of my second year of teaching, District 3 announced that it was sponsoring the Literacy Learning in the Classroom summer institute. All I knew at the time was that there were going to be people from New Zealand talking about their model of teaching. I signed up for the four-day institute hoping that I might get some answers. I had no idea that it was going to change my career path as well as my life.

I will never forget listening to Jan Duncan at that first summer institute. Everything she said made perfect sense. The classroom she described was the one that I pictured in my head. I found myself nodding my head and saying, "Yes, this makes sense" as Jan spoke about assessment, evaluation, planning, and teaching to the point of need. I listened in awe as she spoke about children, teaching, and learning. I sat and thought that I wanted to do it all, but my rational side said no way—it was just too different from what I was doing at the time. I left the four-day institute thinking that I could put into place a few of the things that I had heard about, but I just couldn't do it all.

At about the same time, P.S. 191 made the final arrangements to become a Learning Network school. Upon returning to school in September 1993, my principal, Dr. Elena Nasereddin, asked me if I would like to be a teacher leader for this new staff development initiative. All I knew was that it meant I would get to work with a program coordinator, Jan Duncan, the woman who had left me awestruck that summer. I was terrified, but I said yes.

Jan's two-year involvement in my development as a teacher leader provided me with the support that I needed to turn my classroom into the one I saw in my head. What I did not expect was how much I would change as well. Over the past four years, I have gone from becoming a teacher leader and a facilitator for the Literacy Learning in the Classroom summer institutes to being a program coordinator for The Learning Network. I also remain a classroom teacher at P.S. 191 in New York City. Who would have known that a four-day institute could have changed my life so much?

WHAT IS READING?

At some point during the first summer institute I attended, I was asked, "What is reading?" At the time, I was teaching second grade and I "taught" reading. I was also an avid reader myself. Why then was it so hard for me to come up with a definition of reading? I thought that reading had something to do with the letters on the page and how one would put them together to create words. But what exactly did those words mean and whose meaning was it? Was the meaning created by the letters on the page or was it created by the reader? This single question set me on a journey to find out just what reading is. As I continued to question myself and be questioned by others about reading, I found that one word kept surfacing. That word was *meaning*.

Whether it is the meaning the reader assigns to the letters on a page, the meaning of the words those letters form, or the meaning that is made when those words are strung together into sentences, *reading is the creation of meaning*. I know that it seems pretty simple. In fact, I'm sure that at some point during my first summer institute, someone came right out and told me that reading is the creation of meaning. However, it took a lot of questioning and exploration on my own for me to internalize this understanding, and once I did, my new understanding began to change everything that I said and did. If I believe that reading is the creation of meaning, then I have to question my classroom practice. Does my practice in the teaching of reading reflect my new understanding? Is my main objective to get students to see reading as the creation of meaning, or is it for them to know the letters and words so that they could then "read"? As I began to reflect on my practice, it was clear that I was going to have to make some changes in my teaching.

The process of change is not always easy, but my understandings were deepening as I continued to read and learn more about the process of reading. In turn, the process of change seemed to flow just a bit easier. My new understandings were beginning to be reflected in my practice, but I still could not *articulate* the process of reading or how this understanding was changing my practice. I realized that I still had a long way to go. I also realized that if I was going to change my practice in teaching children to read, it became imperative that I understood just how it is that people do read–another question for me to begin digging into. How do we read?

UNDERSTANDING THE READING PROCESS

My ongoing involvement in The Learning Network has enabled me to continue my learning process. One of the peculiar mysteries of life results when you revisit a professional article or text and discover that you are able to make more meaning out of the same document than before. Such is my view of the reading process diagram and terminology shown in Figures 10.1 and 10.2 (Richard C. Owen Publishers 1997b and 1997c). Each time I study this process, I am able to articulate more.

THE READING PROCESS

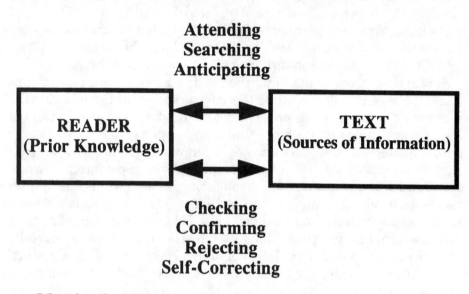

Attending
Searching
Anticipating

READER
(Prior Knowledge)

TEXT
(Sources of Information)

Checking
Confirming
Rejecting
Self-Correcting

Meaning facilitates reading; it is not just the outcome of it.

Attend	Pay particular attention to visual information (to construct the sense of the text)
Search	Look purposefully for particular information
Anticipate	Predict alternatives or probabilities of text on the basis of prior knowledge and information in the text
Check	Reconsider a response against more than one source of information
Confirm	Accept the appropriateness of a response
Self-correct	Provide an accurate response to the text in the light of new information

Figure 10.1. Reading process diagram.

READING PROCESS TERMINOLOGY

	ALSO KNOWN AS:
MEANING	Semantics Sense
STRUCTURE	Syntax Grammatical Pattern
VISUAL	Graphophonics
ERROR	Miscue Approximation Prediction Substitution
SOURCES OF INFORMATION	Cues Cueing Systems
ANTICIPATE	Predict

Figure 10.2. Reading process terminology.

Readers come to a text with *background* or *prior* knowledge. Upon meeting the text, readers are faced with three sources of information: meaning, syntax (or structure), and visual and phonological information. *Meaning* occurs as a result of what the readers know about the world around them as it relates to the text. The use of pictures, diagrams, and charts can help readers make even more meaning. This sense of meaning expands with each word read. As more of the text is read, background knowledge continues to grow and provides the support to maintain meaning. A second source of information is *syntactical*. What readers know about grammar and syntax can help make meaning. Readers can ask themselves: "Does what I am reading sound right?" "Is the grammar correct?" "Do we say it that way?" Again, background knowledge is what allows the readers to confirm or reject what was anticipated. The third source of information is the *visual and phonological information*; the graphophonic information. Yes, phonics. Can people read without the visual information, without the shape of the word, without knowing the letters and the sounds that they make? I would argue that they could read without some of the visual and phonological information, but this source of information must work in concert with the other sources of information in order for the readers to create meaning.

What happens when life-long readers encounter a text? They begin to read based on what they know about the subject matter and about the reading process. Do they know the sounds of the letters in front of them? If so, do they know how to put them into words and sentences that are syntactically correct and that make sense? Life-long readers do. However, in classrooms, teachers are confronted with the challenge of teaching children how to do all of these things. It is not enough to teach a child the sounds of the letters and leave it at that. Sounds in isolation have no meaning. Children have to learn how to look at the letters on the page and make attempts at the sounds with the idea that those sounds must go together to make sense. Reading is the creation of meaning. Visual information is a necessary component of reading, but it must be used along with syntactical information and meaning for it to actually support readers.

Going back to my understanding that reading is the creation of meaning led me to ask myself how *I* create meaning when I read. Any time I become engaged with a text, I bring with me my background or prior knowledge. Prior knowledge about what? At one time I believed that background knowledge focused only on the subject matter of a text. When reading a computer manual, my background knowledge about computers would help me to make sense of the words on the page. I know now, however, that prior knowledge goes a lot further than that. As I read the computer manual, how did I know to look in the index to find out what page to turn to for the information I needed? How did I know how to read the diagrams that helped me set up my computer? How did I know to go back and re-read a passage when it didn't make sense? My prior knowledge of the structure of texts allowed me to do these things. My definition of prior knowledge began to grow as my understandings about reading grew. As a life-long reader, *everything* that I know how to do in order to make sense of a text comes from my prior knowledge.

The diagram of the reading process shows that readers bring their prior knowledge to a text and are met with the three sources of information. How do life-long readers use the three sources of information as they problem-solve their way through texts? They use *reading strategies*. Strategies are those "in the head" processes that readers use as they successfully move their way through a text. When readers get ready to read a text, the reading process has already begun. They are already wondering about what they are going to see and find out. They begin to wonder what the text is going to be about, what it will teach them, or if they will even like it. As they begin to read, they answer those questions for themselves and continue to wonder.

Each time readers read they are first *anticipating* what they believe that text will be, based on what they already know about the information on the page. They also anticipate based on what they know on a larger scale. They begin to anticipate what they think will happen next. They also wonder why an event happened at all. They do this based on their prior knowledge, the information they have already gathered from the text, and from what they think makes sense, sounds right, and looks right.

What happens when *I* am confronted with a challenge and I anticipate something that doesn't make sense, sound right, or look right? As a life-long reader, I rely on my effective reading behavior to help me out. If a word doesn't make sense, I will probably go back and re-read: from the beginning of the word, the sentence, the paragraph, or even further back if I still cannot create meaning. If a word doesn't look right to me, I will often stop to *attend* to more of the visual information—the letters or punctuation, for example. I may make another attempt at that word based on the new information that I am gathering. I also *check* these attempts against other sources of information. Now that it looks right, does it still make sense; does it still sound right? If so, I *confirm* that what I have anticipated is suitable and read on. If my attempt does not seem appropriate, I *search* for more information that will allow me to *self-correct*. This search often takes me back into part of the text I have already read. It may also take me further into the text in order to get enough information so that I continue to create meaning.

How do life-long readers use these sources of information? They do it so innately and interchangeably that it is often hard for them to notice that they are using any of them. As life-long readers, they are constantly asking themselves the questions: "Does that make sense?" "Does that sound right?" and "Does that look right?" They ask themselves these questions most often when they are confronted with a challenge. They also use these sources of information against one another. If they read something that makes sense but doesn't look right, they ask themselves what other word would also make sense but uses the letters they see on the page. As self-monitoring readers, they can substitute one word for another when they are confronted with a challenge. They do this based on what they know about the text from the information that they have gathered. They use their prior knowledge.

It would be wonderful if all students were able to use meaning, syntax, and visual information as freely as effective life-long readers do. However, many teachers are challenged with readers who come to school with tangles, readers who rely on only one source of information, and readers who do not see reading as the creation of meaning but as sounding out the words on the page. Children have to be taught how to use the three sources of information.

The use of these strategies as life-long readers is something that is hard to observe because effective readers use them so proficiently and instantly. Try reading something that is very challenging for you and you can start to see yourself using these strategies. This is because the challenging text causes you to slow down and it is easier to recognize what you do to overcome a challenge. It is these strategies that teachers must identify and learn about so that they can develop their students' understandings about them. They must teach skills in order for their students to employ the strategies that will enable them to create and recreate meaning as they read. The goal, after all, is to create life-long readers who will understand and use these strategies independently.

UNDERSTANDINGS DRIVING PRACTICE

During her visits to my classroom over a two-year period, Jan Duncan's determination and beliefs set an expectation that I wanted to reach. Jan was the one who kept me going, believed in me, and made me believe in myself. She enabled me to make all the changes that I was ready for and continued to support me as I started to question how my instruction was going to change now that I knew all this "stuff."

How would I get all my students on the path to becoming life-long readers who use their prior knowledge, the sources of information in the text, and good reading behavior in order to create meaning as they read? When looking back at what my classroom practice was like before becoming involved in The Learning Network, I realize that my reading instruction was very segmented. We worked from a basal program for 45 minutes a day in reading groups that were organized by ability levels based on informal reading inventories that were done three times a year. I always knew who my "good" readers were, who my "average" readers were, and who my "poor" readers were. Beyond that, I found it very challenging to decide what to do for these readers. The basal manual always had a plan for me to follow, but that never seemed to work for my students, perhaps because the authors of those manuals had no idea about the individual needs of the students in my classroom. I was doing the very best that I could do at that time. I was spending a great amount of time trying to come up with and implement new ideas to reach my students. However, I did not feel that it was working. I was not seeing the kind of growth I believed I should see. My involvement in The Learning Network helped me to focus and reflect upon my understandings and my practice surrounding reading. For the first time ever, I was learning to focus not just on what I was going to do, but more importantly, *why* I was going to do it.

ASSESSMENT AND EVALUATION

What I have learned over the past several years is that instead of planning for my whole class, I had to start planning for individuals. I had to get to know as much as possible about what each student in my class knew about reading and then take each of them from there. It wasn't enough for me to know who the good, average, or poor readers in my class were. That didn't tell me much of anything, and it sure wasn't helping the children. I had to find out what each child could do, what they could almost do, and then teach them right there at the point of need. People often tell me that this sounds impossible. How can you teach each child individually? With an average of thirty children in my classroom, I can't. I group children for reading instruction, but now I group according to needs, not according to general labels such as good, average, or poor. If I have four or five children with a similar need, I have a group that I can work with, with a specific objective in mind. The key is to know my students well enough to be able to find out what they can already do and what needs they have. During my first summer institute, I was introduced to something called a running record. Running records helped to change the way I thought about teaching in general. They also profoundly transformed the way I taught reading.

Running records were developed by Marie Clay, whose book *An Observation Survey of Early Literacy Achievement* (1993) was a great resource for me as a classroom teacher who was trying to learn how best to assess reading behavior. Another resource that propelled me further into my exploration was *Reading in Junior Classes* (Ministry of Education 1985). These two books helped me realize that monitoring and assessing my students' reading must be an essential part of my whole reading program, not something I did at the beginning of the school year, three times a year, or at the end of a "unit." I must continually give myself time to find out what each of my readers can already do. I have come to realize that for running records to be used effectively in bringing students along in their learning, I need to take a running record for each student every three weeks. This gives me the starting points from which I will bring the students to new learning. Through the use of running records, I began to get a view into the minds of my students as they read. I learned to analyze running records to see what my students were doing when they were faced with a challenge in the text, as shown in Figure 10.3. Did they make meaningful substitutions? Did their attempts sound right? Were they using the letters in the words to help them make a guess? Were they making guesses at all? I could also begin to see what strategies the children were using. Did they know to go back and re-read when something didn't seem right? Did they self-correct when something didn't make sense, or did they just go on even though they may have lost the meaning of the piece? From these running records, I began to see what my students knew how to do when they read. I began to find out that they were already doing some wonderful things. I also was able to see some specific needs. I started looking at my students as the center from which I would then move. I began to look for common needs among the students in my class. Upon finding a common need, I had a group of children to work with for reading instruction. What next? How was my reading instruction going to change now that I had a group of children with whom to work?

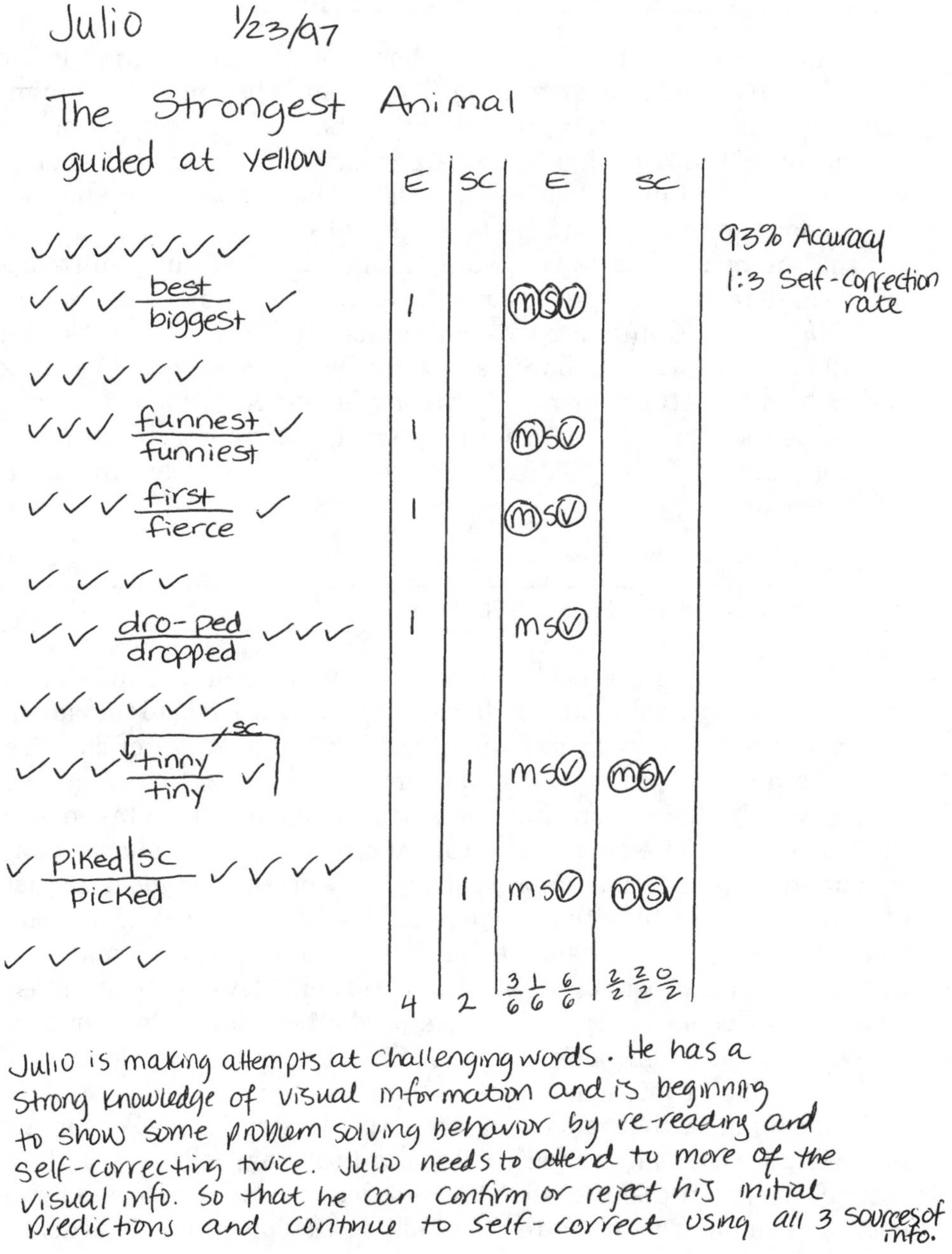

Julio   1/23/97

The Strongest Animal
guided at yellow

	E	SC	E	SC

93% Accuracy
1:3 Self-Correction
rate

✓✓✓✓✓✓
✓✓✓ best / biggest ✓ | 1 | | Ⓜ Ⓢ V | |

✓✓ ✓✓
✓✓✓ funnest / funniest ✓ | 1 | | Ⓜ s V | |

✓✓✓ first / fierce ✓ | 1 | | Ⓜ s V | |

✓ ✓✓✓
✓✓ dro-ped / dropped ✓✓✓ | 1 | | m s V | |

✓✓✓✓✓✓
✓✓✓ tinny↑sc / tiny ✓ | | 1 | m s V | Ⓜ s V |

✓ Piked|sc / Picked ✓✓✓✓ | | 1 | m s V | Ⓜ Ⓢ V |

✓✓ ✓✓

| | 4 | 2 | 3/6 1/6 6/6 | 2/2 2/2 0/2 |

Julio is making attempts at challenging words. He has a
strong knowledge of visual information and is beginning
to show some problem solving behavior by re-reading and
self-correcting twice. Julio needs to attend to more of the
visual info. so that he can confirm or reject his initial
predictions and continue to self-correct using all 3 sources of info.

Figure 10.3. A running record.

PLANNING: KNOWING THE APPROACHES

Prior to the summer institute, I had heard of these things called *shared reading* and *guided reading*. These words become lodged in my head although I didn't have a clue as to what they meant. As my involvement in The Learning Network grew, one of the things I realized was that my reading instruction needed to change based on all of my new understandings. I don't think it was until my second time attending the summer institute that shared and guided reading started to make sense to me. One professional book that helped me was *Reading To, With, and By Children* by Margaret Mooney (1990). This book gave me a foundation of what shared and guided reading were as I began to experiment with them in my classroom. However, what I have also learned is that the way I teach–the instructional approach–is the *last* decision I make. Before getting to this point, I have to select an appropriate resource.

KNOWING THE RESOURCES

After assessing my students using running records, I am able to group children according to similar needs. My next job is to find an appropriate book or text to use with that particular group of children. The book must be one that will allow me to meet my instructional objective, which is based on the assessment samples I have taken with these students. For example, several running records may have shown me that a group of students are relying only on the sounds of the letters when confronted with a challenge. Their anticipation at the word level has the right letter sounds but is not making sense. I may have determined that I want to help these readers develop their understandings of using meaning to make predictions of words they don't know. Therefore, the book I choose must be one in which there is enough support from sources other than the sounds in the words to make meaning, such as a book in which the illustrations closely match the print, a book that is predictable, or a book that follows a pattern. After choosing an appropriate book and determining the level of supports and challenges in the text for this particular group of readers, I then determine the best teaching approach.

USING THE APPROACHES

The approaches of shared or guided reading are tools that I can use to assist me in meeting my instructional objective. Teaching to the

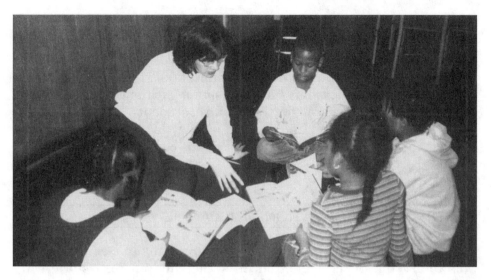

Figure 10.4. A guided reading session.

point of need for a group of learners means having a focused learning outcome in mind. The approach (shared or guided) is the way of facilitating that outcome based on the supports and challenges that are found in the text that I have chosen for that particular teaching episode.

If the book I have chosen has enough support for these particular children to overcome most of the challenges, I can use a *guided reading* approach. In guided reading, the children are reading the text to themselves (see Figure 10.4). I am there as a facilitator as the students problem-solve their way through the text. In guided reading, children are encouraged to question each other as well as the text as they work toward the creation of meaning. I have learned to listen to the students during a guided reading lesson so that I can make decisions about what kinds of questions I might ask. As I listen to what the children are focusing on, I determine the most effective questions I can ask to help students take on new learning based on my instructional objective. Most importantly, however, the children are encouraged to encounter the text and make meaning without worrying about being "right" or "wrong."

If the book I have chosen has more challenges than supports for these readers, I can use a *shared reading* approach. In shared reading, I read out loud along with the children. My voice acts as an additional support so that the readers can overcome all challenges and therefore create meaning. As in guided reading, the use of effective questioning leads the students into discussions that will allow them to take on new learning. Shared reading sets up an environment of total acceptance. There is no pressure put upon the children to read with the teacher, just the expectation that if they feel comfortable, they are free to join in. However, as the teacher, I am focusing my actions on the learning outcome that I have chosen for this group of students. The shared reading approach allows children to take on new learning while gaining comfort in a "reading" situation which builds confidence that they can, in turn, become readers.

READING IS THE CREATION OF MEANING

When I followed a basal reading program, my role as the teacher was to ask questions while and after the children read stories. My questions almost always focused on the story itself. "Which character liked to go to the movies?" "What was her favorite movie?" "Where did she like to go after the movie was over?" If you asked me why I was asking these questions, I'm sure I would have said that I was checking for comprehension. I was focused on the readers understanding the text, not on my understandings of the reader and the reading process. As students left these reading groups, they were not going away with any deeper understandings of what reading was or how they were reading. They had only reiterated and dissected a story to the point of nausea.

Fortunately for my students, someone asked me an eye-opening question: "As a life-long reader, after reading a novel, do you sit down to answer ten comprehension questions?" Obviously, the answer was no. Still, I protested. If I didn't ask the "comprehension" questions, how did I know if my learners are comprehending what they read? It was Jan Duncan, acting as my program coordinator, who brought this point home for me. She asked me what comprehension was. That one question was like pushing over the first domino.

Aha ... comprehension is meaning; reading is the creation of meaning; if the students are creating meaning as they read, then they are comprehending as they go. Of course Jan said it much more eloquently. She said, "Comprehension does not come *at the end* of reading; comprehension *is* the act of reading." Wow!

Does this mean that I don't ask questions when I bring students together for reading instruction? No, it does not. I have to go back to my objective for bringing groups of readers together in the first place. If I want to develop their understandings about anticipating meaning,

I saw the fiercest lion.

Figure 10.5. *The Strongest Animal*, page 7.

my questions are going to focus on getting the readers to articulate to me what they are doing when they confront challenging text. The following dialogue took place during a guided reading lesson using *The Strongest Animal* by Janice Boland (1996). The illustration the reader used is shown in Figure 10.5.

Maria: I'm not sure what that word is.
Teacher: What do you think it might be?
Maria: *First.*
Teacher: Why do you think it might be *first*?
Maria: Because it starts with *f* and I see an r in it.
Teacher: Does *first* make sense?
Maria: No.
Teacher: Why?
Maria: Because it's not the first animal that he saw.
Teacher: I wonder what else we could look at to help us with this word?
Maria: We could look at the picture.
Teacher: How does the lion look in the picture?
Maria: He looks mad.
Teacher: I wonder what word starts with the letter *f* and could mean something like mad?

Maria: Fierce!

Teacher: Does that make sense?

Maria: Yes, because the lion looks mean and he's roaring and that means the same as fierce.

During this conversation, I was able to question the reader. She was able to articulate to me what she did when she came to a challenge. My further questioning focused on getting her to use the meaning provided by the illustrations in conjunction with the sounds of the letters that she already knew. My questions did not focus on the story itself. They focused on developing this student's effective life-long reading strategies. I am confident that when this young reader left this instructional group, she had the understanding in place that using pictures on a page will help her gain meaning when confronted with a challenge. This is very different from letting her leave knowing only that the lion was fierce. At the same time, however, her answers and explanations gave me more than enough evidence that she was indeed making meaning and thus comprehending. There was no need for me to ask any "comprehension" questions.

The challenges of creating meaning become more sophisticated as students become more proficient readers. I observed similar behaviors in previous reading groups of a small group of students and noted in their writing that they were still developing understandings about making comparisons. I selected a piece from a *School Journal* called "Never Ending Teeth" by John O'Brien (1993) because of the clarity of his comparisons. I knew that this piece would be of high interest because of the sharks. I also knew that I could draw on their experience of losing teeth as another support for their learning. I selected guided reading as the instructional approach because I knew that the piece did not contain a significant number of challenges for this particular group. I wanted the students to focus on the challenge of making the comparison between human teeth and shark teeth.

The students worked their way meaningfully through the text while I asked questions that helped them expose the comparisons and unfold the meaning of the piece. The students were confronted with a challenge in the last sentence: "And that's why, every time something goes wrong with my teeth, I envy sharks." The students were stumped with the pronunciation and meaning of *envy*. During the discussion, I knew that it was my job to listen carefully to these readers and to support the problem solving that would enable them to overcome the challenge and leave the meaning intact while continuing to focus on the learning outcome.

Teacher: Let's finish this page; page 23. (Students read silently.)

Carlos: What? I don't get it.

Guillermo: I have a tough word here.

Teacher: What would make sense there? (Pause.) Hold on. We'll look at that word in a second.

Carlos: I *love* sharks!

After the students finished reading, the discussion continued.

Natalie: I sense that, they could lose their whole entire ... all their teeth in a month, and hundreds of sets would grow back.

Teacher: Hundreds of sets ... could you imagine?

Guillermo: At the bottom of the piece, he tries to be like a shark.

Teacher: Oh, yeah, exactly. Let's look at the last word. Guillermo and Carlos experienced a similar challenge. Let's read the last sentence. "And that's why ..."(Guillermo takes over the reading.)

Guillermo: "Every time something goes wrong with my teeth, I envie sharks."

Teacher and Natalie: *Envy*.

Teacher: Now wait a minute. What does that mean: I *envy*?

Carlos: Ooooo.

Teacher: What could that mean?

Carlos: I hate it?

Teacher: I hate sharks? I envy sharks. The sharks don't have to go to the dentist.

Rachel: I *love* sharks.

Guillermo: They're comparing ...

Natalie: They're looking at the difference between sharks and humans.

Teacher: Right. So what could that mean? "I envy sharks."

Rachel: I'm not like ...

Teacher: Hmmmm ...

Rachel: I *wish* I was like ...

Teacher: Yes! Why does he wish he was a shark?

All students in unison: *Because he wouldn't have to go to the dentist!*

Teacher: Exactly. (Guillermo still looks puzzled. Teacher turns to Guillermo.) So if I envy you, I want to be like you. I wish I was like you.

The discussion continued among three other students and the teacher while Guillermo thought aloud to himself.

Guillermo: (Quietly) I wish I was like Albert Bell.

Guillermo was very quiet and was obviously thinking during the discussion. Then he raised his hand.

Guillermo: Ooo ... ooo ... ooo!

Teacher: Yes?

Guillermo: I envy Dante Bouchet.

Teacher: Oh, so now you know how to use the word *envy*. What did you say again?

Guillermo: I envy Dante Bouchet.

Teacher: Who is that?

Guillermo: A famous player on the Colorado Rockies.

Teacher: Great!

New learning has occurred for these students. They have effectively made comparisons throughout the piece, and they have effectively utilized strategies (with support from me) to overcome the challenges that have occurred in the text. During guided and shared reading, my questions must not focus on the text. They must focus on the development and understandings of the child as a reader.

MY JOURNEY CONTINUES

The personal change that I have gone through is a direct result of my involvement in The Learning Network. My classroom is now on the way to being like the one I imagined in my head for so long. My professional growth and my understandings of reading, writing, and learning have enabled me to put into practice that which allows my classroom to be a center for learning for my students. I feel truly blessed to be a part of this process because it has focused on my growth, my new learning, and my understandings. As I continue to learn more, it benefits the children I work with on a daily basis. When I first became a facilitator for the Literacy Learning in the Classroom institute, I remember having some reservations as to whether or not I knew "enough" to do the job. I shared these feelings with Jan Duncan, and her response sent me spinning, as usual. She told me that I could only bring my participants as far as I could go myself. She told me not to worry about what I didn't know, but to focus on all the things that I did know. As I continued to learn, I would be able to bring my participants even further.

This conversation occurred over the summer, and at the time I wasn't really thinking about my third-grade class back in New York City, or about the new group of students who would be smiling up at me on that first day of school in September, but what an impact it has had on them. As my involvement in The Learning Network continues, I am still learning so much. Each September I am able to start at a place that I had just reached for the first time the previous spring. Jan's statement carried right over into my classroom practice. I can only bring my students as far as I can go myself. With the support of Jan Duncan and The Learning Network, there are a lot of children out there who know a whole lot more about being life-long readers because I know a whole lot more about reading, writing, and learning.

ELIZABETH REILLY WELSOME *is both a teacher leader and a program coordinator for The Learning Network. She has been an elementary school teacher at P.S. 191 in New York City for six years. Liz has a Master's degree in education. During the summer she works as a facilitator for the Literacy Learning in the Classroom institutes.*

CHAPTER 11

Focus on Content Areas in the Intermediate Grades

Bonnie Rhodes

*"I've had a major shift in a better understanding of the
literacy process and watched the results in the excitement of
seeing a successful child."*

Karolee Hess
Principal, Phoenix, Arizona

I've thought many times about my own social studies and science learning in elementary and high school. I remember that the teacher was the key provider of information and the student was the receiver of the information. Our roles were well-defined, as was the scope and sequence of our learning. A textbook was provided. We moved from chapter to chapter in order. My responsibility as a learner was to listen, take notes, read, memorize those important facts, and study for the end-of-the-chapter tests. The difficulty with it all was that I wasn't very proficient at many of these tasks, so my social studies and science learning was limited.

In the early 1980s I began my preparation for teaching. I was not disappointed to discover that the scope-and-sequence type of curriculum, supported by teacher's guides, was not the current belief of researchers in education. Instead, I found that curriculum was driven by reading and writing activities related to unit projects. It was very exciting.

In college we learned how to create lesson plans, develop units, and plan projects that developed around daily reading and writing activities. As a student I loved the excitement of developing curriculum, especially when it related to primary children, which at the time was the level I felt confident that I could teach. For an entire semester I explored, collaborated with other students, and developed activities and resources that purportedly supported my development as a teacher.

In 1984, with a first-grade teaching contract in hand, I spent the summer planning projects and activities that would relate to an integrated theme. I had decided that we would study "communities." I knew that I had a variety of materials to support this unit of study. I began recording day-to-day plans of what materials and resources I would need to support the reading or writing. I prepared response logs, authors' folders, journals, and any other organization tools with which I was familiar that I thought would support my students' learning. I spent hours at the library becoming familiar with trade books that would lend themselves to motivating writing activities.

My teacher training led me to believe that if a teacher planned well, learning would be ensured. This is a belief that I still hold, but now I realize that planning for students' learning is based on knowing the learner, not on how many trade books I wanted to "cover" each week. I also had limited understandings of *why* I was I doing what I was doing. I did not know at the time how important an understanding this is to teaching and learning.

So how did I begin to develop new beliefs? How did I come to new understandings? Certainly not by myself. Many people and experiences have played a role in helping develop my beliefs about teaching and learning. I have always considered myself a learner. After my first years of teaching, I took on any innovation or program that came my way as long as it focused on reading and writing. I went to workshops on Saturdays, spent Sunday evenings re-planning activities and schedules, and on Mondays explained to my students the changes that would occur in their learning. For some reason the children continuously accepted the changes. Time after time I made adjustments in my classroom practices without ever questioning why I was doing what I was doing. I never really brought the changes to a conscious level, nor was I challenged to. I was constantly trying to make teaching and learning better but did not allow myself time to think about the implications of the children's learning or my own.

Actually it was through my zest for workshops that I was introduced to the summer institutes, then called Whole Language in the Classroom, in 1990. At the time I had no idea of the impact this four-day experience would have on my future learning. The process of change began to unfold for me. The process of developing my beliefs about teaching and learning on a more conscious level had begun. The workshop (as it was referred to at that time) provided me with the challenge of looking at reading and writing as processes, not as a set of daily activities. The facilitators challenged me to begin thinking about *why* I shifted from one practice to another.

At about the same time that I was starting to think differently about learning, I was also considering teaching older children. I thought that older children would be more independent in their own learning. I know now that independence is something supported and nurtured, not something assigned to a particular grade level. I learned that it is brought about by developing understandings about the conditions that support learning for both the teacher and the students.

In 1993, this change in grade levels led me to change schools. The teachers at my new school, Las Brisas Elementary in Glendale, Arizona, viewed themselves as learners and used every opportunity they had to read, dialogue with one another, and question their understandings. They had a strong desire to learn. The principal, Kay Coleman, was a leader with a vision and understandings about what skillful teaching looks like. She helped create conditions for teachers to become more skillful. The conditions were perfect for the principal to introduce The Learning Network to support our work in teacher development.

CHANGING EXPECTATIONS IN YEAR 1

And so Jan Duncan, a program coordinator for The Learning Network, walked into my fifth-grade classroom to provide support for me as I began Year 1 as a teacher leader. I met the day with great anxiety, as I was unsure of what to expect. Other than occasional visits by an administrator I had never experienced a fellow educator observing me and giving me feedback. I didn't know what it meant to be *supported*. I only understood what it meant to be *evaluated*. I thought that the support I received would show me how to be an effective teacher. I would quickly learn that The Learning Network was about being effective, but it was not about *showing* me anything.

The first time that Jan visited, my students were studying the thirteen colonies. They were reading a variety of texts about the life experiences that people encountered as they came to the New World. I had divided the class into small groups. Each group was assigned to read about a specific colony. They were to write a script that would be used in a reader's theater production. The groups would present their information to each other according to an historic time line.

Jan's visit occurred at about the time the children had completed most of their reading and were beginning to write their scripts. I remember thinking how clever I was to have found a creative and collaborative way for students to learn about social studies. As I looked out over the classroom, scanning to see if everyone was engaged, I assured myself that learning was occurring. The children were immersed in conversations about which characters they wanted to represent as they created their scripts. I was sure that Jan was most impressed with the children's learning. She stayed for about an hour, observing me as I worked with groups of children. She also used the time to ask my students what they were doing. This observation was followed by instructional dialogue.

As the instructional dialogue began, Jan asked me to identify my instructional outcome. I explained that I wanted the students to have a better understanding of the culture of the various groups of people moving from Europe to the New World. So far, so good. Then Jan told me that during her observation, she had asked the children to tell her what they were learning. She revealed to me that most of them were focused on the excitement of a reader's theater production. They hadn't been able to articulate the learning that I thought was occurring. I had planned for them to understand how culture and change influences history. I thought that their scripts would reflect those concepts. Instead, it had become just another reading and writing activity assigned by the teacher. I was disappointed. I had been confident that I had the understandings about teaching social studies and science through reading and writing to bring my students to new learning effectively.

Starting with the Known

An important belief about teaching and learning that Jan led me to understand was the need to know my learners–to base my decisions about students' learning on what I knew about them and what I knew about their experiences. I needed opportunities to become informed about my learners' experiences and not to be in such a hurry to get to that new, sometimes overwhelming, concept. I had to believe that this understanding would come to my learners in time.

Jan asked me to describe what understandings I thought a learner needs in order to bring meaning to a new learning experience, and what kind of support I as a teacher had to provide. She helped me to understand that each student has a unique view of the world. I realized that it was essential for me to support my students' natural curiosity about their own experiences and to provide the time and resources to allow this exploration to begin.

So the children and I began to explore the concept of culture by starting with the known—ourselves. I had to think about what kind of support I would provide. Through my continuing dialogues with Jan I came to understand how important it would be for me to immerse myself in my own investigation alongside my students. This practice would become a powerful tool to help guide me as I planned for my students' next learning experiences. I began by demonstrating to the students my own thinking about reading and writing.

Modeling Writing

Modeling writing was not very effective at first. I had difficulty limiting the sessions to ten minutes, many times drawing them out to twenty minutes or more. My students ended up completely disinterested. There was no response from them at the close of each session. What was going wrong? I went next door to my colleague Marilyn Herzog, who was also being trained as a teacher leader, and watched how she was modeling writing with younger children. What was she doing that I was not? She did not keep them on the floor for thirty minutes, nor did she feel inclined to ask them a series of questions to prove that new learning had occurred. But why didn't she? I went back and watched several more times, each time with a different question in my mind. I became frustrated with the process. I wanted a recipe.

Fortunately my dialogues with Marilyn and Jan continued to develop my understandings about the process of reflection. The power of dialogue, not just with the program coordinator but also with my peers, became the foundation supporting my learning. Instructional dialogue became one way for me to experience reflection. Jan helped develop within me a desire to question and find my own answers to those hard questions. I slowly began to realize that it was not *what* Marilyn was doing, but *why* she was doing it, that mattered.

It was difficult to proceed with my own investigation into social studies and culture while monitoring 35 students. I wondered if some of the pressure I was feeling was shared by my students. I brought them together and asked them how it was going and if they had any suggestions that would make our learning easier. They asked for more time to read and write. From that response I realized how important it was for me to keep going with my own investigation in order to have a sense of what my students were feeling. Because I was experiencing new learning at the same time as my students, I had a better idea of what they were feeling. It was the interaction with my students that supported me as I questioned and examined my own knowledge about reading and writing.

I began modeling writing daily. I knew that it was becoming a powerful demonstrative tool that supported the development of understandings about the writing process and its recursive nature both for myself and for my students. Gradually, as I grew in my understandings about the process that we were all using and why we were using it, my students became more engaged. A collaboration of ideas and perspectives among my learners had begun.

Monitoring my students' draft books–bound notebooks that house all of a student's writing–helped me make more informed decisions about what I needed to demonstrate next. Instead of relying on a pre-planned list of skills to be presented to the class in a predetermined order, I responded specifically to their needs, and my students began to show signs of engagement. I finally began to understand what it means to know your learners. I became more knowledgeable about my learners' strengths and could more clearly determine their next learning steps. I also became more knowledgeable about the reading and writing processes. I was learning what authentic learning looks like.

Modeling Reading

Not only was I modeling writing daily, I also used any opportunity I could to read to the students resources that focused on culture. I immersed them in a variety of genres that illustrated the concept of culture. We read a mixture of poetry, nonfiction books, newspaper articles, and stories. My students began to expect me to read to them daily. When I finished reading a book I would place it on the ledge of the board, and immediately a student would slip it away to his or her seat to read and re-read. The more background knowledge they gained, the more information they wanted to seek out about their own cultures. I also used reading to students as a way of modeling aspects of the reading process. Those important "I wonder" questions came naturally as we created meaning together on each text. I think what surprised me the most as I began reading to students was their limited experience with a variety of genres. I am convinced that immersing ourselves in many different kinds of texts changed many of my students' attitudes about reading.

I no longer viewed reading to my students as just something that I enjoyed. I really needed to think about what I was reading and why. I began to think about the outcomes I wanted to model. What was it that a particular book offered in the way of illustrating certain concepts? To which authors did the students respond emotionally? I had never even considered many of these questions before. Now I no longer pull a book off the shelf five minutes before I read it to the students. I know I need to have a focused outcome. When I read a book for the first time I am very conscious of what I am thinking about. I jot down my "I wonder" questions and make notes of examples of book language that I consider powerful. When I read the text to the children I think aloud about those aspects of the book that I believe are important for my students to hear. I expect that they will think about the outcome I am modeling for them. If I expect this level of engagement then I must be prepared to model and demonstrate particular aspects of the reading process, how the genre works, and conceptual understandings the author is communicating.

Because of my class's exploration of their individual cultures, parents and grandparents began taking an interest in sharing family stories. Some children decided to use the family stories as topics for personal narratives. One family began an intense investigation of their family history. Artifacts were pulled from closet shelves. Children brought them into class and shared proudly. At one point the room was filled with a marvelous display of resources. It was a reminder of what occurs within learners when investigation is supported in a natural way, using personal meaning to guide the learning experiences.

Eventually the students put closure to their investigations and shared their new learning with their peers. Not one student chose to write a script for a reader's theater production. I was not surprised. Why was that? It was because I had given the children the opportunity to make decisions about how to respond to their own learning. I gave them the tools to feel confident and competent. Their decisions about the forms their publications would take were based on their new understandings about reading and writing. There were posters, oral presentations, story telling and, my favorite, an audiotaped conversation between a student and her grandmother.

I did require the students to write a summary of their understandings about the concept of "culture," but instead of sticking them in a folder as an "end-of-unit/evidence of comprehension" artifact, as I might have done the previous year, I used their summaries as a starting point for the next class investigation. The summaries allowed me to make critical observations about the strengths and next learning steps of every student. And so my understandings of the cycle of teaching and learning continued to grow.

Developing Understandings about Learning

We continued to explore important concepts in social studies. We explored the ideas of change, conflict, scarcity, and interdependence, but now we researched our own experiences first. We asked ourselves the hard questions about how these concepts influenced our own lives. The students understood how important it was to understand the concepts in relation to themselves before moving on to investigating history. We successfully applied our new understandings about the teaching and learning cycle to the topic of American history throughout the remainder of that school year.

What was the new learning for me? I learned that it is essential to know my learners and that I must provide students with background experiences when they do not have them. I must start with the known to help develop the unknown. I learned that I must develop my skills as a critical observer of student learning. Most importantly, I found that I need to question my own understandings about teaching and learning continuously, leaving room for reflection and further questioning of myself and my practice.

I learned that I was not the sole provider of information in the classroom. I was not always available for the children to ask questions, so my students began to seek support from each other. A strong community of learners was beginning to develop. They shared their reading and writing and thinking with each other. Those children less experienced in an area went to those with more experience for advice. My old beliefs about teaching and learning had not supported the opportunity for students to learn about and from each other, but now I viewed the change with pleasure.

My students had learned about the processes of reading and writing through the subject of social studies. They had used real events and factual information from their lives and the lives of others to formulate concepts related to social studies. They had taken on the responsibility for their own learning with my guidance. They had learned how to seek out information that would support their new ideas. My fifth-grade students had learned how to work collaboratively and independently.

TAKING OUR LEARNING FURTHER IN YEAR 2

Jan continued to support my learning as a Year 2 teacher leader. I decided to move to sixth grade with my students. I was eager to continue my role in their learning. The first day of school was delightful. There wasn't that long period of adjustment that usually starts each school year because both the students and I had already worked hard to develop our understandings about the conditions for learning (Cambourne 1988). My students knew that it was my expectation that they read and write daily and anticipated that this expectation would not change from the previous year. Many of them took on this responsibility by bringing unfinished books to school that first day, hoping that they would be given the opportunity to read. Those who did not were sent to the library to begin seeking out resources for their independent reading.

During those first days of school I asked each student to begin a list of areas they wanted to explore during the year. We came together as a group, discussed everyone's choices, and posted them in the room as a topic list for the entire class (see Figure 11.1). I encouraged them to add to it when they wanted. I added topics taken from sixth-grade curriculum areas.

I also wanted to get an assessment sample of what strengths they thought they had developed as readers and writers during the previous year. I wanted to see if they viewed themselves as readers and writers. What emerged from their writing was that these students could really express what understandings they did or did not have. They knew where they needed to concentrate their learning (see Figure 11.2).

After the first few days I had enough monitoring notes to start con-

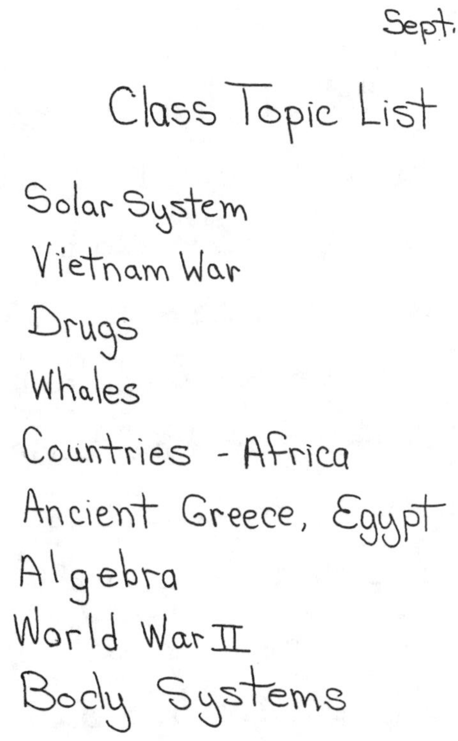

Sept.

Class Topic List

Solar System

Vietnam War

Drugs

Whales

Countries - Africa

Ancient Greece, Egypt

Algebra

World War II

Body Systems

Figure 11.1. A sixth-grade topic list for the entire class.

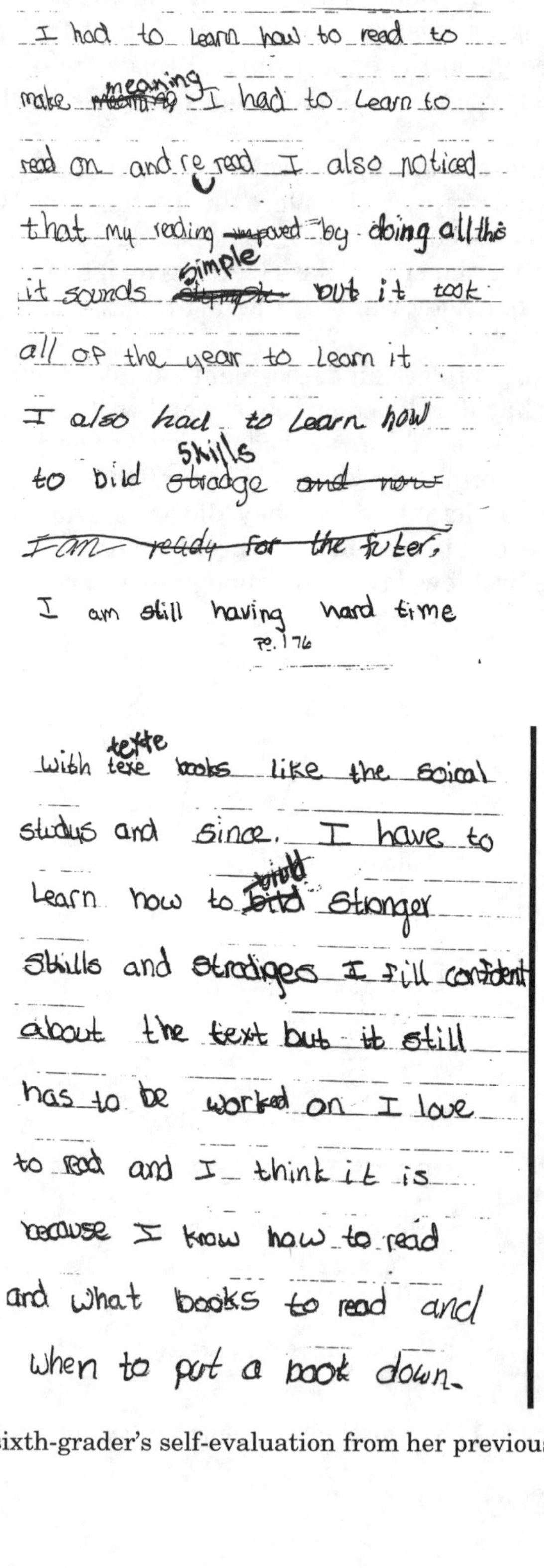

I had to learn how to read to
make ~~meaning~~ meaning I had to Learn to
read on and re read I also noticed
that my reading ~~impoved~~ by doing all this
it sounds ~~simple~~ simple but it took
all of the year to Learn it .
I also had to Learn how
to bild ~~stradge~~ skills ~~and now~~
~~I am ready for the futer,~~
I am still having hard time
P. 176

with ~~texe~~ texte books like the soical
studys and since. I have to
Learn how to ~~bild~~ build Stonger
Skills and stradiges I fill confident
about the text but it still
has to be worked on I love
to read and I think it is
because I know how to read
and what books to read and
when to put a book down.

Figure 11.2. A sixth-grader's self-evaluation from her previous learning.

sidering the students' next learning steps. I was well aware of most students' strengths and could use the information to make decisions about how to organize the day in order to meet their group and individual needs. We discussed what they liked about the previous year and what changes they wanted to make. The most consistent feedback I got from the students was once again the need to have more time to read and write.

Student Planning

I was now ready to develop new planning sheets for the students from the multitude of assessment samples I had collected. I learned that the variety of student planning sheets that we had used the previous year would no longer be useful to us. They were too prescriptive. The students had grown in their independence and were ready to take on more responsibilities. They really had a sense of what engagement feels like and how to immerse themselves successfully in a reading or writing experience. The new planning sheets were extremely simple (see Figure 11.3). Every day the students listed the tasks they anticipated completing and the amount of time each task would take to complete. They updated these when a task was completed. I collected the sheets at the end of each day and used them as a monitoring tool as I planned for the next day.

Many of the topics the class wished to explore were science-related, so we spent several weeks engaged in experiments that would help all of us become familiar with the processes scientists use when they are proposing, testing, and reporting the results of their hypotheses. As the students carried out various investigations I learned what strengths they had and where I would need to focus my planning in order to teach at their different points of need successfully. This challenge actually led me to think more systematically about planning within the teaching and learning cycle.

Teacher Planning

I began planning to meet the needs of my individual learners by thinking about the components of the scientific process of investigation. Based on my evaluation of several lab reports, I listed the names of students who were challenged by particular aspects of investigation. This helped me to determine if I needed to work with the entire class, with groups of students, or with an individual student on a particular concept. This structure allowed me to be specific with learning outcomes (see Figure 11.4). I knew that I was meeting the needs of my

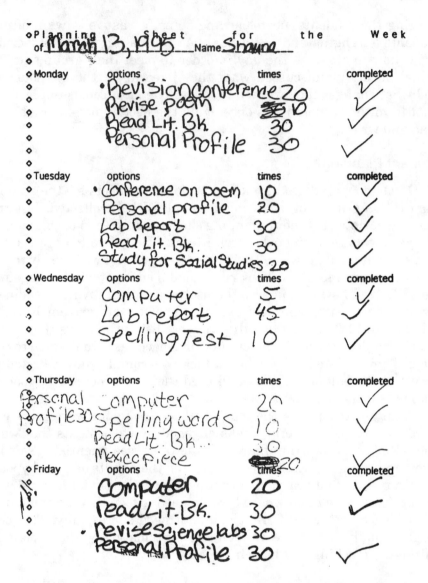

Figure 11.3. A planning sheet for independent learners.

learners without involving the rest of the class in lessons they did not need or for which they were not ready.

I found that as teachers we cannot know where to start planning if we do not clearly understand the processes or concepts we are trying to teach. For example, most of my students understood how to formulate the questions that they wanted to investigate and how to list the materials that they would need for it, but I was surprised by the number of

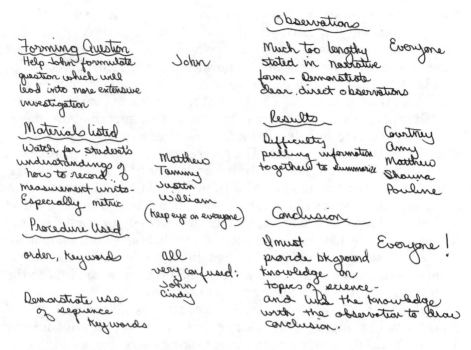

Figure 11.4. Scientific procedure as a basis for teacher planning.

students who did not understand how to sequence and record procedural information. This included most of the class, so I decided to begin my own investigation at that step. I carried out an investigation in front of my entire class, modeling how scientists organize the procedures they use.

A small group of students were confused about how to organize the results they observed. I brought those students together for a shared writing experience. This was a valuable teaching approach to use as it helped me to assess even further their individual responses by listening, questioning, and probing what aspects of the process they did not understand.

I often hear from other teachers that they feel overwhelmed by the amount of skills and information they feel responsible to teach in each area of the curriculum. I used to feel the same way until I began to see the interrelatedness of the processes of reading and writing that we use no matter what subject we are exploring. If, for example, I learn how to write the procedural component of a science lab report, I can use what I have learned to write a procedural piece explaining how to take care of a pet hamster. The words change according to the topic about which I am writing, but the process I use for writing does not.

This does not exempt me from continuously assessing each student's understandings of a particular skill and his or her ability to link the skill between subject areas or genres. When I make such assumptions I am apt to miss an opportunity for new learning to occur.

I have learned that when we study any subject or carry out any investigation there is a certain amount of narrowing of topic that must occur. It is my job as a teacher to help students understand how important it is to be able to bring focus to a particular piece of writing no matter what the genre or topic. The process is the same whether it is a narrative or a report. I did not always understand this and found that some of my students would jump into a piece and find the topic so overwhelming that they would want to give up the entire project out of frustration. Support in defining a topic choice needs to come from the teacher while the ideas are still at the infant stage of development. Teachers must support writers by engaging them in authentic conversations regarding what they are writing and helping them focus on the important ideas that they are formulating.

One student's topic list reflected the broadness of his choices. After several days of exploring his topics he decided he wanted to study the Vietnam War. After several days spent looking for resources and skimming their contents, he approached me and announced that the topic was just too big. I helped him narrow down some of the ideas, but he decided to save it for another time and instead chose to study gun control. As he was an avid hunter, this was a topic that I knew was near and dear to his heart. I did not rush in to help him narrow the topic but gave him some time to apply what he had just learned; time to reflect on and explore his new topic. The time was not wasted for him or for me (see Figure 11.5).

Another thing I learned about learning is how difficult it is to switch gears in the middle of immersing ourselves in a topic. There is nothing worse than someone, usually the teacher, raising his or her voice and asking everyone to please put their reading down so we can begin work on another subject. In a traditional intermediate classroom, the day is segmented into discrete daily periods for reading, writing, math, science, and social studies. I already understood the interrelatedness of reading and writing and was working on integrating those with content area studies, but Jan suggested that I take that idea even further. She recommended that I focus on science for several weeks and then switch to social studies. Most of the time I was able to organize our learning in that structure. Occasionally there was some overlapping, but I tried to find opportunities for my students to immerse themselves in a topic rather than to experience their learning in

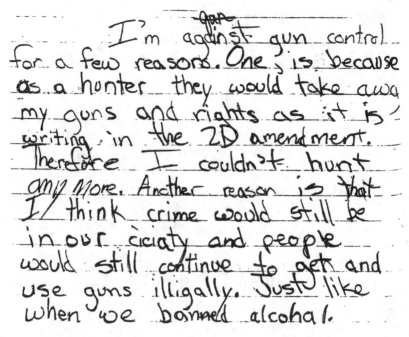

Figure 11.5. Student's narrowing a topic of study resulting in a tightly written essay.

bits and pieces. My learners could plan out over several hours a day what they needed to accomplish and have the time to do it.

Another important aspect of my planning was sharing with my students what I wanted to occur during our long reading and writing block each day. Daily I recorded my plan for this time on the white board, including lists of the small groups of students I would see and why we were meeting (see Figure 11.6). I also listed with whom I would meet during my roving time and what outcome would be expected. The students did not have to wait for the small bits and pieces of time to be handed over to them. Almost all of them planned their time accordingly. I assisted the few who had difficulty planning their time until they became independent. For some students assistance was needed throughout the year.

Focused Teaching

Our next investigation that year was to be an in-depth project for the school science fair. My personal experience with science fair projects typically meant that they were assigned by the teacher but the work was completed at home, and I knew that the parents expected

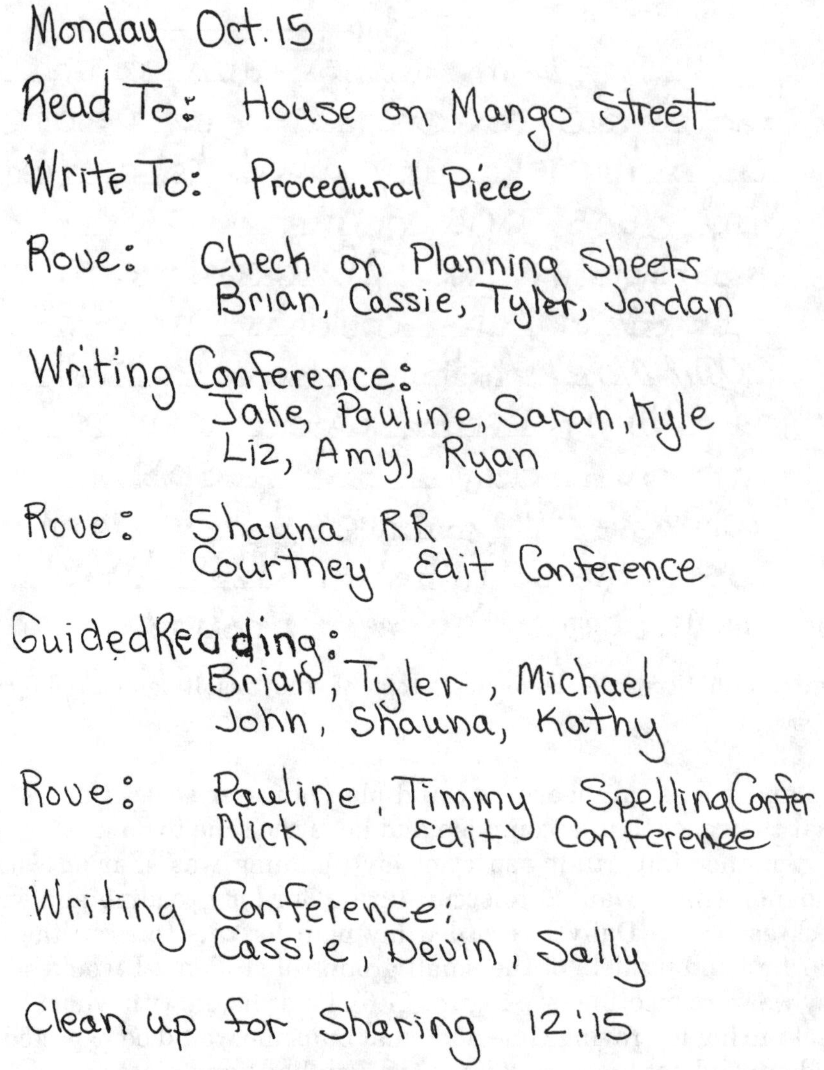

Monday Oct. 15

Read To: House on Mango Street

Write To: Procedural Piece

Rove: Check on Planning Sheets
              Brian, Cassie, Tyler, Jordan

Writing Conference:
              Jake, Pauline, Sarah, Kyle
              Liz, Amy, Ryan

Rove: Shauna RR
              Courtney   Edit Conference

Guided Reading:
              Brian, Tyler, Michael
              John, Shauna, Kathy

Rove: Pauline, Timmy   Spelling Confer
              Nick   Edit Conference

Writing Conference:
              Cassie, Devin, Sally

Clean up for Sharing   12:15

Figure 11.6. A teacher's plan for language arts.

this, as well. Instead, I decided to provide the support the students needed for this project at school. I knew it would be a valuable experience and I had several expected outcomes. The only criteria I required were that each student choose a topic in which he or she was truly interested, that they were able to locate the materials needed for the investigation, and that I was assured that the conceptual level of the investigation was developmentally appropriate for each student. I met with individual students to assess the criteria.

We had nine weeks until the projects were due. I knew that this was going to be a real challenge for students who found it difficult to schedule their time effectively, so this was one of my planned outcomes. I had to provide a great deal of support for many of them. One strategy I used was providing benchmarks or due dates for certain components of the investigation so that they could plan their individual time lines. I gave them monthly calendars to record those important benchmarks. I realized that their daily student planners were still extremely important, but they also needed the support of long-term planning.

As a result of this individual long-term planning, not every student was working on their projects at the same time or at the same stage because that is not what real learning looks like. That is not what we as adult learners do in our own work. As a teacher, I do not find this a challenge. Although I knew that the students would be challenged by the vastness of this kind of project, I wanted them to feel that they still had adequate time to respond to learning in their other subject areas. I did not want them to feel overwhelmed, as some would lose interest quickly.

The mere mention of the upcoming project got the students excited. It did not take long before they began to share their possible topic choices with each other. Resources began filling our classroom shelves. I added past student-published science fair projects to the resource collection.

Many of the outcomes I envisioned for these projects were related to the publication stage of writing, another reason for completing them at school. I had a surface level understanding of publication, and although many of my students were quite creative in their publication formats, I felt that I could expand their visions even further. I began by immersing my students in a variety of posters, business marketing presentations, and past science fair projects. We met in small groups and read the publications. I guided the students as we determined the audience and purpose of each piece and questioned what the writer might have had to consider as he or she developed an understanding of what form the piece would take. I think that sometimes teachers forget to share a variety of published pieces so students can see the multitude of possibilities for their own publications.

I wanted my students to understand that shaping a piece of writing for publication must be considered as part of the meaning making that occurs when we are trying to communicate with others. I was not only concerned about the actual format. I wanted my students to understand that there are certain techniques that can be used when combining visual elements and written text to draw the reader into a published piece. We had to think about where the audience would be in relation to the display boards during the actual science fair. We all used a standard-size board and created a mock plan that would be used for publication (see Figure 11.7). We set a standard for the printed text to be a certain font and size so that it would be large and clear enough to read. I conferred with groups of students before they actually began to draft to ensure that the format of their pieces would meet the standards for our audience.

At the fair, the community was more than impressed with the standard of work that was created by my class. We invited them to

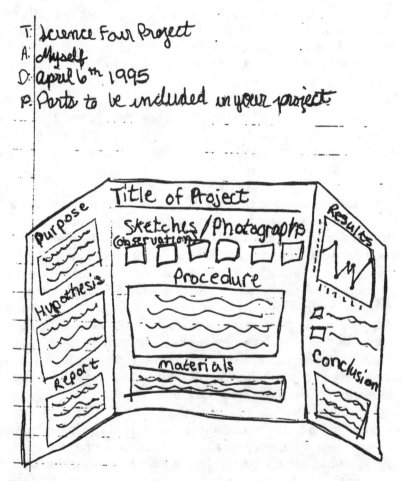

Figure 11.7. Planning for publication at a science fair.

write down any questions they had as they read through the projects. This was exciting to the students. They realized that their audience was really interested in the results of each of their projects. Some children used the questions to further explore their own topics, and all of them demonstrated ownership of the ideas and strategies we had explored. When these students were required to complete a science fair project for their middle school at home, many parents sent notes or dropped by the classroom to thank me for helping to develop the students' understandings about shaping a piece for publication. This is an overall outcome of skillful teaching: students using their newly developed understandings for years to come both in and out of the school setting as life-long learners.

Reflecting on My Learning

So what have *I* learned? I learned that we learn best by doing—by being engaged. Learners come to know that there is a purpose for their new learning. Students need to trust that the processes they are experiencing will be meaningful to their new learning, especially when it seems challenging. They need to be able to access and use what they already know and find purpose for what they are coming to know.

One of my students, Matthew, was learning how to use a particular plan to support his research writing. He was not going to learn how to do this before it was relevant to him. As his teacher, my job was to find out what he did know about planning for research, help him understand the purpose of using a plan, and decide what approach I would use to teach him about how this tool could effectively support him as he began his research. I learned that I could focus my teaching on each learner's needs and next learning steps (see Figure 11.8).

One caution I have for those working with intermediate grade-level students is not to assume that students come to a grade level having developed the skills we think they should have in place. We must

Next Learning Steps: Again I would like Elizabeth to use writing as a way of responding to new knowledge gained by reading a variety of non-fiction text. Elizabeth is still struggling with some of the complexities of writing. She is working hard trying to challenge herself as she supports events in a story with detail. She understands the need for a writer to find personal expression and tries very hard to find that voice. I am very excited to support her as she begins to experience expository texts. I would like to encourage her to find a variety of formats for her writing pieces, as I believe she is quite creative. Elizabeth's strongest characteristic as a writer is her ability to critically assess her pieces.

Figure 11.8. A teacher's plan to teach at the point of need.

never assume anything. As teachers, we have to remind ourselves daily of the power of the teaching and learning cycle, which supports knowing each student's strengths before identifying their next learning steps. We plan according to student needs and what we know about the resources and find the appropriate approach that we find effective. I believe that we can have the highest expectations for our students, but expectations will do nothing for learning if we do not start from the known.

Another observation that I have made over the years with intermediate-age students is their intense need for their learning to be supported in a social environment. They need time to work independently, but this has to be balanced to include feedback and response from their peers. If we do not plan for this kind of flexible learning within our classrooms students may disengage and become passive learners. A room full of engaged students is very contagious to the passive learners. Learning is, after all, a social affair guided by our intense need to know more about the world and the way it works.

So is reading and writing different in social studies and science than it is in language arts? No. We read to gain information and experiences about the world. We write to record our ideas about the world and use a variety of forms to do so. We talk to help make meaning more clear. We do not use these processes in isolation. We internalize the processes of reading and writing as we become more proficient. We gain flexibility in our ability to learn because we have more experiences upon which we can draw. We have the capacity to learn more, and we do so if the conditions that invite the learner into the process are in place.

My work in The Learning Network has helped me to be a more skillful teacher who has come to understand that content-area curriculum is not guided by a textbook or a set of teacher-developed reading and writing activities, but by the students' need to question and examine the aspects of social studies and science that are important to each of them. This does not mean that I do not guide them toward developing understandings related to the important concepts that define science and social studies. I know now that no matter what topic the students explore, there are those essential skills–such as problem solving and communicating–that apply to learning in any subject area. A skillful teacher will work toward developing his or her understandings so that each student's new learning can be supported.

BONNIE RHODES *is a program coordinator with The Learning Network. She was a teacher leader at Las Brisas Elementary School, a Learning Network site in Glendale, Arizona. She has taught at the primary and intermediate levels as well as held administrative positions at the building and district levels. During the summer Bonnie works as a facilitator for the Literacy Learning in the Classroom institutes.*

CHAPTER 12

Focus on Special Needs Learners in the Regular Classroom

Juliana Kwolek and Ellen Lowell

"Growth means change and change involves taking risks, stepping from the known to the unknown."

George Shinn

We are teachers in a fifth- and sixth-grade learning community. Our shared goal is to create an environment where *all* children really do learn together—where students with special needs work alongside their peers all day long. In the three years we have worked together in White Brook Middle School, a Learning Network site in Easthampton, Massachusetts, we have continually and gradually redefined our vision of what is possible for all learners. Although we started with separate classrooms and with students who were receiving instruction in separate special education programs, as we have come together in exploring teaching and learning we now support full-time inclusion and the critical role that instructional dialogue has played in our growth as professionals.

SEPARATE ROOMS, SEPARATE LEARNERS

Juliana: Back to the Classroom

In September of 1993 I returned to the classroom as a fifth-grade teacher after working as a reading specialist for sixteen years. I chose to go back to the classroom, and I chose to take the biggest risk of my professional career. I chose to crawl inside a model of teaching and learning that put the needs of children first and live my belief that classroom instruction needs to change. The words "put your money where your mouth is" were on the tip of my tongue every day. From my experience working as a Title I teacher and coordinator, and doing reading evaluations of students with special needs, I had come to believe that no matter how hard teachers worked, no matter what teachers did, our at-risk or below grade level readers were only marginally successful. They were dependent upon the support of pull-out programs to survive. The majority of students referred to Title I in first grade were still in Title I programs in middle school. I saw Title I as a Band-Aid and special education as a separate program, and thought that we could do better.

As a reading specialist I was requested to evaluate several high school students. These were kids who were failing and who were at risk of dropping out. An investigation of their educational histories revealed that the reading program for these students was changed almost every year since first grade. All of them had begun learning to read in a "phonetic drill for skill" type of approach. When that didn't work, they were put into a sight-word approach in which they read basal textbooks that were supposed to be high interest and low vocabulary. And when that didn't work, we put them in programs in which the creation of meaning while reading was abandoned with text such as "The man ran on the can." Then we learned to teach them phonetic rules by making associations to patterns in words and reading utter nonsense because of controlled vocabulary. I began to think that we were perpetuating a system of educational trial and error. Despite our good intentions and hard work, all of our students were not reaching their full potential. My husband often says, "Let's work smarter, not harder." So I chose to go back to the classroom, embrace The Learning Network, and challenge my own practice.

Ellen: Special Needs in a Self-Contained Classroom

In 1993 I had been a moderate special needs teacher in the Developmental Learning Center at White Brook Middle School for seven years. I was responsible for teaching eight special needs students who didn't fit into a traditional resource room. I had the assistance of two or three paraprofessionals because I taught children who had been labeled as "mentally retarded," "Down's syndrome," "autistic," and "physically and emotionally handicapped." My room came to be labeled as the "retard room" by the other middle school students.

My classroom was an entity unto itself. We were housed in an area that physically segregated us from all the other classrooms, and we even had our own bathroom. Our schedule was carefully designed so that my students would hardly, if ever, encounter other students. We entered and exited the building at different times from all other students. "Inclusion" meant my students ate lunch in the cafeteria, but isolated from everyone else at a separate table. They didn't know anyone and they often complained about being teased by other students in the cafeteria because they lacked appropriate social skills and table manners.

At the time, I thought my classroom was the best possible placement for my students. I believed that they couldn't possibly function in a regular classroom with their age-appropriate peers because they didn't fit in academically or socially. My goal for each student was to attain a third-grade reading level during their four years with me. I thought I was teaching to meet each student's goals and objectives as defined on their Individualized Educational Plans by selectively using dittos, workbooks, skill pads, and thematic units from various publishers. I worked really hard at making learning fun while focusing on developing functional skills.

1993–1994 SCHOOL YEAR: FIRST STEPS

Ellen: Finding a Place for Lee

In the fall of 1993 I had been working with an eleven-year-old student named Lee for one year. He was a quiet, soft-spoken boy who was incapable of initiating spontaneous speech or making direct eye contact. He would often twitch, rock back and forth repeatedly, or walk in circles when confused. Lee had conversations with himself throughout the day. He needed direct adult supervision to complete his work. Lee's parents requested a thorough educational evaluation, which included a psychological, physiological, and neurological profile as part of the annual review of his program. This evaluation was done over a two-month period at a medical center in New England. Lee was diagnosed as having Pervasive Developmental Disorder (PDD) with numerous signs of autism. This report included several recommendations. The most significant was to provide Lee with opportunities to develop his social skills in a non-academic environment, such as art, music, or physical education.

Although I agreed that Lee needed to develop social skills I was concerned that he would never be accepted by regular education students and would become more withdrawn. I visited every fifth-grade art, music, computer, health, home arts, and physical education class. From my observations, these subjects, with the exception of physical education, were taught as academic subjects. I knew that Lee would not be able to meet the academic expectations set for fifth graders. I thought that he needed to be taught at his developmental level in order to be successful. Overwhelmed, I enlisted the help of my principal, Bruce Colling, and he suggested a solution to the dilemma.

Juliana: Making a Place for Lee

Just about the time I was beginning to feel a sense of comfort in my new role as a fifth-grade classroom teacher, I was introduced to Ellen Lowell by our principal, Bruce Colling. I was surprised by the idea of integrating Lee into my language arts block. I had always professed that all children can learn, but I had never known a student with the profound needs that Ellen described. I didn't know what to expect, and I really didn't understand the six-inch stack of special education reports filled with jargon about Lee. I was scared, but saw Lee's integration as an opportunity to test my beliefs and practice.

There were four supports in place for me as I took this step. First, there was The Learning Network, our teacher development program, which was helping me redefine my understandings of teaching and learning through instructional dialogue with our program coordinator, Jan Duncan. Second, there was Ellen, who knew Lee so well, and who was always willing to reflect and problem solve with me. There were Lee's parents, who accepted me as a learner and were eager for their son to be with other kids. And finally, there was my own attitude and willingness to take a risk.

In December of 1993, I began to visit Ellen's classroom to get to know Lee. I felt like I was in a foreign country. It seemed as if there were almost as many adults in the room as students. I tried to take a running record of Lee on the library book he was reading. He seemed to read as if he were playing hopscotch. Throughout the piece, he read a few words aloud and then read the next few silently. When I asked him to retell the story he stared at me. He answered all questions with "I don't know." I was more encouraged when I looked at the writing that Lee had done with Ellen. He could get ideas down on paper and had good control over spelling, sentence capitalization, and punctuation.

Lee visited my classroom for the first time while my students were at music. He walked in about ten steps, stopped, looked around, and read a poem posted on a wall aloud. Then he began to rock from side to side. From talking with Ellen I recognized that Lee was uncomfortable, and that we had better cut the visit short. We had exchanged few words. My mind was filled with wonder. I really wasn't sure how Lee and I were going to communicate.

Ellen and I developed a plan for Lee's gradual integration in my language arts class based upon what we determined were Lee's strengths. Lee would first join my class for thirty minutes a day during our whole group time, when I read to my students and modeled writing in front of them. When Lee became comfortable with this new situation, I would include him for independent writing. We met with his mother to share our plan. She was most concerned with Lee's social development and helping him connect with other kids. I was concerned about his academic growth and meeting his needs as a learner. She agreed with our plan to begin Lee's integration in January of 1994, right after the holiday break. Lee's mother, Ellen, and I agreed to stay in close communication with each other.

Ellen and I also talked about how to introduce Lee as a new classmate to the rest of my class. I was determined to treat Lee like any other student, and decided that there was no need for any special introduction. Before we left for the holiday break, I simply announced that Lee would join our class in January and asked if anyone was interested in being a buddy for our new classmate. Three students volunteered. We agreed that the role of a buddy was to help a new classmate learn the class routines.

In class Lee was very quiet. He rarely spoke, even when spoken to, and he most often responded by shaking his head yes or no. His most frequent verbal response was "I don't know." I never knew what he was thinking. He often rocked in his seat or just sat watching the other students. I could easily see that my first step with Lee was opening a channel between us. I came to understand why Lee's mother was so concerned about his social development.

Even though it was five months into the school year I was still trying to find a room arrangement that met all of our needs. One morning when Lee walked in, the room had been rearranged without his knowledge. He was lost. He stood in the center of the room rocking and talking to himself. One of his buddies rescued him before I could respond. It was then that I began to realize just how valuable peer support was to the success of Lee's inclusion.

In February, Lee began writing with the class and stayed with us for about an hour a day. When I asked him what he was going to write about he said, "Going to my sister's game." This first piece (see Figure 12.1) created a picture of Lee as a writer and a learner that meant more to me than all the test reports in his cumulative folder. When Lee

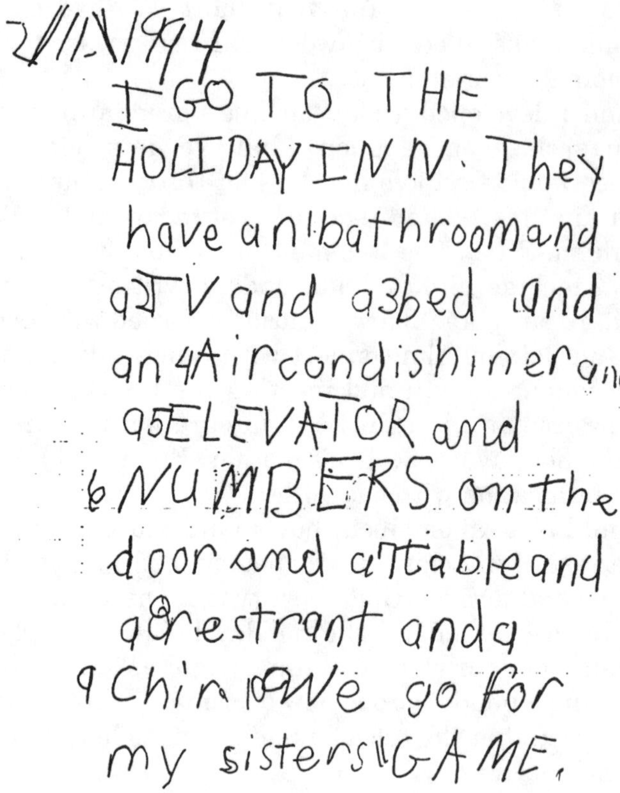

2/11/1994

I GO TO THE
HOLIDAY IN N. They
have an bathroom and
a TV and a 3 bed and
an 4 Air condishiner and
a 5 ELEVATOR and
6 NUMBERS on the
door and a 7 table and
a 8 restrant and a
9 Chin We go for
my sisters GAME.

Figure 12.1. Lee's first piece of writing.

finished writing this piece I observed him numbering each detail to
correspond to the numbers on his web. He could not explain to me why
he put the numbers in the piece. I learned that he could use his plan to
order information as he wrote, and that he needed lots of modeling to
develop his understanding of the writing process.

Lee's next piece of writing thrilled Ellen because it was the first
time that Lee had ever expressed his feelings in words. I saw it as evidence of Lee's ability to communicate an experience. The following is
the text of Lee's draft:

> When I was eleven years old I went to my Auntie Pat's birth-
> day. She has a game downstairs. The only game she has is
> pool. Pool is a game with eight balls. When I was eleven years
> old I wanted to play pool because it looked like fun. My sister
> and some kids wouldn't let me play because they were taking

*turns. They played for a long time. They still wouldn't let me
play. I felt sad because everyone should have a turn. They had
a stool to sit on and I kept on sitting until I played pool. I
played with Mom and then I went home happy.*

By being a daily participant in revision conferences Lee understood that he was expected to answer questions about his writing just
like everyone else. At first I worked patiently to get him to replace "I
don't know" with "I'll think about it." Next, we all learned to pose questions that gave him two choices within the questions. Gradually, Lee
began to respond.

In May we videotaped a revision conference to show his parents
and other support people working with him at a special education team
meeting. The signs of growth were obvious to all. Lee was beginning to
make eye contact with me and the other students when he spoke. Even
though he was very dependent upon me to guide him through the
process of asking and answering questions, he was participating in the
group conference. The signs of stress were also obvious. As Lee sat next
to me, his legs swayed back and forth. His hands covered his mouth
and some of his face as he spoke. Still, Lee was working alongside
other children his own age, doing the same things that they were doing
in writing for the very first time.

In June of 1994, we prepared for field day, our school's annual in-
terclass competition. We all expected Lee to participate with our class.
He signed up for three events and practiced the sack race at recess just
like everyone else. Socially, Lee had come a long way. He loved being
with the other kids and was beginning to fit in.

1994–1995 SCHOOL YEAR: COMING TOGETHER

Ellen: Joining The Network

On the night before the school year was to begin in 1994, I unex-
pectedly received a telephone call from Diane Zink, the director of special education for the district. She asked me if I would be willing to attend a specially scheduled Literacy Learning in the Classroom
institute. I had been amazed by Lee's progress and wanted to learn
about The Learning Network. I also wondered if inclusion could be successful for my other students. I excitedly told her that I'd be there.

After attending the institute, I began changing my classroom practice. I started to read to my class every day, which I had never done be-

fore. Next, I distributed draft writing books instead of dittos and workbooks to the entire class. If it had worked for Lee, I thought it would work for everyone. Then, with the encouragement of the special education director, I joined The Learning Network as a teacher who would be working with a teacher leader. I was delighted to discover that my teacher leader would be Juliana.

As my teacher leader, Juliana observed my classroom practice and facilitated an instructional dialogue with me weekly. I wrote my first action plan on developing my understandings of the writing process. Through dialogue, Juliana helped me to reflect on my practice and to articulate what I was doing and why I was doing it. This type of reflection was something I had never done before. I had always followed teacher's manuals and, as I eventually came to understand, I was following the writing process as if it were a recipe, just as I had followed the teacher's manuals. In order to help me get past this mindset, Juliana said that she needed help, too. We both met with Jan, our program coordinator, for tiered dialogue. This dialogue helped me to realize that there was no recipe for using a draft writing book and teaching writing. I better understood how to determine each student's starting point in writing and not to expect that everyone would begin in the same place. With this new understanding, I reevaluated each of my students and realized that only four of my students were ready for a draft writing book. This dialogue helped me gain confidence, continue to take risks, and believe that instructional dialogue was a valuable tool for developing new understandings.

Juliana: Moving Forward

In September of 1994 Lee and I were promoted to sixth grade. He was now spending an uninterrupted hour and a half per day in my class for writing, spelling, and whole group demonstrations in reading and writing. He no longer needed a buddy. He seemed comfortable and at ease. His rocking from side to side had decreased and he was beginning to laugh at me when I showed a flair for the dramatic. He made new friends with some boys in the class and began eating lunch with them in the cafeteria.

In October, Lee made another significant step forward. The whole class was talking about a story I had just finished reading. I posed a question for their response, and Lee raised his hand. He had never done this before. Lee's one-word response was evidence that he had created meaning and was engaged in our discussion. Ellen and I were both amazed at this dramatic change in Lee's behavior.

As a writer Lee continued to grow. In January we celebrated a major step forward. At a group revision conference Lee shared a piece he had written about the rides at a local amusement park. He defied what all the "experts" said and began to answer questions without support.

Student:	You said you hated the pipeline. Why did you hate it?
Lee:	Because I hated it when it gets darker and darker and lower and lower.
Student:	What is the pipeline?
Lee:	A pipeline is like a water slide. You have to use a tube to go down the pipeline.

My excitement was too much to bear. How did he do it? For me the answer was in our classroom environment. With Lee's immersion in a regular classroom he had begun to learn from the demonstrations of his peers and wanted to be like them. He met my expectations of him because I treated him like everyone else: I expected him to learn and set no limits on how much he could learn. Lee was taking responsibility for his own learning at his own pace. I was certain that all I had to do was continue to build upon what he could do and meet him at his point of need.

In the late winter of 1994 Ellen and I were involved in an instructional dialogue about guided reading. With her new understandings Ellen wanted more time for reading with Lee. We contacted Lee's mother to get permission to shorten Lee's time in my class and increase his time with Ellen. Lee's mother saw this as a step backwards, and said absolutely no! So Ellen and I reversed our plan. Instead of Lee going to Ellen, Ellen would come to Lee with some of her other special needs students and integrate them with some of my students for guided reading. Lee's mother agreed to this novel idea. At the time we saw this plan as a logical compromise and did not realize the impact it would have on the growth of our understandings.

Ellen: Moving into a Regular Classroom

In April of 1995, we took another step. I had been working on developing my understandings of guided reading through observation and instructional dialogue, and for the very first time, Lee and the three other students from my class were going to read in a regular classroom setting. I had selected these students to join Lee because they had common needs. In addition, Juliana and I had decided to integrate two low-progress readers from her class into my guided reading group to help my students become a part of the class and not just a separate group in the corner.

On the first day that I facilitated a guided reading group in Juliana's room, I made an unexpected discovery. My students were achieving success reading a text that presented too many challenges for the students from Juliana's class. I realized that my special needs students would be able to participate in a regular classroom setting. This new understanding forever changed what I perceived as the best educational program for my students.

This experience also made me wonder how I could integrate Laura, a student with multiple handicaps. Since birth, Laura was legally blind, retarded, and a hemiplegic who had recently developed seizures. She was able to write using a computer. She also used a CCTV (closed captioned monitor) that enlarged print to read. The biggest issues for her inclusion seemed to be overcoming her fear and getting all of her equipment to the classroom. Both challenges were resolved because Juliana and I were building common understandings about reading and writing through our weekly observation and instructional dialogue.

Juliana started to bring her class to my room for read to's, modeling writing, and eventually writing conferences. This helped Laura to get to know other students in a familiar environment and thereby eliminated her fear. After a few weeks Laura was interested in going to Juliana's room with her new friends whenever she could. By June, Laura had published her first piece of writing, illustrated by some of her new classmates. She was also able to participate in guided reading discussions because she listened to a tape recording of the text. Through these discussions Laura grew in self-confidence and self-esteem. She began to make predictions and to ask questions. I remember the day Laura's mother observed a writing conference. She left the room in tears of joy because it was the first time she had ever seen Laura work with regular students.

These experiences had a tremendous impact on my teaching and my beliefs. The progress I had seen was overwhelming. I requested a transfer to a fifth-grade position for the next school year. I now believed that special needs students with moderate needs could be integrated in regular education. I wanted to team with Juliana in order to increase our capacity to integrate special needs students. I also chose to become a teacher leader with The Learning Network to continue to deepen my understandings. Lee and Laura joined our new class. Three of my former students were able to move on to vocational programs, and three students with profound needs remained in the Developmental Learning Center with a new teacher.

Juliana: New Understandings

Over sixteen months of school Lee had changed. He now belonged. He wanted to be independent from adults and gravitated to other kids. We were all pleased with his social and academic growth. Over those same sixteen months, I had changed, too. I revised my thinking that all children can learn. I now believed that all children can learn *together*. Lee had taught me well, and it was time to plan for next year.

The special education team thought that Lee should be placed in a seventh grade in September of 1995 to be with more age-appropriate peers. I shared Lee's draft writing book, I am learning to/I can lists, spelling notebook, my insights, and videotapes with his new seventh-grade language arts teacher, but had little to do with his transition. The wheels of our special education process had taken control to design Lee's next steps.

1995–1996 SCHOOL YEAR

Ellen: Adjusting to Inclusion

In September of 1995, Juliana and I came together in our middle school as a fifth- and sixth-grade team with 39 students. More than anything, we wanted the opportunity to create an environment where all students really did learn together. My class consisted of fourteen regular education students and seven students with moderate special needs. Laura was with me full-time and Lee split his day between my fifth-grade class in the morning and his seventh-grade class in the afternoon. Alex, one of my new special needs students, had his own one-on-one paraprofessional because of his needs related to Down's syndrome. I also had the support of a second classroom paraprofessional due to the number of students with moderate special needs in my classroom.

On the first day of school, I observed the seats chosen by my students with frustration. All of the special needs students were seated together in one section of the classroom. I wondered how they would come to accept each other. It was essential that the students share my vision and understand my expectations of building a community of learners. I shared my observation with them and set the expectation that they would all sit next to each other during the year. Together we agreed to randomly change everyone's seat every two weeks. It took a few months for the moans and groans to silence, but eventually they did. I knew that Rome was not built in a day and that we needed time to grow together.

In January of 1996, the outcome of an instructional dialogue with my program coordinator was to explore how effectively I was using my classroom paraprofessionals. The two paraprofessionals were working with my special needs students in a very traditional manner. They corrected papers and worked only with the special needs students. I identified reading and spelling as two areas where their support could improve learning outcomes for all of my students. After sharing my ideas with them, they joined me in shared reading groups to observe. We discussed their observations and the role they could play as facilitators in shared reading groups. They began shared reading daily with a small group of low progress readers to develop the students' fluency and confidence. I selected the resource and monitored student growth. I taught my classroom paraprofessionals to collect words for individual spelling lists (those words from the students' writing in science, social studies, and math that were close approximations to standard spelling). This freed up time for me to do other things. The paraprofessionals also learned to rove and help any student as needed.

Gradually, Alex grew to resent having his own paraprofessional because it made him different from the other students. He became increasingly stubborn and refused to work when the paraprofessional was near him. These negative behaviors escalated dramatically despite our attempts to establish a token economy system combined with time outs. I felt strongly that his negative behaviors would decrease if we treated him like everyone else. In June, when Alex's program was reviewed at a team meeting, the services of his paraprofessional were eliminated.

Juliana: A Catalyst for New Understandings

Lee came back to my sixth-grade language arts class on October 2, 1995. Lee's seventh-grade teacher confided to Ellen and me that Lee was not the same person as the one she had viewed on the videotapes from the previous year. His old behaviors such as rocking back and forth, walking in circles, and talking to himself had resurfaced. My analysis of the situation was simple: the supports that Lee needed were not in place yet. Classroom practice cannot be duplicated by the transfer of a student's work. Each of us needs time and support to develop our own understandings. We had all underestimated the importance of the ongoing dialogue about Lee that Ellen and I had maintained for a year and a half. That dialogue was critical to Lee's successful transition to a new learning environment, as it had enabled us to deepen our understandings of inclusion. That same support was not put in place for Lee's seventh-grade teacher. Again, Lee helped us to learn a valuable lesson.

Although Lee didn't know any of my eighteen sixth graders, he seemed happy to be in my class. The signs of Lee's anxiety soon disappeared, but mine were about to surface. Lee was to be with me for almost three hours every afternoon, double the time I had worked with him the previous year. Initially we spent almost all of that time working on language arts. My first concern was engagement. It was challenging to keep Lee engaged in reading, writing, and spelling for such a long block of time. I became torn trying to keep Lee focused when I was working with small groups. My second concern was Lee's independent reading behavior. Lee read very little. He often re-read what he read the day before and spent a lot of time gazing into space. It was a challenge to help Lee select books to read that appealed to him and contained enough support for him to create meaning. His favorites were books about Amelia Bedelia.

I made many attempts to resolve these issues. The easiest was for me to prepare Lee's daily plan sheet every day. By my listing the activities he needed to do, Lee was able to choose the sequence he followed. This reduced the time Lee and I spent on bookkeeping and lessened the number of times I needed to intervene. In November our team's schedule changed. Social studies was moved to the afternoon, and our time for language arts was shortened. Lee now had two social studies classes, one in the morning with Ellen and one in the afternoon with my class.

That was when I began to question what we were doing with Lee from a different perspective. Lee was fourteen. His age-appropriate peers were in high school. What would Lee do after middle school? What about the development of life skills? Was Lee's program meeting all of his needs? After sifting through much red tape, a special education case manager was assigned to Lee. The case manager designed a program to address Lee's functional needs. She began working with Lee every afternoon. As a result, Lee was no longer in two social studies classes.

It was after a dialogue with Jan, our program coordinator, that I began to explore how to engage Lee by using the shared reading approach instead of independent reading. I learned that reading with a classmate gave Lee the opportunity to talk about what he read, which was so essential for his engagement. I did not need to be the facilitator. I selected the text and met with Lee and his partner for a short time each day. Lee also continued to participate in most of the shared reading groups that I did facilitate. Time for independent reading was limited to very short periods with carefully chosen text. Again, Lee was the catalyst for pushing me to develop a new layer of understanding.

Lee's last piece of writing in my class, shown in Figure 12.2, was about his great aunt, who had recently died. We videotaped Lee work-

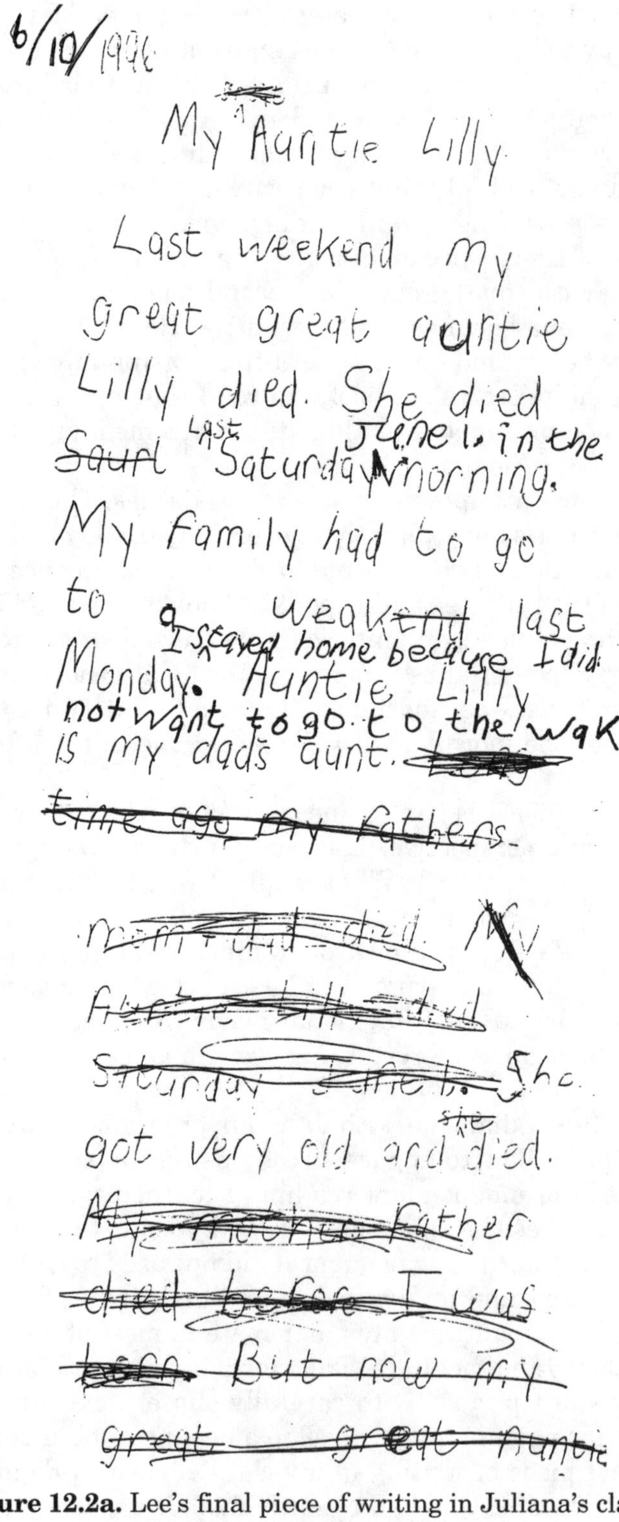

6/10/1996

My Auntie Lilly

Last weekend my great great auntie Lilly died. She died ~~Saurl~~ ᴸᴬˢᵀ Saturday June 1. in the morning. My family had to go to a ~~weakend~~ last Monday. ᴵ ˢᵗᵃʸᵉᵈ ʰᵒᵐᵉ ᵇᵉᶜᵃᵘˢᵉ ᴵ ᵈᶦᵈ Auntie Lilly ⁿᵒᵗ ʷᵃⁿᵗ ᵗᵒ ᵍᵒ ᵗᵒ ᵗʰᵉ ʷᵃᵏ is my dad's aunt. ~~time ago my fathers.~~

~~mom did died~~ My ~~Auntie Lilly died~~ ~~Saturday June 1.~~ She got very old and ᔆʰᵉ died. ~~My mother father~~ ~~died before I was~~ ~~born.~~ But now my ~~great great Auntie~~

Figure 12.2a. Lee's final piece of writing in Juliana's class.

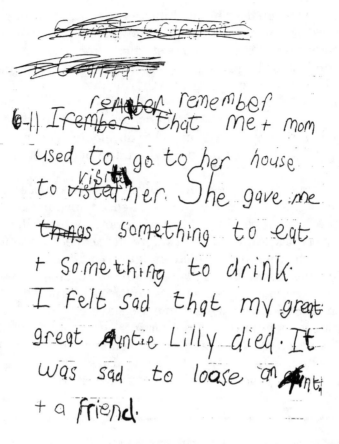

Figure 12.2b. Continued

ing in a peer conference to revise the piece. Lee explained to his partner that his purpose was to identify the parts of his writing that didn't
tell about his topic, Aunt Lilly. What unfolded was surprising. Lee did
not need the support of his peer to identify and line out irrelevant details. Lee's growth as a writer was slow but steady.

Ellen and Juliana: Turning Challenges into Opportunities

In June of 1995, we celebrated Lee and Laura's graduation from
middle school with bittersweet feelings. We had come a long way together in three years. Lee and Laura had become part of the main-
stream. They had experienced all aspects of school life alongside peers
who did not have special needs. Because of them we came together as
learners, stretched our thinking, and redefined our understandings of
inclusion.

For us, inclusion does not just mean a physical placement in a regular classroom, nor does it mean token participation in school and learning activities. For us and our students, inclusion means creating an environment for learning in which all children learn together and accept each other as peers. The growth we made was built upon our ongoing reflection of what we were doing and why we were doing it. For us, inclusion is not a recipe to be duplicated. Inclusion will only be successful when teachers are committed to developing deeper understandings of teaching and learning and where the needs of the learner are paramount.

Throughout our journey, one support has always been in place for us. In the beginning, we had maintained an ongoing dialogue with each other to make Lee's initial inclusion work. When Ellen joined The Learning Network, we began to explore new expectations for our dialogue with each other and with our program coordinator, Jan. Through observation and instructional dialogue we are no longer working in isolation, but have come together in a collegial partnership built upon common understandings. Over time we have come to value instructional dialogue as a powerful tool for increasing our own capacity for meeting the needs of all our learners and empowering ourselves as professionals. Our dialogue remains the seed bed for turning each new challenge into an opportunity for professional growth.

JULIANA KWOLEK has over twenty years experience teaching at the primary and middle school levels. She has worked as a classroom teacher, reading specialist, Title I Instructional Consultant, and as a facilitator for the Literacy Learning in the Classroom summer institutes. Currently Juliana is a fifth-grade teacher and teacher leader at White Brook Middle School, a Learning Network site in Easthampton, Massachusetts.

ELLEN LOWELL has worked with children with moderate special needs for ten years. She is currently a sixth-grade teacher and teacher leader at White Brook Middle School, a Learning Network site in Easthampton, Massachusetts.

CHAPTER 13

Focus on Teaching the Older Learner

Susan L. Goltz

"When I make mistakes, I can no longer blame the curriculum or the child. I have learned to trust the kids more. When you let go, they really fly."

Jill Tinker
Teacher Leader, Phoenix, Arizona

My experience with The Learning Network has been a journey, not an event, as is any effective change. While a seventh-grade language arts teacher at Madison Park School in Phoenix, Arizona, I visited a Learning Network school and I was hooked by the engagement of the students, the energy and purposefulness with which the teacher moved from student to student, and the management system which seemed to ensure that everyone was on task, everyone had a plan, and time was being used wisely. I had no clue what was about to happen to my comfortable classroom philosophies and routines. The transformation in my teaching approaches has been dramatic as I have developed new understandings about my learners, about the teaching and learning cycle, and most importantly, about how good teaching is student driven, not curriculum driven.

COMMITTING TO THE NETWORK

For weeks after that visit I wanted to know more about the classroom I had seen. I kept hearing about successes but no one was able to

clearly explain what The Learning Network was or how I could implement it in my classroom. I was also concerned because the class I visited had sixth graders who were basically in a self-contained environment. My own model of three seventh-grade language blocks a day
looked very different. I remember talking with a Learning Network
teacher from Massachusetts who taught in a middle school. I hoped she
would be able to give me some management clues, but her model was
also a self-contained classroom. Being as stubborn as I am I didn't let
that slow me down. I was asked to be a teacher leader for The Learning
Network. I didn't hesitate at the time. Management and control were
never issues for me, but true engagement was not a commodity I dealt
with on an on-going basis with the vast majority of my population, especially during reading and writing.

I attended the Literacy Learning in the Classroom institute in the
summer of 1995 along with many of my colleagues. I heard a lot of conversation about the Literacy Learning model, the teaching and learning cycle, running records, knowing the learners, knowing the approaches, and knowing the resources. I left at the end of the week with
a sense of overload and the determination to figure out what it all
meant. I was still searching for another upper-grade teacher to discuss
the implementation of this process in my classroom. There was no one
to be found so I decided to stop looking for what obviously wasn't there
and do some ground breaking myself. I read *Dancing with the Pen*
(Ministry of Education 1992) and *Reading in Junior Classes* (Ministry
of Education 1985) and I secretly wondered if anyone in my district or
in The Learning Network realized that I had seventh graders because
the books were all about primary students. I figured that eventually
someone would notice and they would give me the books and basics
that were appropriate to my students. Furthermore, I couldn't figure
out how I was going to be able to do all the things that I felt were expected of me and that I expected of myself with three language arts
blocks a day, a total of about 95 students, and portfolio responsibilities
for fourteen assessments in the areas of reading and writing. I felt that
no one understood my classroom model and deep down I wondered
what in the world I was going to do.

I tried to put The Network out of my mind that whole summer but
it was always there, just below the level of consciousness, nagging at
me. Then, in August, all of the teacher leaders met at the district office
to sort and stamp some of the new materials that had been ordered for
us to use in our classrooms. Sorting and leveling books was a real experience for all of us, but we worked well, if not with much understanding, under the direction of Marilyn Herzog, our program coordi-

nator. Once again I was in the dark about the levels of the books because my students were so much older. Closest to me were a fourth-grade teacher and a third- and fourth-grade multi-age teacher. I knew what it was like to be alone and out on a limb.

When school started I could feel the tension building along with the realization that I was going to be observed by Marilyn in an action plan of my own design within a short period of time. I knew I had better get going but I wasn't really sure how. I very quickly realized that this was different than going to a seminar where if I saw what I liked I came back to class to attempt implementation. It usually took a week or two for me to realize there would be no major miracles happening in my classroom and I generally gave up when I realized it was another program or plan I might use bits and pieces of, but nirvana it wasn't. Instead, The Learning Network was a real commitment that I couldn't rethink on Tuesday after Monday's so-so implementation. I had said I would do this and I really wanted to do it, but I was unsure. I knew that Marilyn was there to help me, my building administrators were incredibly supportive, and I was impressed that the district administrators were also meeting with us monthly to discuss our concerns and our progress and to support us. The other ten teacher leaders in the teacher leader class became fast friends, particularly those in my building, and the feelings of collegiality that developed among two kindergarten teachers, a third- and fourth-grade multi-age teacher, a seventh-grade language arts teacher, and an administrator were amazing. We talked about approaches and understandings, we shared management techniques and planning strategies, we celebrated our successes and worked through our frustrations, and we bonded into a support system that was unlike any other I had known in my professional life. Our weekly meetings became increasingly important, as did the twice a month district level meetings.

CHANGING MY PRACTICE

It became apparent that the concept of "wee steps" on our journey in The Network was not to be. I found myself starting with implementation of some of the physical parts of the philosophy because they were the easiest things for me to do. I began reading to my class on a daily basis. The level of engagement when I did that was incredible. It was a great way to start the day, it got everyone off on the right foot, and the students really seemed to enjoy it. I had always read to my classes, but my reading had been comprised of letters to the editor, short poems, student writing, and on occasion a book or short story that was related to something we had done in class.

I was now reading picture books that I had loved and that my own children had loved when they were young. I couldn't believe how many books I found that I wanted to read to my classes and talk with them about. Furthermore, I couldn't believe they wanted to hear them and they did not feel that they were too easy or too childlike. I was able to talk with my groups about predicting and inferring. We worked to discover themes and develop characters and plot lines, and we did it all within the framework of short, sharp, snappy pieces that I was able to finish reading during one or two sittings.

It was a real awakening for me to realize that so many of the picture books I had always assumed were written for primary students were far too difficult for the lower grades. The concepts and background knowledge needed for understanding were really age-appropriate for my seventh graders. One of the books, *Dear Willie Rudd* (Gray 1993), was especially engaging. It was about a grown white woman from the South who was writing to her long since deceased black nanny. Her message was that if Willie came to dinner at her house today she wouldn't have to eat in the kitchen and she could use the fine china. As a class we talked about the events of the civil rights movement that had changed the world and we also talked about emotions being bottled up. We shared that many of us had things we wanted to say to people who were no longer part of our lives. My students wrote the most wonderful poems and letters (Figures 13.1 and 13.2). It was authentic writing with incredible voice. When everyone who wished to participate was finished we tied the letters and poems to helium balloons and watched them float beyond the mountains up into the clouds. Each of us felt we had done something really special and many of the students said they felt at some level they had reached the people they were speaking to. It was a real event for all of us who participated.

I also began sharing a great deal of myself with my students through my writing. It was a struggle with 90-minute blocks, but I wrote in front of my students daily–pieces about my life, expository pieces about things that disturbed me, letters I wanted to share with them, and poetry about things that were important to me. I had to find a way to balance my time so that I didn't allow their engagement and my enjoyment to eat up a full 90 minutes. I began writing the same piece in little sections in each group. I would start with a plan in my first class and continue my writing in segments throughout the day. My students became eager to read my pieces and to revise them for me as a group. I wrote so much I couldn't believe it. I modeled what writers do and how they do it.

7-Goltz
2-15-96
writing/letter

Phoenix, AZ 85014
February 15th, 1996

Dearest Uncle Robert,

I am writing to you to say I'm sorry. I am sorry for treating you like just another relative when you really were just another angel. Not a real angel, but you were like an angel in the way that you always watched out for me. You loved me, and I treated you like an old present. Like when a kid is done using it, they throw it away.

Well, I let you go seven years ago, and now I'm calling you back. I know that you loved me, and I want you to know; I love you, too.

The last time I saw you alive, you were lying in a hospital bed dying of AIDS. You wanted me to give you a hug, and I wouldn't. I guess it was because I thought I would die too. I was wrong, and I'm sorry. I was only six years old, and I didn't understand.

At your funeral, I didn't even cry too much. I said to everyone, in my little baby voice,
"I know that my uncle loves me, and I know he still does." I guess I didn't understand that I would never see you again.

It's not just me who wants you back. Uncle John does too. He is having some real tough times, and I think he needs a brother to lean on. Did you know, that a few days ago, he drank bleach just to pass a drug test?!! I'm really worried about him, Uncle Robert.

Grandma needs you a lot too; she always talks about you. But, most of all, I need you. You know mom and I were going through some pretty rough times, and I could have used your help. But, it's not your fault that you're no longer alive. It's AIDS that took your life away.

I just want to tell you, I love you!!!!

love,
Sarah

Figure 13.1. Letter written in response to *Dear Willie Rudd.*

THE TEACHER AS A LEARNER

As I saw student interest mount I wanted to know all I could about literacy, about how students learn, about observing and assessing them so I could teach them what they needed to know, not what they already knew or weren't yet prepared to learn. I had talked about individualizing instruction in language arts but once I made sure everyone was reading a trade book they liked I didn't know what else to do. I started my classes in draft books like the ones I had seen in The Network school I visited. I copied the page of draft book standards for students (Figure 13.3) and introduced it in my classroom without giving it

11/18/96
Poem #8

When people die it is so painful
It's like somebody shot a hole in your
that is already weak from hearing
that someone you love died.
Your eyes are so blurry from crying
all day and all night.
The funerals and memorial services
make you so very sad,
When you read about them in the
obituary it makes you want to scream.
It's either they had so much to live for
or their life was full,
But when they die young or old it is
always painful to see them go.
R.I.P.
Vanessa
Desiree
Grandpa Henderson
Grandma Mydear
Bridget
Micheal
Alex
2 pac
Eazy-E

Figure 13.2. Poem written in response to *Dear Willie Rudd.*

a great deal of thought. The ideas were pretty sound and it seemed to be a good place to start. I adopted the idea of the students writing from a topic list of their own design, but early on I was really hung up with teaching genre. When I deemed it expository time in October everyone had to write an expository essay, even though so many of my new learners of English were finally feeling successful and writing personal narratives with great voice and style.

As a result I hit the first speed bump on my journey. It was time for me to be observed by Marilyn. Jan Duncan, a trainer of program co-ordinators, was along to observe Marilyn and I was going to witness a tiered dialogue. Before any of this happened Jan asked me why I was

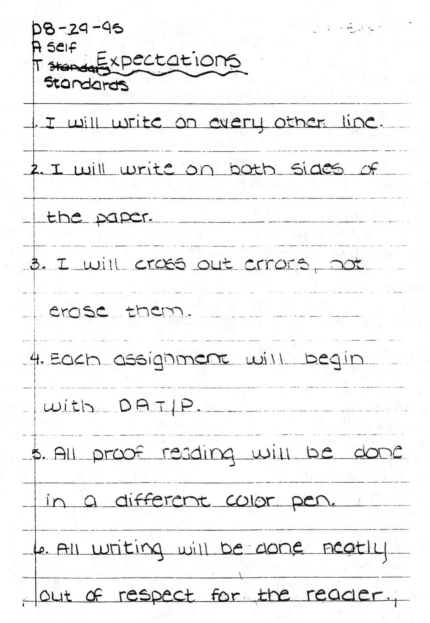

Figure 13.3. A student's draft book standards in Year 1.

trying to teach the concept of an expository essay to students who were attempting to write about things they knew, oftentimes in a language that was restrictive because it was unfamiliar. I remember that day well. I remember thinking and telling her that my district expected me to teach seven genres in reading and seven in writing and provide portfolio samples. If I didn't teach a genre each month there was no way I could cover all of them and allow review time for latecomers and slow bloomers. Based on my understandings at the time it made perfect sense. I could tell that it was not well-received by Jan, whose reputation and celebrity preceded her. She was every bit as awe-inspiring and intimidating as I had been told she would be. Somehow at the summer conference her shadow had not loomed as large, but the specter of this guru sitting in my classroom was scary and I prayed I would not do something stupid enough to cause her to view me as a total numbskull.

During the dialogue with Jan and Marilyn they led me to realize that I could be exposing those students who were ready through read to's and write to's, while allowing those who weren't to continue working on pieces they were feeling good about. I believe that understanding was a real breakthrough for me, and it was only the first of many. I was self-righteous, stubborn, and unconvinced, but I learned from that dialogue and on several other occasions that when I wasn't willful and unbending good things happened in my class. The best I was prepared to do at that moment, however, was to agree to try it their way until November, and if I didn't see students branching out I would do it my way.

Needless to say, all of my concerns were unfounded because the program coordinators were right. The students continued spreading their wings and I didn't have to force choices on anyone. The evidence was there on the ASAP mastery chart I always had discreetly posted in my classroom. It allowed me at a glance to see who had mastered what genre in reading and writing. It was clear from all the stickers on the chart that the students were spreading out and working in a variety of areas. What the chart didn't show was the energy and enthusiasm with which they approached writing. My quick checks on progress showed evidence that those who were ready to move on were doing so and, just as important, those who needed time in narrative or story or whatever were able to spend that time.

I read until my eyes ached. I read books by Don Murray (1987), Donald Graves (1994), and Brian Cambourne (Cambourne and Turbill 1994), and I devoured Nancie Atwell's *In the Middle* (1987). I read and reread the conditions for learning and I tried to create those conditions in my classroom. I felt that I had new understandings and every time I read a book I had a new scaffold to hang the knowledge on. *Dancing with the Pen* and *Reading in Junior Classes* seemed to have been rewritten because they suddenly contained messages I apparently missed during the first readings. I know now that the only thing that changed was my ability to internalize the information because of new scaffolding I was developing through readings, through observations and dialogues with the program coordinator, through tiered dialogues, and through observation techniques I had committed to such as monitoring notes, roves, and revision and editing conferences.

Speed bump two for me came through another dialogue with Marilyn and Jan. They adapted James Britton's saying "Writing floats on a sea of talk" (Britton 1970, 164) and told me that "Reading, writing, and learning float on a sea of talk." I immediately realized that meant my classroom was too quiet. There was not enough exchange among students. My constant efforts to keep the chatter down were actually counterproductive. I also realized that I felt comfortable in a quiet environment and I felt comfortable with the control I managed to have over the noise level. I protested mildly, pointing out that some of my students needed absolute quiet to work. I didn't protest too hard, though, because I knew they were right. A working level of noise was certainly acceptable, it was definitely appropriate, and it could be managed with cooperation from the students. Having matriculated that bump, my journey continued.

That first year was at the same time the most rewarding and the most tiring year of teaching I have ever experienced. I worked harder but, in my estimation, better than ever before. I had to experiment, revisit, and reconstruct on a weekly basis. It was exciting. There were lots of celebrations and there was also a considerable amount of frustration.

I remember a day when I first felt the sense of community in one of my classes. They were the first of the three classes to view themselves as writers and to develop pride in writing and a sense of belonging to a community of writers. They wrote wonderful pieces and they learned to open up and let others in to share their most personal feelings. The other two classes followed later, but not in the same way, though in every group the growth of voice in their writing and the development of style were very apparent. The particular day I am thinking of was when one of my students came up to me after a revision conference and said that she would be attending another conference tomorrow. She usually wasn't so intense about her work. Sometimes I felt she walked through the writing process in her sleep. When she turned to me and said, "I didn't get the help I needed today so I'll try again tomorrow," I knew we had turned another corner. This student had finally joined many of my other students who considered themselves writers and who were serious and sincere about the work they were doing. The attitude of the entire class was reflected in this student's comment.

At about that time planning for new writing pieces became a reflex response for most. They learned, as I had learned, to take the time to plan so that they had a road map for their pieces before they began. Students who were previously having trouble writing paragraphs because many of the topics they were assigned were meaningless to them became fluent writers when encouraged to select topics about which they cared. Eventually they all experimented with the seven genres for which they were responsible. They wrote about topics that were important to them in formats they were comfortable with or at least prepared to learn about. Seeing these students get excited about their work, value themselves as writers, and take risks to share their work was really amazing.

My new understandings empowered me as my students' new confidence empowered them. I was learning how to jump into the writing process, assess and evaluate where they were, and teach at the point of need. I helped my students determine for themselves how they were doing by developing lists of items that they could adapt for their own "I am learning to/I can" pages (Figure 13.4). I learned how to put management techniques in place that allowed me to observe my learners and group and regroup them for various activities with others who were ready for the same teaching points. The vehicles for this type of teaching were small groups, mini lessons with the whole group, and

Date and number drafts
Line out–not erase
Write poems in lines and verses
Use red pencil to proofread
Skip lines
Write in complete sentences
Use quotation marks when someone is speaking
Use a lot as two words
Capitalize the first word in a letter closing
Use the inside heading in a business letter
Use okay instead of o.k.

Figure 13.4. Ideas for students' "I am learning to/I can" pages.

one-on-one interventions with students who needed direct instruction on a particular teaching point. On more occasions than I care to admit I chose the wrong teaching point from the student's writing and I often had to change the "I am learning to" step I had previously designated during an editing conference. As I think back to some of the expectations I actually wrote for my students I can feel my face getting flushed with embarrassment. I have learned from those mistakes and I continue learning, but, yes, I still blush when I think of the mistakes in judgment I made and will continue to make.

STRETCHING MYSELF; STRETCHING MY LEARNERS

As good as I felt about the writing process and our progress, I no longer felt that way about the reading process in my classroom. I knew there was more I could do and more I should do, but I just wasn't sure how to begin. Most of my students could read fairly well, as far as I could tell from the assessments I was using in class. Most of my assessments were summative and knowledge based. Some called for higher-level thinking skills and it was on those assessments that I had the sinking feeling that I was losing students who might have seemed proficient, but who lacked strategies to help them really understand what they were reading in depth. They could "call" the words, but they didn't have the tools in place or the background experience needed to create meaning.

Few of my junior high students enjoyed reading aloud in class; it just wasn't cool. I rarely requested oral reading and when I did it was voluntary. I certainly did not want to embarrass anyone. I was able to discern who my strong readers were from the comprehension they showed on various assessments. I would talk to them about specifics of plot and theme and most of the time they gave the correct responses. I kept hearing from the other teacher leaders that they were beginning to understand reading tangles in their students from diagnosing writing. The prospect fascinated me but I was sure my students' tangles were deeper and more difficult to discover.

I knew I had a few students who had limited understanding and use of visual sources of information and limited sight word vocabularies. With my other learners I needed to work backwards from writing samples to identify reading tangles. My students' writing became a window to their reading. It seemed that I wasn't being paranoid, and I was in fact correct about how well some of their problems were hidden. What I also learned was that by junior high my students had very strong opinions about reading and about themselves as readers and all but the most tangled readers had developed ways to hide their reading problems and keep up the image of success. They had in many ways learned to compensate unless directly challenged.

I began with running records. I could not do these the same way the lower-grade teachers did because I couldn't keep up with my students, even the less proficient readers. I typed text on running record sheets from a variety of *School Journals* (Ministry of Education, various years) and used the prepared sheets to take running records. The task was time consuming, but not so burdensome as to be prohibitive, and it proved to be worth the effort. One insight I gained that amazed me was that one of my brightest students missed many, many words but still came out with a strong sense of meaning. I realized he did not attend to print well, which upon further checking was verified by the fact that he was an absolutely awful speller. He had, from what I have determined, always read books that contained vocabulary that was too difficult for him, but that he could handle from the standpoint of the big picture. He had a strong ability to infer, he was clever about predictions and outcomes, and he could intelligently discuss pieces that were way above his ability if you looked at word-for-word reading. It seemed that he read only the beginnings and endings of words and left out the middles. He spelled the same way. The diagnosis of this was amazing, but the solution was to be more elusive.

After doing running records on those students who I suspected had real tangles I formed very small, fluid groups for reading that were designed to meet a specific problem. Some groups were comprised of students with challenges and were interspersed with students who could provide supports without taking over. The participants and objectives of the groups changed frequently, based on the needs of my students. I had noticed that the students seemed embarrassed about being called on in public to read in small groups, but actually enjoyed participating in the groups themselves. That became apparent when one of my "cool" boys whispered to me on the way to lunch, "When are we going to have that reading group again?" He cautioned me not to tell anyone that he had asked. I worked with one group in each block and by the end of the year we were breaking barriers: my students were reading more willingly and without the high stress levels that were evident early on. When I say stress levels were evident early on, I must make it clear that they weren't evident to me.

You guessed it: speed bump three; enter Jan and Marilyn. After an observation Jan commented that she was not seeing the same joy on the faces of my seventh graders as on the younger students, most specifically during reading. I dismissed it as being an "age thing," but then something happened that I couldn't ignore. Marilyn sat beside me during a guided reading lesson and I watched my students. I saw them put their heads down on the desks, closing themselves off from the group. I saw hands that were tearing paper and twisting hair, nervous habits that were unconscious and were definitely heightened by being in the group. Marilyn asked them what their experiences had been in previous years when they had been brought together in reading groups. They shared in one- or two-word responses that the teacher had always made them read aloud; that they had continually been told they were wrong when they didn't read a word correctly. Other students had made fun of their errors. The teacher had asked them questions and reprimanded them for incorrect answers. It was no surprise that these students found reading in small groups a painful and unpleasant experience. I realized that the first thing these students needed to understand was that reading is supposed to make sense, the job of the reader is to create and recreate meaning, and that all readers may not create the same meaning from the text. I spent much time during the next few months using a shared reading approach with these students, taking the responsibility for the reading by reading aloud pieces to them and encouraging them to create the meaning. I know now that it is my responsibility to help the students understand that reading can be as meaningful an experience as writing. I may be tempted to blame the teachers of the lower grades for not doing this, but I can't absolve myself of the responsibility of helping students create meaning as they read.

FROM THE NETWORK TO MY CLASSROOM

Educators in The Learning Network frequently refer to the Gertrude Stein quote "Just when you think you're there, there's no there there." To me, this means that this journey I am on is never-ending and that my colleagues and I are committed to a lifetime of learning. It means that my understandings are constantly being developed and expanded. It means that I have empowered myself with an ever-widening base of knowledge about the approaches that are available, the resources I can use, and the learners I am trying to reach. I have committed myself to reading books and articles by the experts in my field and to refining and expanding my practices. To me it means that I will continue to grow as a professional. My expectation now is that I am a better teacher today than I was yesterday and I will do an even better job tomorrow. That concept is exciting to me and bodes well for the students I will face in the years to come.

In this second year of my involvement in The Learning Network I have a seventh- and eighth-grade multi-age class. It is really a wonderful way to work in this literacy program. Half of my students understood the management routines on the first day of school and therefore I have been able to really delve into problem areas in writing (Figure 13.5). Since I am working with teachers in the afternoon I am teaching only one student block this year. I have to plan a 150-minute block for language arts and social studies and I am responsible for only 35 students. The teachers who are working with teacher leaders have two blocks with anywhere from 60 to 65 students total. In either case it is a lot easier than working with 95 to 100 students and their draft books, but numbers should not discourage anyone who wants to employ the principles of the Literacy Learning model. I did it and so can everyone else. It looks a little different in my classes than it does in the

---

Expectations

1.   I will write everyday and I will finish my pieces.

2.   I will write about topics I care about.

3.   I will take risks as a writer, trying new genre and new topics.

4.   I will write on every other line in my draft book.

5.   I will line out rather than erase.

6.   I will number and date all my drafts using DATP

7.   I will follow the steps of the writing process.

8.   I will proofread in red pencil

9.   I will take care of my draftbook and not draw or doodle.

10. I will make decisions about what is working and what I need to work on in my writing pieces.

11. I will not skip any pages in my draft book.

Figure 13.5. Draft book standards developed by the teacher and students in Year 2.

kindergarten and third- and fourth-grade multi-age classes, but The Learning Network does not attempt to create a model classroom and clone it. It attempts to help teachers develop understandings about learners, resources, and approaches.

In Year 2 of my Network involvement and in my working with colleagues in their classrooms I know I have already learned a lot. I am still writing in front of my students, but I have a new discipline in modeling writing which has resulted from my understanding of the many different ways modeling may be used. I am demonstrating the elements of various genres in my plans and my published works while sharing my thoughts and feelings. I believe that my modeling is much more effective and I am giving my students valuable information in a way that is painless and purposeful.

My confidence in how to teach the writing process, how to model it, and how to manage students actively in their routines is growing daily. I am working on new and improved ways to deal with individualized editing points with each student while at the same time trying to model good revision strategies so that they can stretch each other as they work independently in revision groups (Figure 13.6). I have taken on individualized spelling lists as a new component of my literacy program.

Teacher Pledges:

1. I will write and finish pieces.

2. I will prepare and present mini lessons based on what you need to know next.

3. I will provide a class environment in which you'll feel free to complete tasks.

4. I will be your editor, once you have proofread.

5. I will give you help in finding new topics.

6. I will make sure you have adequate publishing opportunities.

7. I will make sure that no one disturbs or distracts you while you are writing or conferencing.

Figure 13.6. Standards set by the teacher for herself in Year 2.

It is early in Year 2 and I have small reading groups going. As an upper-grade teacher I have once again assumed responsibility for teaching reading. For many years I assumed that as a junior high teacher exposing my students to literature was my primary job. I believed that the strategies for making meaning were taught early on and for the most part were in place in my students. I did not know how to work with students who needed help. I am now trying to help seventh and eighth graders respond positively to a reading approach that has been pretty negative for some of them and pretty new for me. I don't ask anyone to read aloud and I don't ask questions that require an answer that can be judged wrong or right. Even with those changes the structure of a reading group is not easy to deal with. I feel that I have a better handle on many issues this year, but the more I understand the more I know there is to know. I use all the approaches of reading to, with, and by. I feel that guided reading is a crucial tool for assisting some students to understand pieces that have challenges for them and for learning new reading strategies. It is also a great approach for those who have trouble with a particular genre. It is a way to delve deeper into text. Guided reading is dependent on my awareness of each student's skills, experiences, and interests, determining the supports and challenges offered by a book, and accepting the role of supporting learning rather than directing it. It helps students set purposes and allows them to analyze what they think in an open environment. There are no right or wrong answers, but there are lots of ideas that we read further and discuss to confirm or reject. It provides students with a forum to test their silent reading ideas and develop them. I am the guide or facilitator, and I work hard not to do all the talking.

I believe that The Learning Network arms teachers with the understandings and the tools that give us the power to be in charge of an essential element in this teaching and learning business. That element is the quality of instruction that occurs on a daily basis. Student attendance, a high rate of transiency, the lack of an early literacy-rich environment, socioeconomic dynamics, and the amount of parent involvement and support are factors we all face and seek to improve. In reality, however, the only area we as teachers can really control is the quality of teaching we provide. The Learning Network is helping me meet the challenge to be the best I can be for today, tomorrow, and in the future. It is staff development at its most effective. It is my district making a conscious decision to provide quality to its consumers. It is my commitment to quality education.

SUSAN GOLTZ returned to teaching in 1990 eager to learn more about reading. She is currently a teacher leader and a multi-age seventh- and eighth-grade language arts teacher in Madison Park School, a Learning Network site in Phoenix, Arizona.

PART III

Changing the School and the District

CHAPTER 14

Getting the Whole School on Board

Romelle Parker and Deborah Jinkins

"Even if you want to go back to the way you used to teach (and believe me, from time to time I've wanted to go back) your kids won't let you."

Cecilia Crabb
Teacher Leader, Phoenix, Arizona

How one goes about bringing the whole school on board for anything depends on where the school is beginning and where it is headed. The principal plays a critical role in evaluating where the school is in relationship to a projected goal and in determining what it will take to move the school community toward that goal. Although Forest North Elementary and Wells Branch Elementary, both in Round Rock Independent School District, a large suburban district in Texas, came into The Learning Network together, the two campuses came from different starting points. As principals on these campuses, our experiences of how we got into The Learning Network, what understandings have guided our path in expanding The Learning Network on our campuses, how we implemented the Literacy Learning model, the pitfalls we have encountered, and how we plan to sustain continued professional development have been quite different.

STARTING POINTS: A DUAL PERSPECTIVE

No one enters the change process from the same point of origin. Our campuses, although in the same district and joining The Learning Network at the same time, came from two very different perspectives.

The Forest North Perspective: Small Starts

Forest North Elementary School serves approximately 450 students in preschool through fifth grade. The students come from a primarily white, middle-class neighborhood. In the spring of 1992, two significant events occurred at Forest North. The school district named me, Romelle Parker, as the new principal. I was to replace the former principal of thirteen years, who was moving to a new campus. During that same spring, a Southern Association of Colleges and Schools accreditation team visited Forest North and recommended that the highly structured phonetic approach used to teach reading be replaced with a more developmentally appropriate reading program. The report created several factions among the teachers. Some continued to favor the structured phonics approach and were incensed with the Southern Association report. Some preferred a traditional approach using basals, spellers, and ability-leveled reading groups. Still others argued for a "whole language" approach that would be more supportive for the Reading Recovery® program. The faculty struggled over the next two years to find common ground and to develop a unified language arts program. Changing demographics in our school community and the lack of success many students experienced in both the phonics-based and traditional approaches to reading complicated our struggle.

Looking for answers, during the 1993-1994 and 1994-1995 school years we focused school-based staff development programs on cooperative learning, using the writing process, current brain research, and various learning theories. Teachers were encouraged to take Round Rock Writes, a three-week summer writing institute sanctioned by the New Jersey Writing Project. Some teachers took Early Literacy Training based on Marie Clay's work and the Reading Recovery® model. Early childhood and kindergarten teachers participated in High Scope training, which advocated instructional practices based on Lev Vygotsky's "zone of proximal development" theory (Vygotsky 1978). We had a lot of important pieces, but had not put them together into a unified plan of action or training.

It was in my search for better staff development in reading that I first heard about The Learning Network through a colleague, Chuck Ament, principal at Wells Branch Elementary. Chuck and I discussed the possibility of writing a joint staff development grant proposal to attend the Literacy Learning in the Classroom summer institute. As we talked about the grant, the initial idea expanded from having just a few people attend the institute to seeking funding to join The Learning Network. A great deal of time was spent on the phone talking with Phyllis Greenspan at the Richard C. Owen Publishers, Inc. New York office to figure out just how this idea looked in action and in financing.

I spoke with three teachers, one in kindergarten and two in first grade, to see if they would be interested in attending the summer institute with me and becoming teacher leaders. All three expressed interest in the training, even though they knew that winning the entire faculty over would be a difficult task. We wrote the grant proposal and received enough funding to attend the institute, join The Learning Network, and purchase a collection of Ready to Read books. In the summer of 1995, Jennifer Bordic, Connie Munley, Jennifer Bassetti, and I attended the Literacy Learning in the Classroom summer institute in San Antonio, Texas. Jennifer Bordic and Connie Munley accepted the challenge of the teacher leader positions. We first met and worked with Angel Stobaugh, our program coordinator, at the institute.

Forest North entered The Learning Network through a back door. We did not have a whole faculty buy-in to The Network concept. In fact, the idea had not even been presented to the whole faculty. Joining The Learning Network and training two teacher leaders had been presented to the Site-Based Decision Making Committee (SBDM), and the members had approved Forest North's proposal to seek funding for participation in The Network through a grant. The plan at the point of entry was to explore The Learning Network as a means of upgrading staff development in teaching language arts. If the concept proved to be beneficial, we would have the seeds of change planted with the teacher leaders and could nurture the process of developing additional teachers over time.

The Wells Branch Perspective: A Broader Base

Wells Branch Elementary is a true "neighborhood school" serving 610 students in preschool through fifth grade. While the school is not considered a high minority campus, the 1995 District Curriculum Audit described Wells Branch Elementary as "the most culturally diverse" of the twenty elementary campuses in the Round Rock district. The majority of the students come from middle-income families.

In 1992 Wells Branch Elementary received the Texas Successful Schools Initiative Award for increasing the student performance scores on the statewide assessment test. This funding allowed the principal to send the majority of the faculty to the summer institute (then called Whole Language in the Classroom). Coincidentally, this was the event at which the staff met Chuck Ament, their new principal and my predecessor, for the first time. Teachers were very excited about the potential for the Literacy Learning model because one of the kindergarten teachers had traveled in New Zealand and shared her experiences and observations. As so often happens with teaching innovations, however, this model was not put in place during the school year. Teachers made some steps to implement a few aspects of the model, but nothing that could be termed a "campus-wide initiative." The model was essentially another notebook on the shelf. During the next two years, little was done with regard to instruction and implementation of this model of teaching and learning literacy. The faculty did begin to talk about reading instruction, focusing the campus improvement plan on two main topics: 1) natural learning; and 2) authentic assessment, both central to the Literacy Learning model.

In the fall of 1994, Chuck Ament and Romelle Parker, the Forest North principal, wrote a grant requesting funding for involvement in The Learning Network. The grant was awarded and Wells Branch selected two teacher leaders to lead the campus in this literacy teaching and learning initiative. A first-grade teacher and fifth-grade teacher, Kristi Jordan and Millie Bishop, agreed to serve in the role of teacher leaders and to begin their year of intense training.

Before the year ended, Mr. Ament resigned, leaving the teacher leaders to attend the institute with a third teacher. Within three weeks I, Deborah Jinkins, was named the new principal of Wells Branch, but was now behind the curve, having not attended the summer institute. Fortunately, I had done significant research into the literature about literacy development. This background knowledge enabled me to focus on the implementation of The Learning Network staff development model rather than expending energy learning the basics of literacy development. And so, Wells Branch came into The Learning Network with a large number of teachers having attended a summer institute at some point, two strong teacher leaders, and a principal eager to learn and become a part of The Network process.

UNDERSTANDINGS GUIDING OUR PATH

As our faculties embarked upon the new adventure in The Learning Network, some basic beliefs and understandings guided our path. First of all we recognized, as did Thomas Sergiovanni, that "changing the basic theory of schooling ... requires a rethinking of our most common, entrenched, and fundamental education beliefs, structures, practices, and behaviors" (1994, xii). We also recognized that the campus principal plays a critical role in the change process not only by providing the leadership or vision necessary to initiate change, but also by setting expectations and providing support to sustain it. Change, however, does not come without costs or consequences. The leader must anticipate what the costs will be at the onset and during the entire process for individuals and the institution as a whole. Thoughtful leaders should consider the consequences of successful implementation of an initiative as well as the consequences of failing to successfully implement the anticipated change. The weighing of pros and cons in the change process reflects the core values and beliefs of the leader.

Frequently, change literature speaks about the leader as a visionary who sets the driving expectations for the institution. As principals, we, too, believe it is the role of the leader to articulate the vision and define expectations. The leader must individualize expectations for adult learners in the learning community, just as teachers must individualize expectations for learners in their classrooms. To individualize expectations, leaders need to know the people with whom they work and understand what supports and challenges are needed to move individuals along a continuum of change toward the beliefs and values that support the vision.

Leaders make decisions every day that affect their ability to be successful and effective. It is possible to be successful but not necessarily effective. If a leader is successful in achieving a goal, but in pursuit of the goal has steamrolled or alienated a number of his staff, the leader has not been "effective." In what Paul Hersey and Kenneth Blanchard (1978) define as "coercive or top-down change," the leader uses his or her position of power to affect group change, hoping it will channel down and transform individuals. While this approach achieves superficial results and may be necessary in certain circumstances, the distrust and resistance created impedes real, long-term change. If, however, the leader uses his or her position of power to empower individuals through increased access to knowledge and information, he or she creates "participative change" and increases the likelihood that individual attitudes and behaviors will change. As individual attitudes and behaviors in the organization change, group behavior transforms. Over time, the critical mass needed for complete transformation can be achieved.

The process of transformation occurs in three stages—orientation, disorientation, and new orientation (Brueggemann 1995; Ricoeur 1970, 1971, 1976). In the *orientation* stage, the leader comes to know and respect each staff member as an individual in regard to attitudes, beliefs, practices, and needs. Considering these aspects about each individual, the leader determines the degree of "challenge" each individual needs to keep them moving in the change process and what kind of support they need to be successful in the change. The degree of challenge should be strong enough to move the individual into the *disorien-*

tation stage, which causes them to question previous practices and beliefs. When the leader provides the necessary support in terms of resources, training, and personal encouragement, the individual can risk making change. Successful attempts to change practices help the individual internalize new practices and develop a *new orientation* for beliefs and practices. The tension between challenge and support is the point of creativity. An imbalance between challenge and support where challenge is too heavy overwhelms the individual and results in a manifestation of destructive and subversive behaviors. On the other hand, when support is too heavy in the equation, stagnation occurs. Defining the expectations for change is reasonably easy. Providing meaningful support is more difficult (Jinkins and Jinkins 1991).

Traditionally, teacher support for needed change has come in the form of "sit and get" workshops. Typically, these workshops are one- to five-day isolated experiences in which the teachers receive multiple cookbook-style ideas for improving student performance. What is often missing from these training events is the teachers' understanding of *when* and, more importantly, *why* to use these strategies. Teachers return to school, pull out the new activity, and attempt to use it in class. When the new strategy fails to produce the desired outcome, the teachers discard it and revert to the tried-and-true practices of the past. Dead-end staff development experiences leave teachers feeling betrayed and frustrated.

Many teachers today are unable to cope with the diverse student populations and social conditions they encounter because teacher education programs have failed to prepare them for the multiple contingencies of real world teaching. According to Linda Darling-Hammond, "students are not standardized and the tasks of an effective teacher are not routine." Consequently, professional development programs must aim to "transform teaching so that it focuses explicitly on student understanding and learner-centered practices" (1994, 14). Teachers need to be freed from the factory model of teaching (Schlechty 1990), in which one size of instruction was meant to fit all learners, and be given the autonomy to plan and evaluate their own teaching based on their knowledge of diverse learners and multiple instructional approaches. Teachers who have clear understandings of how students learn and an in-depth knowledge of subject matter are empowered to deal with the increasing demands created by changing demographics in the schools and ever-higher standards for students. It is what teachers know and are able to do that has the most influence on what students learn.

Where can the teacher turn for help? We believe that teachers can find help in collegial dialogue and collaboration with their peers.

Teachers with more information and experience in an initiative, such as teacher leaders in The Learning Network, provide teacher support by making observations of classroom practice and facilitating reflective instructional dialogue. Providing time after school once a week for interested faculty members to discuss as a group what they are reflecting on encourages teacher interactions and increases the probability that the conflict and disorientation necessary for transformation will occur. With each successive group discussion, beliefs, values, and practices shift from individual preferences and judgments to the more powerful shared beliefs, values, and judgments of the collective. Quality learning organizations, according to Peter Senge, "invest in improving the quality of thinking, the capacity for reflection and team learning, and the ability to develop shared visions and shared understandings" (1990, 287). However, as Judith Warren Little cautions:

> *The content of teachers' values and beliefs cannot be taken for granted in the study or pursuit of teachers' collegial norms of interaction and interpretation. Under some circumstances, greater contact among teachers can be expected to advance the prospects for students' success; in others, to promote increased teacher-to-teacher contact may be to intensify norms unfavorable to children (1989, 22).*

Little's caution reaffirms the importance of the principal's role in maintaining the vision and setting the expectations for change.

PUTTING BELIEFS INTO PRACTICE

Just as the point of origin for joining The Learning Network was different for Forest North and Wells Branch Elementary Schools, so would the actual process of bringing these new beliefs into the classrooms differ.

The Forest North Approach: Continuous Dialogue

Participation in The Learning Network occurred simultaneously with other professional development initiatives at Forest North. In the spring of 1995 and prior to Forest North's entry into The Network a few faculty members attended training in using whole faculty study

groups as a form of staff development. The staff development committee liked the study group idea and believed that it offered an opportunity to build collegial relationships on campus and create a community
of learners. When the committee presented the study group concept to
the faculty, 78 percent of the staff members voted to use study groups
to accomplish our campus-based staff development during the 1995-
1996 school year. In order to create more time for study groups to meet,
campus administrators agreed to schedule campus meetings only on
Wednesdays and to limit faculty meetings to one Wednesday per
month.

When Jennifer Bordic, Connie Munley, Jennifer Bassetti, and I attended the Literacy Learning in the Classroom summer institute in
San Antonio during the summer of 1995, we began to talk about how
we could share what we were learning and thinking with the faculty.
We felt as if our hands had been tied, first of all because faculty meetings had been reduced to only one per month, and second because the
focus of the study groups was yet to be determined by the faculty. We
valued the study group idea, however, and believed that providing
teachers with the time to talk about what really matters–teaching and
learning–was vital to our faculty and to our students if we were to
come to common beliefs about teaching reading and writing. Belief systems cannot be mandated from the top. We knew that we could establish our own study group and continue learning. Bordic, Munley, and
Bassetti believed that they could share their new understandings with
their own grade-level teams at weekly planning times.

During the staff development days at the beginning of the 1995-
1996 school year, we used the problem-solving model depicted in Figure 14.1 to guide our thinking in the development of the campus improvement plan. The information we analyzed included student
performance data on the Texas Assessment of Academic Skills (TAAS),
student writing samples, and discipline records. The analysis indicated
that while math scores had improved significantly over the past year,
reading scores had declined. Test results showed that word meaning
and summarization skills were particularly weak, so the faculty chose
these two areas as targets for improvement. When the faculty discussed strategies to improve student performance in the target areas,
ideas for formatively assessing student progress in word meaning and
summarization were lacking. Staff development in running records
and other reading assessments was needed, along with strategies for
teaching reading comprehension.

Approximately one month after the development of the campus

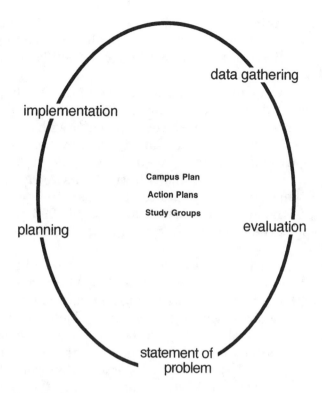

Figure 14.1. Problem-solving cycle used by Forest North Elementary.

improvement plan, the faculty of Forest North met to discuss the formation of faculty study groups. Based on spring and summer training in whole-faculty study groups, the staff development committee proposed that the faculty consider student performance data and choose a study group focus for the year based on the area needing the most improvement. Clearly this area was reading. Roughly twenty percent of the faculty had opposed the study group idea in the spring and now expressed their dissatisfaction with having to study a particular topic. Believing that professional development ought to be meaningful to all participants, the staff development committee and I altered the original study group plan to allow groups to choose topics relevant to their particular professional needs. Approximately two-thirds of the staff chose to focus on reading while the others chose topics such as integrating math and science, sign language, and building resiliency in children. The largest group formed around the idea of exploring the Literacy Learning model (known on campus as LLN) with Jennifer Bordic and Jennifer Bassetti. Kindergarten teachers formed a group to further their thinking about student writing with Connie Munley. Three other reading groups began their studies by reading *Dancing with the Pen* (Ministry of Education 1992) and *The Whole Story* (Cambourne 1988).

Study groups nurtured the seeds of new understandings and encouraged collegial dialogue on campus. The gentle winds of change, however, frequently found themselves confronted with storms of resistance. Some staff members resented having to use their valuable time to attend study groups. Others feared they too would be "forced" to implement the Literacy Learning model in their classrooms. Despite the suspicions of some and the resistance of others, study groups stimulated interest in the model. During the summer of 1996, ten additional teachers attended the Literacy Learning in the Classroom summer institute.

A major support for me was the training and insight provided by Angel Stobaugh, our program coordinator. Angel taught me how to notice the strengths in both students and teachers. As I went to teacher leaders' classrooms with Angel and worked alongside her and the teacher leaders, I gained insight into how children develop literacy. During the instructional dialogue sessions, I learned new techniques for helping teachers reflect on their own practice and come to new understandings. Angel frequently stayed until late in the evening, talking with me and guiding my own learning.

In addition to the stimulation provided by Angel and the study groups, Forest North was fortunate to gain Liz Sims as an assistant principal during the fall of 1996. Liz had served as a teacher leader in Hutto Independent School District, Hutto, Texas and was a tremendous support to me and to the teacher leaders. Although the critical triangle of The Learning Network requires only one campus administrator, usually the principal, I heartily recommend that all campus administrators be a part of the process, including observation and instructional dialogue. The time that administrators give to an innovation emphasizes the value the innovation holds for the entire campus. It is important not only to "talk the talk," but to be able to "walk the walk."

Liz and I worked together to reinforce with the faculty the importance of planning for instruction and having the conditions for learning in place (Cambourne 1988). We set these expectations through individual teacher conferences, team meetings, staff memos, and newsletters. We assessed and evaluated teacher understandings by reviewing unit plans and lesson plans and through formal and informal classroom observations. We found that curriculum topics or TAAS objectives drove instruction more often than the evaluation of individual student's needs and next learning steps.

Realizing that getting the teaching and learning cycle (Figure 14.2) in place was critical to the improvement of student performance and the expansion of Learning Network ideas, Liz and I intensified our efforts the following year to facilitate teacher understandings in the areas of assessment and planning. Teacher handbook sections on unit planning and lesson planning were updated. In addition, staff development before the opening of school focused on the use of the teaching and learning cycle in the preparation of unit plans and daily lesson plans. A copy of the graphic organizer used for unit planning is shown in Figure 14.3. The "challenge" evidenced by the unit plan format is the expectation that formative assessments will be done to evaluate student progress throughout the unit, not just at the end. The "support" comes through grade-level efforts to develop formative assessments and through faculty meetings in which curriculum coordinators and colleagues help generate additional ideas for assessment.

In June of 1996 ten teachers attended the Literacy Learning in the Classroom summer institute along with Jennifer Bassetti, Jennifer

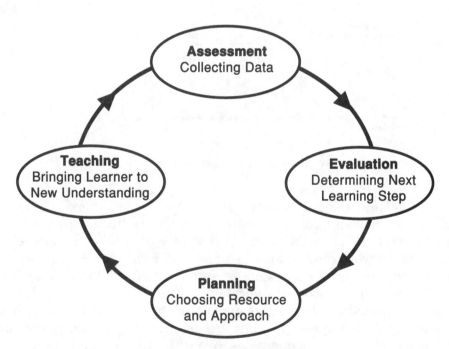

Figure 14.2. The teaching and learning cycle.

Unit Plan of Instruction 96/97
_________Nine Weeks

****

Grade Level:________________________________

Unit Topic:________________________________

Duration of Unit (days, weeks):__________________

Content Integrated:
Science_____
Social Studies_____
Math _____
Language Arts_____
Health_____
Art_____
Music_____
Physical Education_____

****

I. Curriculum Standards Addressed: (Integrate & code)

II. Performance Expectations Specific to Unit: (Integrate & code)

III. Key Instructional Strategies/Learning Activities: (Refer to Best Practices)

IV. Formative assessments:

V. Summative Product/Performance for Assessment and Crieria for Evaluation (i.e. rubrics, analytic scale, test, etc.)

Figure 14.3. Unit plan organizer.

Bordic, Connie, Liz, and I. Teachers were not asked to make a commitment to implementation and continued training with the teacher leaders until the end of the institute. At that time, the teachers were asked to reflect on what they had learned and to determine if they were willing to put their new understandings into practice and to continue their growth with the support of the campus-based teacher leaders. Teachers who wanted to receive the support of the teacher leaders had to commit to attending weekly group discussions, maintaining a monitoring notebook, writing action plans, being observed in their classrooms by the teacher leader, the principal, and occasionally the program coordinator, and reflecting on the understandings that drove their practice in one-on-one instructional dialogue sessions with the teacher leaders.

During Year 2 in The Learning Network, nine of the ten teachers who had attended the institute began implementing the Literacy Learning model, with three teachers in kindergarten, one in first grade, one in second grade, one in third grade, two in fifth grade, and one special education teacher working in inclusion classrooms. Jennifer Bassetti, Jennifer Bordic, and Connie Munley continued the implementation process they had begun in Year 1. An Academics 2000 grant provided funding to hire an additional full-time teacher at Forest North. This allowed our two teacher leaders to share a classroom and be released fifty percent of their time to work with the other teachers. Jennifer Bordic and Connie Munley could observe in another teacher's room or conduct an instructional dialogue without disrupting the continuity of instruction for children in their own first-grade classroom.

Special education teacher Patti Starke went to the Literacy Learning in the Classroom summer institute and continued her development in Year 2 through the teacher leaders and group discussions and instructional dialogue sessions. Patti implements the model in one inclusion classroom alongside Jennifer Bassetti. She also worked in a fifth-grade classroom with a new teacher, Brenda Lambe, who had not yet attended the institute. The sharing Patti and Brenda did as they collaboratively planned for language arts instruction built Brenda's understandings and were bringing her into The Network.

Weekly group discussions are still held to increase teacher and administrator understandings. The dialogue sessions are open to all faculty members, but teachers who have committed to The Learning Network are expected to attend along with Liz and me. At first some of the teachers working with the teacher leaders confided to them that they were afraid to voice concerns or questions with Liz and me present. The teacher leaders pointed out that Liz and I were learners in The Network, just like everybody else, and that we needed a forum to raise our questions, too. In dialogue sessions and in the classroom, we are all learners together.

Jennifer Bordic, Connie Munley, Jennifer Bassetti, Liz, and I meet in our own "LLN" study group each Monday afternoon. During that time we continue our own learning by discussing books or articles we have read, analyzing student writing, revising daily planning ideas, or considering complicated running records. Bassetti in particular has some students in her second-grade classroom who are experiencing tangles. We frequently assess their progress, discuss their next learning steps, and brainstorm possible instructional strategies to use in accelerating their progress. We also discuss where the teachers working with the teacher leaders are in their learning and what topics might be useful in group discussions to promote deeper understandings and better practices. These weekly study group sessions have helped to sustain the enthusiasm and motivation of the core group at Forest North.

Dialoguing with Ann Mace, our program coordinator for Year 2, has also strengthened our understandings. By discussing a teacher's strengths and approximations prior to tiered dialogue, the teacher leaders, Ann, and I are able to pinpoint learning steps for each teacher and to appreciate growth. Ann has also been helpful in suggesting ways to work alongside teachers to get them moving and keep them moving. Through Ann we have experienced key understandings about how to use student draft books, monitoring notebooks, and lesson plans to assess teacher growth.

Student success is the best source of support for The Learning Network and Literacy Learning in the Classroom. When teachers using the Literacy Learning model lead previously tangled readers and writers through the maze and into fluency, it gets the attention of other teachers. In addition to noticing student achievement, teachers notice the enthusiasm and renewed vigor that Learning Network teachers have for their work. As any cruise line knows, it is much easier to get folks on board a smooth sailing ship than it is to get them on a sinking tub!

The Wells Branch Approach: Authentic Leadership

As the new principal appointed to Wells Branch just as it joined The Learning Network, a high priority for me was to establish myself as an authentic leader at the school. Three elements of authenticity are: 1) shared perceptions; 2) a sense of heart; and 3) competence (Jinkins and Jinkins 1991). The first of these, *shared perceptions*, ties directly to the culture, beliefs, and values of the school. I believed it to be imperative that early on I learn the history of the school and the community. During my first week on the campus, I met with each grade level team. I used this time to ask questions such as: "What moments or events have defined this school's way of being?" "What words or phrases would you use to describe Wells Branch?" "What should never be changed about Wells Branch?" "Who are the most significant people in the formation and history of Wells Branch?" The information gleaned from these conversations was invaluable as I began to make initial observations of faculty interactions, both in small settings and in the system as a whole. Through these observations I discovered, as many leaders have, that the stated beliefs and values were not necessarily the demonstrated beliefs and values. Next, I began to "dip stick." In private conversations, in groups of two or three, and sometimes in curriculum committee meetings with representatives from all levels, I began to check the depth of understandings of faculty members with regard to literacy development, personal attitudes and beliefs, and perceptions of the learners at Wells Branch. Through classroom observation, I saw that instructional practices were consistent (for the most part) with the current understandings and attitudes the teachers had voiced. I began to have an understanding of the Wells Branch culture and value system.

To continue establishment of shared perceptions, I set about clearly and succinctly stating my beliefs and values about children and the importance of their learning to read and write in the first years of school. I shared with the faculty that the research is clear: students who do not read by the end of first grade remain "at-risk" throughout their school careers. Since we are the adults in the situation, we have reasonable control over the structures, procedures, and practices that will be used in our schools. Consequently, we are responsible to create learning environments in which every child experiences relevant and focused instruction every day. We have the power to make it happen. It is our responsibility to make it happen. Anything less is non-negotiable. Through clear statements to this effect, the faculty came to know me, my beliefs, and my values.

At the same time that these conversations and observations were taking place, I was also becoming familiar with the processes of the Literacy Learning model. First, I learned the theory behind the teaching and learning cycle and the conditions for learning (Cambourne 1988), which in my mind are the cornerstones of the model. I realigned my language and understandings in terms of the Literacy Learning model to reduce confusion in dealing with teachers, teacher leaders, program coordinators, and parents. Shared perceptions were strengthened by this consistency of language.

In considering the second element of authenticity, *a sense of heart*, I knew that in the beginning the faculty was wondering: "Does she like us? Does she accept us?" This is a most troublesome aspect of leadership. Generally, leaders enter a new position with hundreds of ideas and possibilities running through their minds. It is very difficult to communicate acceptance and understanding of the individuals within the organization while at the same time articulating a new vision and very often setting an entirely new course. I made it a priority to notice the strengths of individual teachers and the program as a whole and then to communicate appreciation for their efforts in written notes, as celebrations in faculty meetings, and the like.

In addressing the third element of authenticity, *competence*, I was faced with establishing myself as a competent leader as well as a competent teacher. Faculties need a leader who can organize routines and procedures that enhance the efficiency and effectiveness of the program. They want a leader who understands and is competent in the classroom. The question here is twofold: first they ask "Does she know what she's doing?" and then they wonder "Why should I listen to her when it comes to teaching?" I began establishing my competence by making myself available to teach, to read, and to participate as fully as possible in the instructional setting at all grade levels. As teachers began to accept me as knowledgeable and skillful in the classroom, they more readily accepted my suggestions and advice and saw me as a viable resource in seeking solutions for concerns about individual students. I could now turn my attention more fully to the teacher leader training and preparing the campus for implementing the Literacy Learning model through the professional development model offered by The Learning Network.

A basic tenet of leadership is presence. My active and on-going presence in all aspects of the implementation phase of The Learning Network would communicate my values and expectations. Observations made of the instructional dialogue between Angel Stobaugh, the program coordinator in Year 1, and Millie and Kristi, the teacher leaders, resulted in the deepening of my own understandings of the teaching and learning cycle as well as clarification of effective strategies for broadening the acceptance of the model across the campus. In conversations with Angel, I sharpened my understandings of the conditions for learning, the teaching and learning cycle, and of the importance of having these in place for the adult learners with whom I would work.

Implementation of the Literacy Learning model at Wells Branch would begin by establishing strong teacher leaders. I facilitated this by learning about and applying the teaching and learning cycle myself. During frequent observations in the teacher leaders' classrooms, I assessed and evaluated the practice and understandings of these two teachers. In conversations, I modeled the inquiry process, addressing issues identified by each teacher. On-going instructional dialogue and support enhanced the professional growth and understandings of the teacher leaders during this year. Growth in other teachers was encouraged through topic discussions in faculty meetings, staff development sessions, and time spent with our program coordinators, Angel Stobaugh and Ann Mace.

The teacher leaders and I did not, however, see the faculty embracing the process as quickly as we believed they would considering that the majority had already attended a Literacy Learning in the Classroom summer institute. The attitude of many teachers seemed to be: "We're already doing this." In dealing with this avoidance behavior, my approach was to assess each teacher's practice and validate any signs of implementation or understanding that I noted. At the same time, my own understandings of the conditions for learning began to fall into place. I analyzed which of the conditions were in place in the total campus context and determined that by: 1) establishing expectations; 2) holding teachers responsible for basing their practice on their understandings; and 3) providing specific response to their efforts, I would be able to impact the implementation process more profoundly. I reinterpreted the attitude of "We're already doing this; it's nothing new" to mean "We're ahead of the game; let's raise the bar."

Consequently, instead of sending only eight teachers to the Literacy Learning in the Classroom summer institute as we had originally planned, we sent *all* of our kindergarten, first-, and second-grade teachers, our special education resource team, and any upper grade teachers who wanted to attend. Nineteen teachers, two teacher leaders, and I, a total of twenty-two educators, attended the 1996 Literacy Learning in the Classroom summer institute. The expectation was set. All primary teachers would work with teacher leaders during Year 2. The Literacy Learning model would be the focus for language arts instruction at Wells Branch.

Another challenge awaited the implementation of literacy learning at Wells Branch in the form of school culture. Terrence Deal (1987) describes school culture as "an all encompassing tapestry of meaning," which is "transmitted from generation to generation." According to Deal, much effort is expended by the group attempting to protect the existing ways the school does things. This was true at Wells Branch. Deal goes on to suggest the use of "transition rituals" to recreate school cultures and consequently to decrease resistance to an innovation by connecting it to elements of the existing culture. Transition rituals call for connecting existing beliefs and value systems to proposed change through heroes and celebrations.

The early work of discovering the school's culture served me well at this point. I was able to demythologize inaccuracies in the history and to recount the many successes and achievements of the school. We set about celebrating the heroes. The instructional resource room we established was dedicated to Lucille Harmon, the kindergarten teacher whose journey to New Zealand had begun the exploration into literacy learning at Wells Branch. Today, teachers across the campus use materials from the Lucille Harmon Book Share Room.

Initially, the shared values of the faculty were articulated by creating a strong connection between the school's involvement in The Learning Network and the two previous administrations, which were trusted and highly valued. When more of the faculty accepted me as a leader, I tied the innovation to my personal beliefs and values. Teachers began to read, observe, and reflect, and the understandings of teaching and learning in the area of literacy began to deepen. Almost spontaneously, the teachers began to share a new set of values and beliefs based on these new understandings. As the teachers transform, so does the school's belief system and culture.

Specific objectives and plans for implementing the Literacy Learning model were set early on in the process. Before school began, the two teacher leaders and I made a list of issues the teachers would face as the implementation phase began. We planned brief presentations for faculty meetings. During the fall of 1995, most of these presentations dealt with the teaching and learning cycle or a specific element from the cycle (e.g., assessment; planning). The teaching and learning cycle drove our approach for developing our campus improvement plan. We evaluated the state assessment data by student and by teacher in order to focus planning on specific needs. Instructional approaches such as reading to students and modeling writing were evidenced in campus improvement plan strategies. Connections between literacy learning and teacher practice were being made.

As Year 1 progressed, Angel Stobaugh, our program coordinator, spoke at faculty meetings, worked with teachers in organizing the instructional resource room, conducted training for the faculty on how to evaluate the supports and challenges in resources, and in some cases, observed in classrooms other than the teacher leaders'. At about this same time, Millie and Kristi invited their peers to observe them during instruction. Several teachers took advantage of this opportunity. As a result, many teachers began to "play at the model" and seek out dialogue with the teacher leaders regarding the *why* behind the teaching and not so much on the specific approach selected.

By March of 1996, we had finalized registration for the summer institutes and scheduled biweekly study groups based on readings from *Reading in Junior Classes* (Ministry of Education 1985) and *Dancing with the Pen* (Ministry of Education 1992) that were conducted by the teacher leaders. We learned early on that for many teachers there were two critical issues. First, most of the teachers did not grasp that teaching must begin with individual, on-going assessment and subsequent evaluation in order to determine and plan for the next teaching step. They were still looking for a scope and sequence; they wanted to be told what to teach next. To help them internalize this crucial aspect of the teaching and learning cycle, the teachers leaders and I modeled this assessment and evaluation process in dealing with them as adult learners. The second issue was the realization that meaningful change in behavior comes from a transformed belief system. The belief systems of teachers are changed by new knowledge, reflection, and time. For the teacher leaders and I, this meant pressing teachers to ask "Why?" at every juncture. Sometimes it seemed as if we were unrelenting in this. In the end, it paid off. Teachers began to "get it."

At the Literacy Learning in the Classroom summer institute, the teacher leaders and I made observations and anecdotal records of teacher comments, responses, and behaviors at the various sessions and discussions. Through informal conversations over lunch and at breaks, we sought to alleviate the anxiety teachers were feeling with regard to what the new understandings would mean for them. At the end of the week, the teacher leaders and I reviewed our monitoring notes. We assessed and evaluated each teacher. We considered the appropriate approaches for each adult learner and any potential challenges or supports of which the teacher leaders needed to be aware. Then we developed individual plans for the teacher leaders to use with each teacher. At the start of the school year a schedule was developed for teacher leader observations to occur once every two weeks. After the first six weeks observations were accelerated to one per week. Teachers were expected to submit a new action plan and reflections on their instructional dialogue sheet on Thursday after dialogue. I checked through these on a random basis to see who was turning them in, if they were moving on to new topics, and what understandings were developed in the instructional dialogue sessions.

We consistently worked on the development of more effective and efficient group meetings and dialogue sessions. In the beginning, the teachers working with teacher leaders needed time to process a lot of information. By mid-year a focused teaching point for each dialogue session was developed based on what the teacher leaders identified as common issues or concerns from a topic suggested by a single teacher. The new format for group meetings is: 1) celebrations; 2) concerns; and 3) the focus, such as assessing teaching points from running records, determining group members from assessments, or determining the level of supports and challenges in a resource.

Time is always a critical issue when implementing an innovation of this magnitude. Traditionally, the daily planning time for teachers occurred during the fifty minutes when their students were in classes such as art, music, drama, or physical education. In order to recover additional time for teachers to reflect, read, and observe in classrooms, art was taken off this daily rotation. Each class was scheduled for a fifty-minute art period each week. During art time, teachers observed in other classrooms, analyzed assessments, or read from professional literature. Teachers noticed what strategies, approaches, resources, and monitoring techniques were being used and often dialogued with peers about why particular approaches were chosen.

As a leader on the Wells Branch campus, I try to remember two things: 1) change affects specific individuals, and it is on individuals that my primary focus must be placed; and 2) as leader I am also the interpreter. Just as the Interpreter in *Pilgrim's Progress* leads Christian through the images of his spiritual life to face the decisions and consequences that lie in store for him (Bunyan 1988), as principal, I lead the faculty in the reflection of who we are, what has been accomplished here in the past, what we are about now, what we can become in our future, and how best to get there.

PITFALLS ENCOUNTERED ALONG THE WAY

Since most innovations in education come in the form of a new program or method that dictates "how to do" classroom practice, it is sometimes difficult for teachers to accept that the Literacy Learning model is a way of understanding how students learn and letting that understanding guide practice. Consequently, when educators in The Learning Network try to communicate with peers about the Literacy Learning model, the other teachers are usually listening to hear *what* to do, not *why*. Teaching is about students and their needs, not about cookbook methodologies. When Learning Network teachers resist suggesting a recipe for classroom practice, teachers not yet trained suspect that their peers are holding out and being secretive.

Some teachers resist a practice that requires them to think through their understandings about teaching and learning and plan for each individual student in their classroom. Focusing on the next steps of individual students is especially challenging to those teachers who work from a deficit model rather than building on students' strengths.

Suspicion about The Learning Network comes in yet another form. If teachers see The Network as an innovation being pushed on them by the administrator, their resistance will be focused on the perceived imposition of authority rather than on new understandings about teaching and learning. Teacher leaders are often seen as agents of authority and become targets for the barbs of discontent and insecurity.

In a social environment where education is under constant attack not only from within but also externally by parents, politicians, and the media, reflective practice can be threatening. Constantly asking oneself "Why am I doing what I am doing?" seems a little masochistic at first. Questioning an understanding or a practice tends to put teachers on the defensive. To diffuse this defensive posture, more time is needed for self-reflection and the sharing of ideas and understandings through dialogue and collaboration with peers. School leaders have to communicate that reflective practice challenges ideas, not individuals.

SUSTAINING THE MODEL: WHERE DO WE GO FROM HERE?

The responsibility of keeping the vision of The Learning Network alive and supported falls to campus administrators. One major source of support comes through funding to purchase materials and to provide release time for teacher leaders to attend focus meetings and to work alongside teachers on campus. So far, Forest North and Wells Branch faculties have been successful in receiving enough local, regional, and state grants to pay for two years of full participation in The Learning Network, to purchase materials for a fully equipped instructional resource room for kindergarten through fifth grade at each school, to allow sixty teachers to attend Literacy Learning in the Classroom summer institutes, to allow teacher leaders and campus administrators to attend the annual Learning Network conference, and to provide release time for teacher leaders. We continually investigate sources of funding that can provide on-going training, materials, and release time for teachers.

In addition to financial support, however, teachers undergoing such radical change need moral support and personal encouragement. Often teachers implementing new ideas find themselves and their ideas challenged by peers. When this happens, campus administrators have two roles to play. First, we must console and encourage the teacher being challenged. Second, we need to confront the challenger, find out why there is a need to challenge, and deal with it. Often the challenger feels threatened by the changes taking place on campus. All teachers need to know they are valued and play an important role on campus.

A third area of support for The Learning Network comes at the district level. For The Network to thrive and grow it must be consistent with district beliefs and practices. It is the responsibility of campus administrators to articulate The Learning Network principles at the district level. We have endeavored to achieve this task by sharing at principals' meetings, presenting grant proposals to the school board, and serving on district-level curriculum committees for language arts and reading. Having The Learning Network and the Literacy Learning model accepted on a broader scale than the individual campuses adds clout and facilitates bringing the skeptics on board.

Finally, and most importantly, for The Learning Network to continue and for our schools to become self-winding, "teachers (individually and collectively) must develop the habits and skills of continuous inquiry and learning" (Fullan 1993, 81). As administrators we must commit to finding time for teachers to learn from each other and from outside resources. We must ensure that resources are available and that the conditions for learning are in place for *all* learners.

ROMELLE PARKER is the principal of Forest North Elementary, a Learning Network school in the Round Rock Independent School District, Austin, Texas. During her 25 years in public schools she has served as a teacher, librarian, and administrator. Romelle is completing a doctorate in Public School Leadership.

DEBORAH JINKINS was principal of Wells Branch Elementary School, a Learning Network site in the Round Rock Independent School District, Austin, Texas when she wrote this chapter, and recently moved into district administration. An educator for eighteen years, she has taught elementary, middle school, and high school students. She is completing a doctorate in Curriculum and Instruction. Deborah has presented workshops and conference sessions on reading instruction, curriculum development, assessment, and leadership.

CHAPTER 15

Organizing the Instructional Resource Room

Ann Mace

"Does the piece achieve what it claims? Does the author fulfill all the promises engendered by the title and text? Is the message genuine? Does it avoid the sham, the misleading, the prejudiced, the stereotyped, and the superficial?"

Margaret Mooney
"A Good Book is a Good Book Anywhere"

I first came from New Zealand to the United States in September of 1994 to work in New Jersey. I joined Richard C. Owen Publishers a year later as a facilitator for the Literacy Learning in the Classroom summer institutes and as a program coordinator for The Learning Network. I had come through the New Zealand school system as a teacher, assistant principal, and advisor to schools.

EXISTING ORGANIZATION OF READING RESOURCES

As I traveled to various schools across the United States I found a variety of scenarios regarding the selection and use of books for reading instruction. When I made my first visits to classrooms in New Jersey I was surprised to find many teachers using only basal textbooks for reading instruction. There were other teachers who had added some trade books to their basals. There were still others who had quite a variety of trade books in their classrooms. Some teachers had small reading books, which they used mainly for independent or home reading, not for instruction.

Those who had trade books often had only one copy of each title and sometimes these titles had been replicated in several classrooms. Teachers who had a set of these books referred to them as "my books" because they had been allocated the money to purchase them. In other schools there was a variety of sets among rooms and the teachers were beginning to share them naturally. One New York teacher who had changed to a lower grade level had no books in her room when she arrived. She was expected to buy them herself or to scrounge from other teachers who were reluctant to part with any of theirs. Many other teachers I have met have bought books for classroom use with their own money. In New Zealand the school takes full responsibility for the purchase of instructional reading texts.

Although I knew that basals were still widely in use in the U.S., I wondered why anyone had taken eight wonderful, individual picture books and bound them in one cover to put into the tiny hands of a six-year-old. I read *Report Card on Basal Readers* by Ken Goodman (Goodman et al 1988) to find out their history. I discovered that they were written in the 1920s for teachers who were relatively untrained in the theory of teaching reading. I wondered if the teachers with whom I was working knew that.

During my entire teaching career in New Zealand I was involved in the selection, buying, and storage of books for classroom use. A resource room—a central storage area for shared instructional reading materials—had always been part of my teaching life, so it was a shock to see that this wasn't the case in the U.S.

An instructional resource room is one sure way of having a single organized place in a school to store books used in reading instruction. Having books housed in one place where they can be shared makes budgeting easier and money go further. It assures both a variety of resources for learners and easy access to them by teachers.

Schools in the U.S. vary in the quantity and quality of resources for the teaching of reading and writing. As teachers' understandings about teaching reading and writing grow, they are finding it necessary to choose the right texts to scaffold new learning. They begin to re-look at the texts available to them in their schools.

WHAT IS AN INSTRUCTIONAL RESOURCE ROOM?

An instructional resource room is simply a small, centrally located room that houses all reading material used by the school; a well-organized, wide range of small books, big books, picture books, audio tapes, anthologies, collections, periodicals, and poetry cards. Rather than keeping books in classrooms for only that particular class of students to use, all books from all classrooms are stored in one place and all teachers have access to them. This is a great advantage as they have a wide variety of books from which to choose.

In New Zealand, teachers are provided with a core series of reading books published by Learning Media, a department of the government-run Ministry of Education. Ready to Read books and School Journals make up the original series. They now have been added to by a variety of others, some series in the native Maori language and some series in other languages, as understandings develop and as the population changes.

Additions to these series arrive during the school year. I remember looking forward to the new editions when I had prior knowledge of their arrival. Sometimes I had been involved in the trialling of a book so the children and I felt as though we had ownership of it, and we eagerly looked for any changes, especially if we had made recommendations for revisions.

The books were always stored in a book room, often a storeroom or closet, somewhere within easy reach of the classroom teachers. New Zealand teachers believe that children learn best from a variety of *real* quality books so the books provided by Learning Media weren't the only ones we used, but they provided structure for our collection. Books from other publishers were put alongside those from Learning Media when the budget allowed. Publishers' representatives often called on us, and some teachers attended conferences where new books were displayed. We weren't very good at choosing in the early years, but we became better with practice.

Now schools budget very carefully to purchase books based upon students' and schools' needs. Teachers have a better understanding of what a good book looks like and are guided by the criteria set out in *Developing Life-long Readers* by Margaret Mooney (1988). Good books have charm, magic, impact, and appeal. They avoid stereotypes and do not patronize the reader. They are age appropriate and conceptually appropriate. They are authentic, credible stories covering a range of genres. The small books that form the bulk of the material usually contain a single story, eight to sixteen pages long. The illustrations are very important. They support emergent and early readers in particular as they gain meaning from the text.

SETTING UP THE RESOURCE ROOM

In my position as program coordinator for The Learning Network, I have had the opportunity to assist many faculties in establishing instructional resource rooms. At Oakman Elementary School, a Learning Network site in Dearborn, Michigan, a group of teachers and I made a start in setting up a resource room. When I arrived at the school I found an almost empty room attached to the library. It was beautiful, with windows at one end letting in light and old oak shelves around the walls. Before I arrived all the junk had been cleared out and the shelves were crying out to be filled.

Schools that don't have a room such as Oakman did can usually find a small room somewhere in the school, usually full of unused equipment and books, which can be transformed. Hutto Elementary School in Hutto, Texas has moved from their first, small resource room to a much larger one as their collection has grown. They are now adding multiple copies of articles—short, sharp, snappy pieces that they have used with older readers—in three-ring binders with plastic pockets.

A quantity of adjustable metal shelving is required to meet the needs of the school (see Figure 15.1). You will also need file or magazine boxes, blank self-stick labels with which to label the boxes, and markers. Some schools also use colored dots to label the books. Boxes are available from different sources, so shop around for competitive prices. A school will need at least one hundred boxes to begin. The number depends on the quantity of books the school already has and the size of the school. Several titles may fit into one box, but they shouldn't be squashed in too tightly.

It is advisable to have mending equipment available and for teachers to know how to effectively mend books. A table for resting and sorting books on and even a comfortable chair in which to sit and read is helpful. Good lighting is necessary. Professional resource books, book catalogues, and charts can also be kept here.

LEVELING

At Oakman Elementary, a shipment of books had arrived from Richard C. Owen Publishers and we were eager to open them. First we had to make sure that we had all the necessary equipment: boxes, boxes, and more boxes in which to store the books; and labels, markers, and colored dots to label them.

When we set up a resource room, we use nine levels, which are designed to cover three main developmental stages of emergent readers, early readers, and fluent readers, and four for older fluent readers. Figure 15.2 shows the leveling bar that appears on all Books for Young Learners and also represents the structure of the resource room.

Figure 15.1. Empty shelves at Bluebonnet Trail Elementary, Manor, Texas.

The emergent stage has only one level. The early stage is divided into four levels, as is the fluency stage. The Ready to Read books also use nine levels, which are designated by colors. Magenta represents the emergent stage. The early stage is designated by red, yellow, dark blue, and green, and the fluent stage contains orange, light blue, purple, and gold. Most readers move through these stages from ages five to seven. As the lower elementary teachers in Oakman were the teachers ready to use the resources, we decided to leave the organization of the

EM	EARLY			FLUENT			
S	G	I					

Figure 15.2. Books for Young Learners leveling bar.

books for older readers until later. They were placed on the allocated shelves as we found them. At a later date, the fourth level would be divided to cater to the interests and concepts relevant to seven- to eight-year-olds, eight- to nine-year-olds, nine- to eleven-year-olds, and eleven- to thirteen-year-olds. Books, periodicals, newspaper clippings, brochures, and pamphlets would be added as teachers found them.

The labor force was divided and the work began. The shelves were temporarily labeled with the color names. Boxes were opened and wrapping was removed from the packs of books. Storage boxes were assembled. Temporary labels for the boxes were hand written.

As books were unpacked they were placed into boxes, labeled, and placed on the appropriate shelf. The smell of new books helped the level of excitement grow. People came to see what we were doing and to bring books from their classrooms (see Figure 15.3). Over two days

Figure 15.3. Books to be sorted and leveled in Bluebonnet Trail Elementary.

books appeared and were roughly leveled and placed on shelves. The dots would be put on later. The levels would be decided on more firmly as the books were used with students.

The Books for Young Learners and Ready to Read books form a framework around which to place other books. This system of leveling is built around the supports and challenges found in books to suit the normal progression of readers (see Figure 15.4). Some schools have adopted the Reading Recovery® numeric system, but it is too narrow for use in classrooms. It is specifically designed to accelerate tangled readers who get extra help daily from trained Reading Recovery® teachers. There are resources such as *Books for Ready to Read Classrooms* (Richard C. Owen Publishers 1994), soon to be replaced by *Choosing and Using Books for Young Learners*, to help level books from other publishers and collections.

At Barton Elementary in Dallas, Texas we simply picked one Ready to Read book from each color level and laid them out in order on tables. The participants at the leveling session (see Figure 15.5) methodically picked up a book from another collection, read it to determine which of the Ready to Read books it was similar to, and placed it on the table. As each book was boxed another member would check the approximation and if it was all right, the process would continue. If he

Figure 15.4. Temporary labels to identify supports and challenges in texts.

Figure 15.5. Participants at Bluebonnet Trail Elementary leveling and boxing books.

or she thought it had been placed at an inappropriate level another member of the team was consulted and eventually an appropriate level was agreed upon.

Two other things happened during that session. Some books were discarded because they were found to be totally inappropriate for the understandings the teachers now had about quality books for children (Mooney 1987). Secondly, some of the faculty realized that some books were more suitable for shared reading than for guided reading. More understandings were developing.

After the books are leveled and boxed, they are coded with stickers that correspond to the leveling bar. An *S*, *G*, or *I* written with marker on the sticker or colored dot shows the teacher which instructional approach is recommended for that particular level of development. S is for shared, G is for guided, and I is for independent reading. Any leveling done is not set in concrete. Levels should be checked as the books are used in guided reading situations in the classroom and confirmed with the use of running records.

Schools usually box books in sets of five or six for shared and guided reading. Guided and shared reading groups should not be too large, and each child plus the teacher should have a copy of the same book. A separate section of the shelves houses books for sharing (reading to) and bins of books for independent reading. At Bluebonnet Trail Elementary School in Manor, Texas, big books, poem cards, and song charts for sharing have been hung on a rail in another area. Books for reading to children other than library books are placed on shelves above them.

All schools will need multiple copies of each title, usually about six per every hundred students. Most titles will be placed in both shared reading and guided reading sections. Several titles will fit in a box if magazine boxes are used. On the front of the box the title, the recommended approach, and the level is shown. Some schools also indicate how many copies of each title are in the box (see Figure 15.6).

For each level several bins of books for independent reading should be assembled. Twenty to thirty single titles should be in each box. Teachers can then take the books to their room and keep them for up to two weeks. If the children need more time on that level then they can be replaced with books from a different box, which will contain some of the same titles and many different ones.

A check-out system needs to be decided upon. Most schools provide teachers clothespins with their names written on them, sometimes

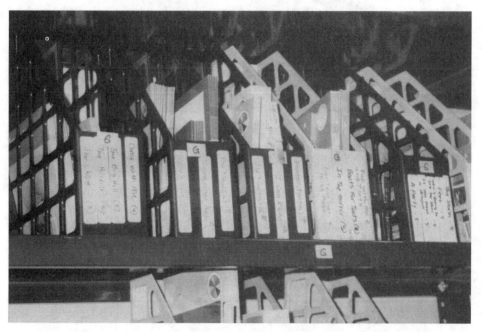

Figure 15.6. Sets of books for guided reading at the emergent level.

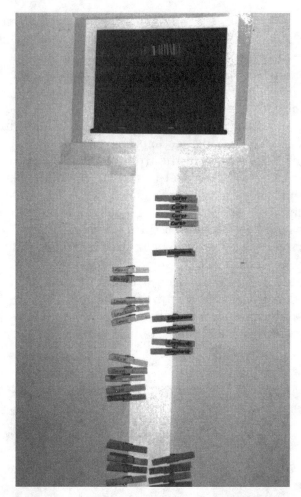

Figure 15.7. Clothespins as a check-out system at P.S. 191 in New York City.

painted brightly for easy recognition, to pin on the box from which they have borrowed a set of books (see Figure 15.7). If the labels are placed vertically on the front of the box, the check-out clothespins can be placed exactly on the title. This allows for easy return and for other teachers to see who has a title they may need.

EXPANDING THE COLLECTION

Once the resource room is set up with whatever books a school has already, the school can begin a focused purchasing plan to fill any gaps.

An organized resource room makes it easy to see the gaps immediately. After a year or two, replacements for favorite titles must be considered.

Many schools put their books on a database. It is helpful when purchasing because they can pull up a field by level or publisher. They can then see exactly what they have and the gaps they need to fill. This also helps in budgeting.

How does an instructional resource room impact on a school's budget? In P.S. 191 in New York City the teachers are all given $100.00 to spend at the publishers' court on staff development day. In the year prior to their involvement in The Learning Network they bought their books independently, and when they talked about them over lunch, they discovered that several of them had purchased the same titles. With the support of The Network the following year, the teachers decided to pool their money. The books they purchased went into their resource room to be shared among all of their classes. Teachers in P.S. 191 are collaborating on resources much more than ever before.

USING THE RESOURCE ROOM

Teachers in Learning Network schools use the teaching and learning cycle to organize their daily planning and teaching. They use running records and observational notes as assessment tools to decide the next teaching point for each student. As a result of their evaluations, students with like needs are grouped together. Then the teachers head for the resource room to select the appropriate books for the groups they will meet with that day. They choose resources to meet the needs of the individual learners and the supports and challenges each book offers that will scaffold the new learning they have planned. The teacher then decides on the approach with which to use the text.

Running records and assessment during the most recent guided reading session showed Tami, a first-grade teacher at Boone Elementary in Austin, Texas, that Stevie, Arturo, James, and Maria were gaining in confidence as readers and using all sources of information. However, when they used visual information to help approximate a word, they didn't always look at the whole word. These children tended to use only the beginning letters of the word on which they were stuck. Tami wanted a text in which the readers had to problem-solve to overcome challenges. For this particular group of learners, Tami chose *Blackbird's Nest* (Harvey 1985) from the Ready to Read collection because the children really had to think in terms of meaning and look through the chunks of letters in the word. She went to the resource room and borrowed five copies, clipping her clothespin onto the box so she could easily return them.

After she chose this book, Tami selected the approach of guided reading. She knew that these readers' strengths would provide the supports they needed to overcome most of the challenges. She also thought that they would need to do some work when they encountered unknown words. Tami's role would be to ask questions to uncover the challenges, then provide enough support to scaffold new learning.

On page 2 the text reads: "Four speckled eggs in a blackbird's nest." Tami thought that *speckled* might be a challenge for this group. It was. Maria approximated *specked*. James told her where to put her fingers to help with chunking it.

On page 4 the text reads: "Four bare babies in a blackbird's nest." James approximated *naked*. Maria left the word out and commented that the baby birds in the illustration had no feathers. James got the word *bare* and kept it to himself. He then tried to help Maria. He asked her what a word that meant "no feathers" would be. He realized the importance of her doing the problem-solving herself.

Tami could also have chosen *Nothing in the Mailbox* (Ford 1996), a text from the Books for Young Learners collection. She may do so for the next guided reading with this group. It is a story about a boy writing letters to people. Tami anticipates that meaning may break down as the readers encounter challenges such as *uncle*, *cousin*, and *president*. She expects that her students will make approximations of these words based on meaning (what would make sense) and picture clues. They will check these approximations using the visual information. The challenges will be easily overcome with Tami's support.

A skillful teacher such as Tami learns to choose the texts and the teaching approach carefully. She can draw from the varied range of books in the instructional resource room. She evaluates her assessments in order to plan for effective and focused teaching. The teaching and learning cycle continues as the teacher collects assessment information during the reading of the book. The monitoring notes taken during the guided or shared reading will assist in further planning. The teacher is not only assessing the students for further learning needs but also herself as a teacher.

CONCLUSION

The instructional resource room does many things for a school. It is not just a storage area for books. It is a learning ground for teachers.

They begin to collaborate more and more on what they need to under-stand as teachers and discover what works best for students. They learn about the supports and challenges that books offer children. They continue to learn about the reading process and how children learn to read. They come to be better judges of what makes a quality book and have higher expectations of resources. They are more dis-cerning of how each dollar is spent. They strive to build a balanced col-lection of books to meet the needs of the vociferous readers their learn-ers become (Figure 15.8).

Figure 15.8. A full and balanced collection from Oakman Elementary, Dear-born, Michigan.

In my role as program coordinator in Learning Network schools I have seen instructional resource rooms at their beginning stages, when the teachers had few understandings about books and approaches to teaching reading and writing. As the resource rooms have grown, so have the teachers' understandings, and vice versa. I have seen the collaboration of teachers who once kept to themselves and I have seen many young children blossom as life-long readers due to skillful, focused teachers using a variety of quality reading resources to meet their needs. The model of The Learning Network, which builds a philosophy of teaching and learning, has created this.

ANN MACE is a program coordinator for The Learning Network and a facilitator for the Literacy Learning in the Classroom summer institutes. She has worked in Texas, Michigan, and New York. She came through the New Zealand education system as a teacher, an assistant principal, and an advisor to schools. She has just had her first children's book, New York City Buildings, *published as part of the Books for Young Learners collection.*

CHAPTER 16

Creating District-Wide Change

Kay Coleman

"It's exciting to be in a room where people are high on teaching, learning, and kids. The energy is back where it needs to be. Every day you're a better teacher."

Margie Kessler
Administrator, Phoenix, Arizona

I had the perfect job. I was principal of a beautiful new elementary school in the midst of a gorgeous area on the outskirts of Phoenix, Arizona. I had been able to selectively staff the school based upon the desire of every faculty member to be a life-long learner and evidence of their skillful teaching. All staff members knew from the beginning that we were to be a Learning Network school. We had a wonderful first year. The community was very supportive of the faculty and excited about our work in knowing our learners, knowing our resources, and knowing the approaches needed to take each student to the appropriate next steps in learning. We had made great strides in setting a foundation for a self-winding school through our work with Jan Duncan, our program coordinator from The Learning Network. I knew the district well: I had served as teacher, staff developer, director of curriculum and instruction, and principal. I had literally grown up as an educator in the district.

Despite all this, here I was thinking seriously about taking a job as assistant superintendent in a district in which I knew no one, which had a reputation of being extremely conservative, and which seemingly measured its success only by norm-referenced standardized tests. As I sat in my office on the last day of that first magical year at Las Brisas Elementary School I thought of all those things and I cried because I knew what I needed to do, and yet I wondered how I could leave the people for whom I cared so deeply—the teachers, the students, and the parents who I loved and who had shared their lives with me. We had lovingly planned and purchased and worked around the clock on many occasions to open the school on time. Our regular staff development that focused on developing consistency, quality, and high expectations for our students was invigorating. As a faculty we had struggled to put our beliefs about teaching and learning into the reality of our daily work with students. We had labored to make the school a significant place in the lives of the children and the community. We had walked our talk, and we knew how rewarding and how tough that could be.

I had always believed that school improvement came "school by school .... one school at a time," but during that first year in Las Brisas, I had come to realize that these words spoken to me by Larry Lezotte, an effective schools researcher, several years before in a visit to my district were true. Larry told me in all of his work with school improvement around the U.S. he had found that "school by school .... one school at a time" was true for school improvement, but with one small hitch: if the district is not supportive of the improvement initiatives in the school, in the end the school will be greatly slowed down, if not stopped. I knew that Las Brisas was a target because our district administration was not on board. The cartoon of the monkey hammering down the nails in the floor as they continue to pop back up frequently came to my mind. There was a desire on the part of the district to keep all the schools at the same level, and Las Brisas was a place that would continually pop to the surface. Our nail just would not stay down.

So I made the lonely and hard choice to take on a new challenge. I knew clearly that the way in which I would do the business of assistant superintendent in my new district would be radically different than what I had previously experienced as principal. I have always believed that being a good school administrator meant remembering what it was like to fill the other roles within the system—student, parent, teacher, principal—because it is through the people in those roles that productive change happens in our schools. Although I had been successful in each of those roles, I had no idea what was ahead of me as assistant superintendent in the Madison Elementary School District in Phoenix, Arizona.

I had studied the literature on staff development, organizational change, curriculum and assessment development, effective schools, and literacy development in students. I had a fair understanding of how to facilitate and support teacher development in small groups and with individual faculties. But suddenly, in this new district—where I knew only a few people and certainly couldn't fall back on the relationships developed over the years with staff—I found a new culture, new players at the table, and new politics, and it was time for the "rubber to meet the road" in my professional practice.

ASSESSMENT AND EVALUATION OR WHERE WE WERE

I quickly came to understand that my time for getting the pulse of the district was limited. The superintendent and the governing board wanted to see productive change for our students and they wanted it quickly. Madison, with its 5,000 students, 240 teachers, and seven schools, had been a "lighthouse" district in the state for over a hundred years but had progressively slipped. Student achievement was still high, but certainly not in the first or second position in the state as it had been. However, there was still a perception among the staff and community that the district was at the top of the state in student achievement and educational opportunity, which meant to many that we just needed to keep doing what we had been doing. This perception needed to become the focus for our early work if we were to see improvement within the system.

Richard Beckhard and Wendy Pritchard have provided a useful way to think about resistance to change. The formula is

$$C = (D + V + F) > X$$

where

C = Change;

D = Dissatisfaction with the status quo;

V = Vision of the desirability of the proposed change or end state;

F = First steps in arriving at the V;

X = Cost of changing.

Factors D, V, and F must outweigh the perceived costs for change to occur. "If any person or group whose commitment is needed is not sufficiently dissatisfied with the present state of affairs (D), eager to achieve the proposed end state (V) and convinced of the feasibility of the change (F) then the cost of changing (X) is too high and the person will resist the change" (Beckhard and Pritchard 1992).

Based on my understandings of change within organizations we needed to have a good assessment and evaluation sample that clearly defined the dissatisfaction (D) with the present state of affairs. So the search for the facts began, with the goal of having a clear picture of "where we were" completed within six months.

During the summer of 1994 I found that:

♦ the district had few curriculum guides;
♦ staff development was extremely limited with a reported lack of interest;
♦ funding for curriculum development and staff development was nonexistent;
♦ any work to support curriculum and staff development that was being done was done on the backs of a core group of teachers who were either not paid or paid a minimal sum in the summer to keep things moving.

Within days of my appointment, I requested a listing of strengths and concerns about the district from each administrator, board member, key teachers, and community members. I scheduled meetings with as many of those people as possible during the summer months. With the beginning of the school year I walked through all district classrooms with building administrators. I used Brian Cambourne's conditions for learning (1988) to help me analyze what I was seeing in classroom practice.

We conducted an analysis of how we spent our federal and state funds for our most at-risk students and what the educational outcome was for those students. As we looked at our Title I students over time it was clear that they were not making progress academically–in fact, they were losing ground. As the number of students with whom we were least successful continued to grow within our district we expanded the number of instructional aides in the schools. Those instructional aides frequently were the people held responsible for teaching our most at-risk students. However, the data were clear: at a local and a national level instructional aides were not making an impact on the academic achievement of students.

During the fall of 1994 the governing board approved a request from our superintendent for a curriculum audit conducted by the National Curriculum Audit Center. Our goal for the audit was to be honest with ourselves and the community; to take stock of teaching and learning in the district, and begin to take the steps necessary to return this good district to the "lighthouse" district that it had once been. We wanted to fully meet the needs of each individual child and in the process to raise the expectations and standards for the academic achievement of all of our students.

The findings of the audit and the informal assessment samples were not a surprise to anyone within the system, but certainly put the issues on the table for discussion and solution. The recommendations were far reaching, including suggestions for improving the culture, curriculum, instruction, and assessment practices used in the district. The report called for system-wide improvement reflecting a new attitude—one of continuous improvement throughout all areas of the school district.

PLANNING: THE PUZZLE PIECES

In those first weeks of school in 1994, during my visits in classrooms throughout the district, I frequently heard questions and statements that troubled me:

"So what will we be doing with reading?"

"You know we only use second grade materials if children are in second grade. We can't use anything else."

"What about math? This is the year for new books. When will we get them?"

There seemed to be a belief that the superintendent and I would issue edicts and things would change in terms of curriculum and instruction in district classrooms. The assumption seemed to be that the teaching staff were under our authoritarian control. I heard stories of teachers hoarding old textbooks and hiding them so that they could use them with their students when administrators weren't around. This left me with a terrible unsettled feeling. The professional staff of this district appeared to feel that someone outside their school was supposed to make all the decisions. There was an empowerment issue here and there was certainly a lack of trust and much of that lack of trust was centered on me.

Building Relationships and Building Procedures

It became clear to me that people needed to see quickly that I was a person of integrity, that I could be trusted, and that I cared about the needs of students and teachers. I knew of no other way of accomplishing that than to "walk my talk" and begin to work with teachers on tasks that needed to be done to get the district back on track. During that fall, work began in earnest to establish curriculum policy and initiate multiple curriculum committees that had real work to accomplish. Classes were offered which included study groups using several thought-provoking professional books. Resources were allocated to allow those working on curriculum committees to attend state and regional conferences along with their study of the current literature in their content area. Although I was told it wouldn't work, people did apply to be on committees and one-third of the teaching staff registered for district classes. The study group idea didn't take off until the second semester, but the seed for valuing dialogue was planted. It was a good year of hard work, and with that work came the mutual respect that develops when people work together on tasks that are challenging and they know in the end that they are better educators because of their study and dialogue.

Reflecting on that year, I am increasingly convinced of the power of relationship building as an administrator. It is through those relationships that we develop a professional culture for shared empowerment within a district. We must learn that:

> *Highly successful leaders practice the principle of power investment: They distribute power among others in an effort to get more power in return. But their view of power investment is sophisticated; they know it is not power over people and events that counts but, rather, power over accomplishments and over the achievement of organizational purposes. They understand that teachers need to be empowered to act–to be given the necessary responsibility that releases their potential and makes their actions and decisions count (Sergiovanni 1987).*

Observing: A Picture is Worth a Thousand Words

Assessment and evaluation data about the district were shared with administrators, teachers, board members, and the community, along with the challenge that as a district we needed to find a way in which teachers in our system could be supported in using the teaching and learning cycle shown in Figure 16.1 to truly meet the needs of *all students* on a daily basis. This was the V of our formula.

Observation in a Learning Network school was an important part of our planning. It is difficult to visualize what this means for children and teachers without seeing it in action. I had become convinced as a principal in a Learning Network school that this was the most effective model I was aware of in supporting the development of skillful teachers who understood that, in the words of Gertrude Stein, "there's no there, there," and that continual improvement is what we are about in our profession. But this was not my decision to make. The instructional leader of a school, the principal, is key to making any initiative work

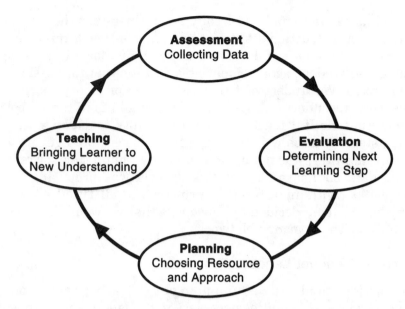

Figure 16.1. The teaching and learning cycle.

within a school. So, our observations started with the administrators of the district. Principals were invited to observe various models of teaching that were occurring in the area, including a Learning Network school. As principals became increasingly interested in The Learning Network I invited board members and other district office administrators to observe, and principals began to ask teachers to observe. It was important to have a large group at all levels to be part of the conversations about any changes we were anticipating within the system. Without fail, every person who observed had the same reaction by the time they walked out of a Learning Network school: "This is the kind of school that I want my child in." Discussions regarding the implications were frequent and in-depth across the district between teachers and principals, principals and principals, principals and the district administration, and any other configuration that could be initiated. We invited Jan Duncan, our program coordinator at Las Brisas, and Marilyn Herzog, who was at the time a teacher leader, to talk with us about the implications for a school and a district if we were to take on this model of staff development. During this time it became apparent that principals and teachers from several schools were increasingly interested in the Literacy Learning model and in The Network.

Funding

Our next challenge was funding. Because of changes in requirements for districts receiving federal dollars the time was perfect for us.

The administrative team had already determined that there would be a reduction of instructional aides in our schools over a three-year period because of the lack of data, at a national and local level, supporting increased student achievement as a result of paraprofessionals in the classroom. We understood that in a "time of plenty" paraprofessionals were a wonderful convenience for the adults in the school, but we knew that skillful teachers with the ability to identify the next learning steps for each child on an ongoing basis would get us to our goal. This, however, was not a "time of plenty," but a time for results.

The data on Learning Network schools was promising. In the spring of 1995, with input from the principals at all Title I schools, the administrative team decided by consensus that we would focus our Title I funds on The Learning Network.

Selection of Teacher Leaders

We decided to identify a minimum of two teacher leaders on each campus who had the qualities necessary to be leaders and were willing to take on a professional challenge. The qualities that we looked for in our teacher leaders were that the teacher:

♦ sees self as a learner; is open to new learning and new understandings;
♦ seeks professional challenge; knows that developing new understanding involves the challenging of old ideas;
♦ is able to express thoughts clearly in discussion and in writing;
♦ expects learning will occur for both students and teachers;
♦ knows the learner and strives for learning outcomes for all;
♦ has respect for and is respected by colleagues;
♦ displays leadership qualities and works comfortably alongside adults;
♦ has a strength of commitment (Richard C. Owen Publishers 1995a).

The Literacy Learning in the Classroom summer institute of 1995 was a great experience for the 45 teachers, administrators, and board members who attended. We were able to learn together and spend those four days dialoguing with each other to make sense of the content of the institute. We began to formulate a common vocabulary around teaching and learning. I recall being so proud of our participants at the end of those days. Some had come with apprehension, but the apprehension had changed to beginning to believe that we all had something to learn about knowing the learners, knowing the resources, and knowing the approaches.

Resources: Books and Time

During the institute, teachers were busy listing all the resources that they needed to begin implementation of this approach to teaching. They were quite convinced that they needed to have a specific type of easel, lots of chart tablets, and draft books for their students that looked like those that they had seen in classrooms in which they observed. "Oh, and by the way," they reminded me that they needed a resource room of leveled books in each school. Having lived through this implementation before I knew they didn't really need exactly those easels, those chart tablets, and those draft books, but I also knew that those physical resources consistently seem most important to teachers as they begin implementation and there was no way I was going to get in the way of progress. It is important in the early stages to provide teachers with those materials that they feel are critical in making their lives easier.

On the other hand, the "oh, by the way" regarding the instructional resource room of leveled trade books was a necessity. From a fiscal standpoint, if every business manager understood the power of a shared resource room in a school and how much money could be saved, we curriculum people would have more than enough money to make this happen in each of our schools. The challenge, of course, is for faculties to learn to value such a shared resource. As teachers, for years we have all hoarded resources due to an inadequate supply of instructional materials. As administrators, we need to be cognizant of a lack of trust that exists among teachers that their colleagues will be responsible for the shared books, and we also need to demand accountability from each teacher so that trust can develop around sharing resources.

The instructional resource room allows teachers in a school to share a great variety of wonderful trade books to support children at all levels of reading ability. I have found that many of our classrooms and schools contain sets of literature which have been purchased over the years that are duplicated from room to room in the school, and they all sit unused except for two weeks out of the year. This kind of waste in our tight budget times is foolish. The other problem that we have found with those literature sets from our book flood years is that they frequently have been used with all the students whether or not they were providing the appropriate level of supports and challenges. By knowing our learners and knowing our resources we are able to be more fiscally responsible and certainly more instructionally responsible.

Time is another resource for which we have to plan carefully. Teacher leaders need time in the summer to develop the resource rooms of leveled literature. During the year they need time to meet with their teacher leader class twice a month in focus meetings. On at least one of those occasions, school and district administrators need to meet with the teacher leaders to be certain that we are all learning together. In our district we have a lunch meeting with all the teacher leaders, the principals, the superintendent, the assistant superintendent, the directors of special education and educational programs, and our program coordinator. Teacher leaders also need time to meet in a learning and dialogue mode weekly with the principal(s) on their own campus. This time is spent discussing professional reading, challenges in implementing the model in their classrooms, and school-specific topics and planning school-wide inservice programs.

Another time and funding resource that must be planned to support the teacher leaders working alongside their colleagues in Year 2 is part-time release for each teacher leader. Title I funds are a good source, although some districts are able to allocate these funds from maintenance and operation funds. If this model of teacher development is to be effective, the release time is critical. We cannot expect teacher leaders to observe and dialogue with their colleagues during preparation periods, lunch periods, or before and after school.

Full faculties need planned time to work together on a regular basis to define their shared beliefs and values regarding teaching and learning and to learn together. Monthly staff development meetings of three to four hours are powerful opportunities to develop the shared vision for a school. What this undoubtedly means for the administrator is that he or she needs to be willing to take the time to put into writing the administrivia that frequently occupies faculty meetings so that the focus of faculty meetings can be teaching and learning.

Principals need to plan for time to shadow the program coordinator when he or she is on campus each month. Shadowing is time-consuming because it takes a good portion of one day of every month, but we have watched our principals become stronger instructional leaders through these experiences. It is through shadowing, the weekly instructional dialogue sessions held with the teacher leaders, and the regular staff development meetings and the monthly focus meeting with the teacher leader class that principals expand and deepen their own understandings of the Literacy Learning model.

District administrators also need to plan time for shadowing the program coordinator, attending teacher leader focus meetings, observing in classrooms where teachers are putting into practice the Literacy

Learning model, attending the institutes, and participating in dialogue sessions with teacher leaders to develop their own understandings and abilities to articulate why they are doing what they are doing relative to literacy. Time for reflection and dialogue will not occur without being planned for and valued by the administrators.

IMPLEMENTATION OF THE "WEE STEPS"

Many of our teachers were fortunate in the first year because as they left the four-day summer institute with all the enthusiasm that was generated they walked into a two-week summer program designed to give kindergarten through second-grade students who were identified as being at-risk academically an opportunity to get a jump-start on the year. It provided them with time to get a jump-start on practicing some of the strategies about which they had just learned. What a wonderful coincidence this was for us. The following Monday in nearly every jump-start classroom students were using draft books, teachers were modeling reading and writing with read to's and write to's, running records were being taken on students, and small groups of students were engaged in shared and guided reading. The jump-start experience allowed teachers to think through and coach each other on classroom organization and strategies. We now try to schedule our Literacy Learning in the Classroom summer institute shortly before our jump-start program so that we can provide an opportunity for teachers to practice their new skills before school starts.

As the school year began in the fall of 1995, I watched with amazement as teachers took on their new understandings and children began to blossom. I also watched with concern as I saw a great number of teachers trying to do everything at once. Many were successful. The teacher leaders were in the best of all situations because they knew they had support coming from their program coordinator, Marilyn Herzog. They in turn attempted to support their enthusiastic colleagues as best they could in that first year. It is important that administrators have a clear picture of the overall needs of teachers in times such as these. Administrators need to encourage teachers to take those "wee steps" that Jan Duncan talks about rather than taking on too much and being unsuccessful. Continual "wee steps" add up to giant leaps in professional practice over time.

As we struggle with implementing skillful teaching strategies in the classroom, the days of the parachuting specialist who drops in and provides us with "wisdom" and then leaves us on our own are a thing of the past in districts involved in The Learning Network. We have found that the parachuting specialist is a waste of time and money for all but two to five percent of teachers. We have learned from the work of Bruce Joyce and Beverly Showers (1995) the importance of skillful teachers working alongside their colleagues in a coaching role. The Learning Network takes that coaching to a new level with the instructional dialogue that is so powerful in building shared understandings of the teaching of reading and writing.

During the summer of 1996, 140 teachers, administrators, and at least one parent from each school attended the institute. This began our second year of implementation. The second year was marked by teacher leaders beginning to work alongside their colleagues on a weekly basis. The language of our teachers has changed and become more precise as they talk about what their students are doing in reading and writing. Parents are thrilled with what they see happening for their children. The topic of many meetings in which parents are involved is what is happening in the classrooms across the district where teachers are part of this professional network. The comments sometimes come with tears as parents describe the joy they have as they watch their children grow and excel.

When I walk into classrooms today, children are engaged in reading and writing, there is evidence of student responsibility through planning, there is evidence of assessment driving instruction, there is evidence of planning for individual children, the environment is comfortable and conducive to learning, and children are using the resources in the room and in the school (library, other teachers, and so on) in their learning. These classrooms are becoming a center for learning with teachers who are becoming more skillful each day.

When I go into faculty meetings in these schools I see teachers who are interested and engaged in learning and faculties that are striving to redefine their vision of what they want for their students. These faculties are developing into communities of learners who are increasingly dissatisfied with the status quo. The goal of continually refining their practice is evident in their conversation and action. They are realizing that where they are is an okay place to be ... but not an okay place to stay. Continual improvement is becoming a norm.

When I meet with teacher leaders I see professionals who are continually challenging their own and each other's understandings about teaching and learning. Their roles shifted dramatically in the second year as they began to work daily with their colleagues in coaching and facilitating their growth in classroom practice. They have gained a more global perspective of their schools and their vision for curriculum and instruction in the district has greatly expanded. They understand the Literacy Learning model and serve as continual reminders to administrators that the teaching and learning cycle is just as appropriate to the learning of adults as it is to the learning of children.

When I talk with principals I hear the excitement, passion, and vision that they hold for their schools and their community. They are articulate as they talk about the learning of children and adults. They are serious about walking their talk. For some, the idea of retirement that a few years ago was enticing is not quite so enticing any more—at least until their schools are well on board as self-winding communities focused on the needs of each individual child.

REFLECTIONS: LEARNING OVER TIME

My personal learning has been great and cumulative. There are many similarities between bringing a district along the road to literacy and bringing a school along the road. The main difference is that, at a district level, we have many more learners to know and many more resources to know and be able to find. I believe that it is our responsibility as district leaders to support the schools and to help build the capacity of each school community to more closely meet the needs of children. Yes, there is pressure and an expectation of accountability for results with our students, but with that pressure principals and teachers must feel great support.

My learning about creating district-wide change can be summarized as follows:

- Take time to understand and value the culture of the system.
- Build relationships and trust through real work.
- Value teachers and promote their professional growth.
- Be willing to state what you believe and value.
- Promote collaboration at all levels of the system.
- Walk your talk.
- Provide the "pictures" of what we can become through observation and dialogue.
- Provide pressure and support for refining practice and continual improvement.
- Use your position to make things happen to support the needs of teachers and schools so that they can support the needs of children.
- Remember that everything we do is for the benefit of our students.

My learning is ongoing. But in the words of one of our teacher leaders at the end of her first year, "I had no idea what I was getting into ... but this has been the most incredible professional experience of my life–and the hardest." As we evolve as a district, I know that we have the pieces of the puzzle moving into place to once again be a "lighthouse" district that has teachers, administrators, and students who are fully engaged in rigorous learning and continual growth.

KAY COLEMAN is assistant superintendent of Madison Elementary School District in Phoenix, Arizona. She has been an elementary principal, director of curriculum, instruction and assessment in a K-12 district, director of staff development, a staff developer, a reading specialist, and a classroom teacher. She has been active in a number of professional organizations, including past president of the Arizona affiliate of the Association of Supervision and Curriculum Development.

CHAPTER 17

Poking and Prying with a Purpose: Exploring Research on The Learning Network

Darcy Bradley

"Pausing to reflect is a luxury. Having the opportunity to look for common threads, I am now able to plan from reflection."

Peggy Grubel
Teacher Leader, Phoenix, Arizona

Research is a loaded term with many different meanings for users and producers of it. For some educators, the term research is terrifying, implying that what we do in our classrooms or schools is either right or wrong, black or white, consequential or inconsequential. For others, research belongs to the scientist who works in some mysterious and distant laboratory; when an experiment is completed, the scientist writes up the findings for a small body of other scientists. In the broad educational spectrum that spans grade school to university, other perceptions are that researchers at universities are the producers of knowledge and teachers in the K-12 arena are the users of it. In other words, a few of us will be knowers and producers of knowledge and a whole lot of us will be doers and users of it. What does research really mean and what implications does it hold for the development of teachers and students in The Learning Network?

The origin of the word *research* is Old French, meaning "to seek out" or "to search again." Gifted African-American writer Zora Neale Hurston has referred to research as formalized curiosity–a poking and prying with purpose into ideas and actions that interest us. I have been curious about The Learning Network since my first exposure to it in the summer of 1993 when I attended a four-day institute, then called Whole Language in the Classroom. Since that time I have been doing my own purposeful poking and prying into the theories and practices that drive the structure of The Learning Network in order to enhance my teaching and knowledge of children, novice teachers, and experienced teachers. The reason I bother to poke and pry is that my affiliation with the educators–past and present–who built The Learning Network into its current iteration has been as influential on my attitudes, understandings, and practices in literacy learning as those I experienced through my doctoral studies at The Ohio State University and the intensive training I participated in as a Reading Recovery® Teacher Leader. In this chapter I focus on the seeking that has been done so far, what still needs to be sought, and what might need to be searched again.

A BRIEF PERSONAL HISTORY OF POKING AND PRYING, SEEKING AND SEARCHING

In thinking about research, I have to relate a journey that began for me in 1988 with an early intervention program called Reading Recovery (Clay 1993b). Reading Recovery combined theory and practice so productively and profoundly that it has since affected every aspect of my teaching life. The program was developed by looking carefully at the best primary classroom practices in New Zealand and doing meticulous research on what skillful readers do as they read. The Reading Recovery lesson framework was developed over time through much trial and error by experienced and knowledgeable teachers and the brilliant Marie Clay, one of New Zealand's best known literacy researchers and theorists. Long before any formalized research was attempted by Clay, she and a handful of the best educators were "seeking out" the efficient ways to reach the most emergent readers and writers. As I learned more about Reading Recovery, I began to understand something much bigger than the program itself: productive researching (and teaching) comes from using common sense, asking skillful and useful questions, taking time to observe, consuming well-done research carefully, and letting those interested and invested in whatever you are doing know what you are finding out.

From 1992 to 1995, during my tenure as a Reading Recovery® Teacher Leader, I appreciated more deeply how reading and writing are strategic "in-the-head" processes that can be "taught for" but not taught, and I began to see the change process that same way. I noticed that some of the children who had successfully exited the Reading Recovery® program were not perceived by some of their classroom teachers as proficient readers and writers. While Reading Recovery® teachers were making shifts in their understandings of the reading and writing process, instructional behaviors, and how children learn, I realized that many of the classroom teachers were not. Reading Recovery® teachers were supported with weekly classes and multiple visits from a Teacher Leader. Classroom teachers who had Reading Recovery® students in their classrooms typically did not receive such support. Could this lack of support be a factor in how some classroom teachers perceived Reading Recovery® students? I wondered why a child could appear to be a proficient young reader and writer in one setting and not another. Since most Reading Recovery® teachers appear to undergo a transformation in their understandings of learning theory and the processes of reading and writing, did the classroom teachers' understandings have to change as well?

When I attended the 1993 International Reading Recovery Conference in Columbus, Ohio, I wrote summaries on the major conference speakers for "The Running Record," an international journal published periodically for Reading Recovery teachers. It was there that I first heard Jan Duncan speak about "Laying a Foundation for Literacy Learners." Over a thousand people, including me, stood and applauded for several minutes when Jan concluded her compelling speech on what it meant to be a skillful teacher who provided that essential "good first teaching" in reading and writing. When I heard Jan say that a challenge for us was "to provide the kind of teacher development that will enable Reading Recovery® to function alongside classroom teaching founded on a common philosophy and motivated by the same goal of developing students as life-long readers, writers, and learners" (Bradley 1993, 2-3) I thought that this was a woman with clear vision about literacy learning and perhaps some answers to my questions about the teacher perception of those Reading Recovery® children in the primary classroom.

That summer after hearing Jan, I attended the institute with some classroom teachers and Reading Recovery® colleagues. I was reminded that Reading Recovery had developed from skillful classroom teaching in New Zealand. I was reminded that the running record (an assessment tool for recording reading behaviors of students) was used as an assessment tool in the New Zealand classroom long before Reading Recovery was developed and implemented. As I listened carefully to the whys and hows of literacy teaching and learning from K-12 classrooms where teachers appeared to be highly skilled in engaging students in sound literacy practices, I wondered how I might take the knowledge I had gained from Reading Recovery® about young learners as strategic and independent problem-solvers and apply it to a larger population—not only children in the classroom but classroom teachers and preservice teachers. I also remembered the challenge of changing my own attitudes, understandings, and practices related to literacy learning and teaching. Even as I valued what I had learned about literacy from my graduate studies and superb initial training at The Ohio State University, I reconfirmed that I would be refining my knowledge of literacy learning and teaching for the rest of my career.

In 1994, I began to work as a facilitator for the Literacy Learning in the Classroom summer institute that I had attended the previous summer. There was certainly some worthwhile "poking and prying" to be done there. Also, I searched for a job where I could work with novice and experienced teachers, work with children in a general education primary classroom, and conduct more classroom research.

I left Reading Recovery® in the summer of 1994 for a job in a university teacher education program. I wanted to be able to investigate what was happening not only in the university classrooms involving literacy training for novice teachers but also to work with children and teachers in public school classrooms. One of the gifts from Reading Recovery® training is my strong belief that skillful educators—wherever they are on the learning continuum—need to link theory and practice. They need to link *knowing* with *doing*. Since 1994 I have been intrigued by the innovations and power of The Learning Network for helping educators and children become more accountable for learning.

PRINCIPLES FOR SUCCESS

What are the principles for success of The Learning Network and what do they have in common with other current successful programs? The Learning Network is a thorough staff development plan for all school personnel who impact students. The Learning Network is designed to work across all grades and subject areas. Understanding the nature of learning and literacy development is the umbrella over this model for professional change. The Learning Network is a "two-year, site-based, professional development investment that focuses on literacy and the growth of skillful teachers" (Richard C. Owen Publishers 1996c, 2). Five principles drive this promising professional development system: the learning needs of students drive instruction; effective teachers are skillful and knowledgeable teachers who can articulate how theory drives their practice; change takes time; change needs to be school-wide; and teaching and learning is a cyclic activity (Richard C. Owen Publishers 1996d, 5).

Although there are many models for staff development and school improvement, three appear consistently in the literature: James Comer's School Development Program, developed in 1968 at Yale University Child Study Center; Robert Slavin's Success for All, created through Johns Hopkins in 1987; and Henry Levin's Accelerated Schools, developed at Stanford University in 1987. While it is not the scope of this chapter to review all of the similarities and differences between The Learning Network and these three models, some observations can be made.

The Learning Network shares several common elements with Success for All, the School Development Program, and Accelerated Schools. Most notable is the element of developing the entire school as a learning community with members of that community sharing a consistent philosophy of teaching and learning. Most of the implementations of all the models have occurred in elementary schools with high at-risk populations. All four of these models require an investment in an outside entity (a change agent) until the school can function successfully on its own through a self-governance system. There is an emphasis on reading and language skills in each of the programs, and each of the models allows for a collaborative approach to change. Differences exist, however, between each of the models as well.

While the four models stress the importance of literacy learning and literacy development, The Learning Network is not a scripted literacy program like Success for All, nor is any curriculum acceptable, as it is in Accelerated Schools and the School Development Program. With specialized individualized training, teachers in The Learning Network learn how to make teaching decisions based on their knowledge of learners, their knowledge of resources, and the teaching and learning cycle. The Learning Network seeks to improve *how* the curriculum of the state, district, and school is delivered.

Reading Recovery® is used as an additional comparison. It is not applicable to the entire school faculty in the same sense as The Learning Network, Success for All, Accelerated Schools, and the School Development Program, but it does have similarity to The Learning Network in the approach to professional development and the emphasis on the student as a strategic learner. Marie Clay based the format of Reading Recovery on sound theoretical underpinnings from reading, writing, and learning and the practice of skillful primary classroom teachers. A structure for reading and writing is in place, as it is in The Learning Network, and teachers must make productive teaching decisions based on the needs or the cutting edge of knowledge of the learner. Reading Recovery is successfully implemented in all of New Zealand, many parts of North America, and some parts of Australia. Although this program is aimed at a very small population of low-achieving children in their second year of formal schooling, the staff development piece of Reading Recovery is exemplary. In the U.S., teachers are intensively trained in the assessment and evaluation elements of Reading Recovery® and begin to work with children almost immediately. Each week these teachers meet to watch their colleagues teach children. These teaching sessions are vehicles for developing understandings of theory and practice that drive the Reading Recovery program. A Teacher Leader facilitates these sessions and also makes periodic visits to the Reading Recovery teachers. The purpose of these visits is to further the Reading Recovery teacher's understandings at the point of his or her specific need.

Reading Recovery Teacher Leaders receive a year of special training before they implement a training class for teachers. This training is much like the training that they will provide themselves the following year: they work with children; they meet as a group under the facilitation of clinical and theoretical instructors; and they report back to their school districts. The instructors of the Teacher Leaders are well-versed in the politics of change processes, reading, writing, and cognitive theory and practice, and have in-depth knowledge of Reading Recovery procedures and practices.

What The Learning Network has in common with all of the above successful programs is an understanding of the importance of developing staff-wide philosophical harmony and allowing teachers time for change. One thing that separates The Learning Network from other staff development programs is that the theory that drives classroom practice is identical to the theory that drives the practice of teacher development. What may be the most distinctive contribution of The Learning Network is the expectation that classroom practice will be observed and dialogued about purposefully and concisely with the classroom teacher involved, and that the focus of the discussion will have been determined by the classroom teacher. Although each of the other three models has a coaching or mentoring component, a major difference in The Learning Network appears to be the component referred to as *instructional dialogue*. Different from peer coaching or mentoring, instructional dialogue occurs between the change agent (i.e., the program coordinator or the teacher leader) and a teacher. The focus of the instructional dialogue originates from a weekly action plan made by the classroom teacher. The teacher's action plan and the observation provide a vehicle for this dialogue. This dialogue occurs after a classroom observation by the program coordinator or teacher leader. In this observation, the classroom teacher has taught a lesson during which the teacher leader and/or program coordinator has been present. The purpose of the instructional dialogue is to use the recently taught lesson as an experience for developing and deepening understandings about teaching and learning. The dialogue is focused and concise, resulting in a new understanding about theory and practice for the classroom teacher (see Chapter 2). In the research we do have, teachers frequently mention the positive impact instructional dialogue has on their learning.

While there are many exemplary facets of The Learning Network, several existing hallmarks are the critical triangle, the long-term commitment to training and development of school personnel, the theoretical framework that guides school practices, and instructional dialogue.

CURRENT AND PAST RESEARCH ON THE LEARNING NETWORK

What does the current and past research on The Learning Network indicate about its effectiveness? The Learning Network began in 1993 with fifteen schools. At the time of this writing, 68 schools in ten states across the U.S. are part of The Learning Network. Although there is a minimal amount of what we might call formal research and little of it has been published, studies that are available provide provocative insights on the power and promise of The Network. Although most of the research focuses on the change process for educators, several funded studies also include data on student outcomes. Available studies are summarized below.

The Aurora, Colorado Study

One of the most recent, comprehensive, and perhaps most promising studies on The Learning Network is the RMC Research Corporation's study entitled "The Balanced Literacy Approach in Aurora: Evaluation of the Implementation in Four Schools" (Billig et al. 1996). This descriptive study was funded by the Aurora School District's Title I program and sought to address questions about implementation effects and establish baseline data on student achievement. The study was conducted in four schools in the Aurora, Colorado school district, three of which are at various stages of implementing The Learning Network.

Research questions focused on length of training received by various staff members, to what extent critical components of The Learning Network are used in the classrooms, how the amount and type of training and exposure to the model relate to implementation, and what outside factors might affect the implementation. This study also attempted to evaluate the relation between implementation of The Learning Network model and student achievement.

Written surveys, interviews, and documents were used to collect the data for analysis. The survey and interview questions were constructed by program coordinators from The Learning Network and Title I administrators with assistance from the project researchers. The documents used for analysis included demographic and descriptive information about each of the four schools, standardized test scores (disaggregated by school, grade, and subject matter), and school improvement plans.

Although data were not collected directly from actual classroom practice and relied heavily on self-reported information, many findings are promising in support of The Learning Network. It appears that teachers with the most exposure to and experience in the model are best able to implement the sophisticated practices that are associated with it. The biggest factor in teacher change appeared to be the one-on-one instructional dialogue between teacher leader and classroom teacher, which is a distinguishing feature of The Learning Network. Also of note is the finding regarding years of teaching experience and instructional change: "Any changes in classroom practice were attributable to teachers' exposure to the model, not to their years of teaching. This supported the hypothesis that teachers can change their classroom practices regardless of their teaching experiences" (Billig et al. 1996, 30). The researchers who studied The Learning Network in the Aurora School District recommended continued support for it, stating: "even though the impact on student achievement is not yet clear, it is evident that teachers have changed their classroom practices in ways that are beneficial to children" (45).

One school in the Aurora School District has the longest history with The Learning Network. Montview Elementary, one of the four schools in this study, has participated in The Network since the fall of

1992. The data on student performance at Montview bears a closer look for several reasons. When Montview became part of The Learning Network, its students scored the lowest in the district's standardized test scores. Over the past four years free and reduced lunches have jumped 23% (to 82%). While the Caucasian and African-American population has remained relatively stable, the Hispanic population has increased by over 500%. The student population is currently about one-third Caucasian, one-third African-American, and one-third Hispanic. In the 1995-1996 school year, with a 67% increase in English as a Second Language students, an increase in students in poverty, an increase in student population, and an increase in the transiency rate, Montview's Title I teachers identified that students made 13.6 NCE gains in reading, 18.8 NCE gains in basic math, and 17.1 NCE gains in advanced math (a 2.0 NCE gain is the district and national standard expectation). The fourth-grade Iowa Test of Basic Skills (ITBS) scores for Montview increased from a range of 4.1 to 4.6 grade equivalents in 1994-1995 to 4.4 to 5.0 grade equivalents in 1995-1996.

As part of the ITBS testing, Montview students have also participated in a standardized integrated language arts performance assessment since 1994-1995. The achievement data from the past two years is particularly promising. This performance assessment was first administered in the spring of 1995. This test takes one and a half hours to administer and measures students' performance at responding to an expository text passage. The text passage is written at the fourth-grade level and requires students to respond in two different genres: summary writing and persuasive writing. In the first year, Montview fourth-grade students ranked at the 73rd percentile. In the second year, they performed at the 82nd percentile, which was the highest ranking performance of all 26 Aurora School District elementary schools. When Montview fourth-grade test scores were reported by ethnicities, African-American students were in the 82nd percentile, Hispanics in the 75th, and Caucasians in the 89th. The African-American students scored higher than any other group of African Americans in the district. The Caucasian students outperformed all other district Caucasians. The Hispanic fourth-graders were the second-highest of all district Hispanics.

The Aurora study highlighted Montview and stated that the school "overall showed substantial increases in student achievement over the past three years. Montview's growth over time appeared to be related to the implementation of [The Learning Network]" (Billig et al. 1996, 38).

Itterly's Study on the Mentoring Role of the Teacher Leader

Kathy Itterly (1995), along with Nancy Allen, Betsy Conz, and Nancy Harrington, teacher leaders in the Northampton, Massachusetts School District, secured funding from the Massachusetts Field Center for Teaching and Learning through the University of Massachusetts at Boston for a small action research project on the role of the teacher leader in implementing theoretical and practical changes at the classroom level. This study was conducted during the second year of Learning Network implementation in their district.

Itterly examined the role of the teacher leader as a change agent, how The Learning Network professional development processes could be enhanced, and if a common theory and practice of literacy learning could be developed school-wide. Interviews and journals were used to collect data from the four teacher leaders in the project and a survey was distributed to teachers participating in the project. The research team transcribed the taped interviews, analyzed the data for patterns of response, and developed categories of responses.

The findings from this study suggest that the support, format, and personnel provided by The Learning Network can help develop a community of teacher/learners who begin to use a common literacy theory and practice. The researchers stated that "the process will continue with reading and learning as the foci" in their school-wide improvement plan (Itterly 1995, 18). Itterly and her colleagues found that implementing the practices and working within the structure of The Learning Network was challenging and identified five stages that occurred during the second year of implementation. They identified the five stages as naive optimism, discouragement and uncertainty, crisis intervention, rejuvenation, and realistic optimism (see Chapter 3). At the end of the year, the teacher leaders in this study stated: "We have become much more informed about the change process through research and experience. We are better prepared to meet the challenges which we know await us. We have 'toughened' up but most importantly, we have become more knowledgeable. We have learned not to personalize so many of the setbacks which are inevitable. We have, in fact, added the element of realism to our optimism" (10). The Itterly study concluded with recommendations for strengthening their schools' implementation of The Learning Network, many of which were acted upon as they entered their third year of being a part of The Learning Network.

Kussy's Study on the Superintendent's Role in Transforming Instruction

Kathy Kussy's (1995) single case study focused on her role as superintendent in the Easthampton, Massachusetts School District in creating the conditions necessary for teachers to move from teacher-directed to learner-centered classrooms in the first year of implementation of The Learning Network in a K-8 system. As a participant/observer, she examined the actions she took in this role and looked for evidence of lasting and deep structural school reform.

One of the important findings from Kussy's study was that when she engaged herself in the same learning and teaching processes she supported for teacher leaders, she provided powerful examples in educational leadership, administration and management, and communication. Because Kussy engaged herself as fully as the teacher leaders in the professional development training from The Learning Network, she demonstrated the value she places on life-long learning (Kussy 1995, 94).

Kussy found evidence that dramatic shifts in classroom practices occurred in the teacher leaders who participated in her study. She reported that changes were highly personal and individualistic. She noted that "when teacher leaders could articulate the beliefs driving their practice, a change in practice occurred" (Kussy 1995, 97). She found that the teacher leaders in the study "were no longer teaching 'curriculum' or wedded to particular methodologies; they were teaching students. They no longer relied upon a single resource or program, but rather had developed the expertise to meet the individual needs of the learner and to personalize instruction at the point of need. The purpose of all instruction was meaning; the content was the mechanism for authentic investigation and communication" (98).

With an apparent deep understanding of the change process and her visible involvement as a co-learner in the professional development facilitated by The Learning Network, Kussy appears to have positively affected many layers of the school district: students, teachers, parents, other administrators, and the school board. In the first year of implementation she saw that "excellence and equality can be achieved in our classrooms and schools. I have now seen it happen and know it can be accomplished" (Kussy 1995, 103). She felt that the active engagement of the superintendent as learner was critical in the success of the first year of implementation of The Learning Network.

Readsboro Studies on The Learning Network Implementation

Readsboro Central School District in Vermont is one of the smallest Learning Network schools. Approximately one hundred students attend primary and intermediate school. About 50 percent of the students qualify for free and reduced lunches. When Readsboro joined The Learning Network in 1992, they also committed to do a three-year study supported by the state of Vermont and conducted by RMC Research to assess and evaluate the growth and development of teachers' understanding of the model and the impact of the implementation. Although the studies are not longitudinal, the findings were strong enough each year to recommend continued interaction with The Learning Network as a staff development model. In the last year of the study, RMC Research (Seagar and Graham 1996) attempted to measure the impact of The Learning Network implementation on the school staff, student learning, school organization, and the wider school community. Although a study was conducted each year since 1992, I have only included information on the 1994-1995 school year, as the studies were not set up to be longitudinal.

In this descriptive study, data was gathered via individual interviews and written surveys with all staff members and a review of standardized test results and report cards on Title I students. The written survey looked at behaviors of faculty as they related to classroom practices expected as a result of implementing The Learning Network model. Faculty also kept tally sheets on running records administered to individual children throughout the year.

The findings show that teachers who had the most exposure to the model and support from the program coordinator were most comfortable and congruent with the implementation expectations. When the researchers analyzed the data, three separate and distinct groups emerged: those with the most exposure to the model (three years), those with moderate exposure to the model (two years), and those with limited exposure to the model (one year or less). As in the Aurora study, length of time as a teacher was not as important as length of time a teacher was exposed to the model.

Although teachers reported increased enjoyment, participation, and engagement by Title I students in reading and writing, the standardized test information from the California Test of Basic Skills (CTBS) and Vermont Portfolio Assessment showed no significant changes in Title I student performance.

Duncan's Study on Consistency in Teacher Understandings about Literacy Learning and Teaching in Learning Network Schools

Peter Duncan began an exploratory survey study that looked at the consistency of teacher perceptions about literacy teaching and learning. This unpublished study was conducted at Montview Elementary in Colorado, one of the oldest and most successful of The Learning Network schools. Duncan asked eight open-ended survey questions to faculty and staff about their attitudes toward, behaviors about, and understandings of literacy teaching and learning. Preliminary findings suggest that there was a high level of consistency on questions that focused on classroom practice and less consistency in respondents' expressed understandings about the processes of reading, writing, and learning. In other words, teachers were more consistent in the practices instilled by support and experience with The Learning Network and comparatively less consistent when articulating the theory that drove their practices. In contrast, when Duncan used the same survey in non-Learning Network schools, the data appear to tell another story. In schools where a range of classroom practices exist, dramatically lower rates of consistent responses across all of the questions appear.

This study suggests that practices of teachers can be consistent across a continuum when certain supports are in place. It may show that while there will be inconsistencies across practices and being able to articulate the understandings that drive them, in schools where The Learning Network is operating there is not such a wide range between inconsistencies. It also suggests how slippery and difficult understanding and articulating theoretical principles can be.

Bradley and Button's Study on Emergent Kindergarten Writers in Two Models of Early Literacy Kindergartens

The intent of this study by Darcy Bradley and Katie Button was to compare and contrast the literacy learning and teaching occurring in two kindergarten classrooms: one involved in the Early Literacy Learning Initiative (ELLI) developed and supported by The Ohio State University and the other involved in The Learning Network. The children's writing is the vehicle for observing literacy learning and is the primary focus of this research. Samples of children's writing were collected over three points in time during the 1995-1996 school year for analysis of convention usage and message quality. The teachers in the project administered Clay's observation tasks of early literacy achievement at the beginning and ending of the school year (Clay 1993a). Growth trends are being analyzed from the pre-test and post-test scores. In addition, two videotapes were made of whole group writing instruction at the middle and end of the year, and pre- and post-year interviews were conducted with each of the classroom teachers about the theory that drove their practices.

Preliminary findings show that both sets of children showed growth in their understandings and use of the conventions for writing. The average length of a piece of writing grew by the end of the year. Children in The Learning Network kindergarten tended to show a greater knowledge of the writing process than children in the ELLI kindergarten. Both teachers in this study demonstrated a high level of understandings about teaching reading and writing.

WHAT CONTINUED POKING AND PRYING NEEDS TO BE DONE?

More research on The Learning Network is needed. A particular research challenge for The Network is that it is not a university based innovation for school improvement and staff development. Most highly regarded school improvement programs such as James Comer's School Development Program, Henry Levin's Accelerated Schools, and Robert Slavin's Success for All have been well-researched, well-funded through grants and university salaries, and written about prolifically by their innovators, their innovators' colleagues, and the innovators' graduate students. Reading Recovery®, while not a school improvement program but one with an exemplary staff development component for the teachers in it, was imported from New Zealand, and is sponsored and made available in the U.S. through The Ohio State University. Universities typically enjoy a tax exempt status. University faculty often have access to large sums of grant monies, research bureaus, and have time and an expectation for being innovators. It is not surprising that they often lead the way in creating and disseminating innovations.

In contrast, publishers are not often associated with school reform movements; they are more likely to be perceived as entities who offer short-term workshops for teachers in order to increase book and resource sales. When commercial organizations attempt to enter the domain of staff development and curricular reform, they may be regarded with "profit motive" suspicion by the public. The Learning Network, however, is beginning to gather promising data on school change and student achievement that will likely produce the same kind of exponential growth experienced by Success for All, Accelerated Schools, and the School Development Program. A reason for this growth may be the strong understandings of literacy and learning development that drive the theories and practices promoted in The Network. An analysis of some of the literature on cost factors and the conceptual frameworks that drive the aforementioned three school improvement innovations (Ascher 1993; King 1994) suggests that The Learning Network may be accomplishing its goals as productively and/or cost effectively as Success For All, Accelerated Schools, and the School Development Program.

The little research that exists on The Learning Network has mostly been unpublished and/or funded by school districts or small local or regional grants. But what makes Richard C. Owen Publishers, Inc. a bit different from other publishing companies is a commitment to implementing and supporting long-term school-wide change. An affiliation with a university could be a research advantage for The Learning Network; access to research monies, personnel, and people who are trained to do research could provide valuable information about this innovation.

A first logical step is to publish the research findings that are currently available so that a wider audience is familiar with The Learning Network. Often a function of publication is to generate interest from other researchers. Very little of the research is reaching an outside audience. What is written about and published in the educational arena is what is frequently attended to by educators.

How and why teachers change in their understandings and practices is an important aspect for research. If the change of the teacher's understandings is critical to making changes in classroom practice, then it makes sense to study the attitudes, understandings, and behaviors of teachers and how they change as the teacher grows. One influence on research has occurred as a result of the Literacy Learning in the Classroom summer institutes. For instance, some of the teachers in the current Master of Education program at Western Washington University where I currently teach were influenced by this four-day experience. Several teachers who attended the institute commented on how the theoretical background developed in their university course work helped them access more of the information offered in the institute. Their action research studies document the power the institute can have to help teachers focus on a particular aspect of classroom practice they wish to improve. For example, one teacher, whose action research focused on spelling, found a way to organize her second-grade spelling program as a result of the institute. Her research documents dramatic spelling gains for all of her students, based not only on her deepening understandings of the writing process and spelling development, but how to organize and manage a successful individualized spelling program.

Some schools have begun to use the Concerns Based Adoption Model (CBAM) to measure how well teachers are adopting an innovation in the classroom. This survey can be used to gather data on where individuals perceive themselves in relation to an innovation. The CBAM is used at different points in time to measure the common concerns teachers experience during the implementation of an innovation. Assumptions that underlie the CBAM are: change is personal and involves changing individuals before the organization will change, and when specific concerns can be identified, the change agents will be more able to provide needed support and assistance (Warger et al. 1988).

In The Learning Network, there are already many data collecting instruments in place. Most educators involved in The Network utilize weekly action plans and have regular meetings with other members of the group. These instruments and settings provide rich sources for information and data gathering. A researcher can attach him- or herself to a group, video- and/or audiotape sessions, and analyze what occurs. Monitoring notes that teachers write on each student's learning can be used for comparative studies on novice and more experienced teachers in the model. Running records and summary statements can be used to show changes in teacher understandings. Since teachers are already video- and audiotaping some of their teaching interactions, a time on task and/or a content analysis over time in the school year can be completed. Action plans of novice and experienced teachers can be analyzed for content and compared.

Because instructional dialogue centered on teacher action plans is a critical component in The Learning Network, those interactions need to be studied. Program coordinators and teacher leaders take careful observational notes of the teaching interaction. The notes help the teacher leader focus on the teacher's own learning outcome. What follows is an example of observational notes taken by Marilyn Herzog, a program coordinator and trainer of program coordinators in The Network. The non-italicized notes are the original notes Marilyn took as she observed a teacher leader working with a group of children in a guided reading session. The bold notes show what questions Marilyn formulated as she observed in order to guide the teacher leader to new learning after the observation. The italicized notes show Marilyn's analysis of the teacher leader's understandings. The teacher leader's action plan for this observation was on helping her students develop a better understanding of checking for meaning by using the pictures in the text.

Teacher (T): The title of this book is *Going Outside*. Does the cover give you any hints?
How was the learning outcome determined?
Excellent text selection, which was a former action plan. Using pictures to assess background knowledge.
T: Read pages 2 and 3 (students read silently). What do you think? (Students respond.) What makes you think that?
Student (S): Well the girl up here on page 2 ...
Evidence of S using pictures for support and confirmation.
T: What do you think will happen next?
S: There will be other animals and other people.
T: What's giving you that notion?

S: Well, this box shows the girl with her cat ...
Use of picture to anticipate.
S: I don't get this (reads aloud): "She feels ex ... ex ..."
T: How can you tell her feelings?
S: Well, up here (points to picture) she looks really tired.
When faced with a challenge, T takes S back to meaning through picture.
T: Let's go back and re-read ...
S: (reads) "She feels ... excused? ... and thirsty." That doesn't make sense. "Excused" doesn't mean "tired."
T: Hmmm ... So, we're thinking of a word that means "tired." Let's look closely. (Writes the word *exhausted* on white board.) This is tricky. What do you notice?
S: There's *-ed* at the end.
T: (says slowly) Ex ... haus ...
S: Exhausted!
T: How did you know?
Great assessment sample for T .... what assessment sample did you obtain from this reading group? Did you write it down in your monitoring notes? (None observed.)
S: Well, it sounded like exhaust ...
S: And it had *-ed* at the end.
S: And she looked tired. When my mom is tired she says, "I'm just exhausted."
Reinforcing checking meaning with visual information.
T: Good for you! Now let's re-read to see if it makes sense.
Back to meaning within the text.
What information about learning and teaching would a careful analysis of those interactions reveal?

Another important avenue for research is, of course, student achievement and performance. It is logical to think that students' standardized test scores will improve when quality innovations are actively supported and internalized by school members. In fact, Success for All, Accelerated Schools, and the School Development Program have provided evidence for overall gains in test scores at many of their sites. Data from The Learning Network's Montview Elementary in Aurora, Colorado shows dramatic gains in most curricular areas as measured by standardized tests and the highest district test scores in 1996 on a performance writing assessment.

Other schools are showing encouraging results from standardized test data. In a Learning Network school in Tallahassee, Florida, spring 1997 data using the Kaufman Test of Educational Achievement shows all 29 kindergarten students tested reading at or above first-grade levels. This reading subtest takes about fifteen minutes to administer individually and measures letter recognition, high-frequency word recognition, and comprehension. To measure comprehension the students read a series of directions and do the actions of those directions. The directions increase in difficulty and complexity for each test item. The average kindergarten score was a 1.93 grade equivalent, with a grade level equivalent range from 1.1 to 7.3. Twenty percent of the kindergarten scores were at 2.0 or above. The average first-grade score was 2.94. Thirty percent of the first graders scored 3.1 or above. The average second-grade score was 3.24, and over 50 percent of the students scored at 3.0 or above. This test will provide baseline data for this school. What will longitudinal collection of this data reveal? If an experimental research study is designed and implemented as a comparison in non-Learning Network schools, will there be any significant differences in the data?

However, standardized test scores are not enough to document student achievement and performance. Benchmark reading passages can be established for use at each grade level and data from running records and retellings can be collected over time and analyzed. Because all children in Learning Network schools are expected to write every day, the students' draft books can be analyzed over several points in time, as in the Bradley and Button study (in process). Draft books can be analyzed for both qualitative and quantitative information. For instance, control and growth of spelling development can be studied. Writing can be systematically evaluated through six-trait writing analysis (e.g., organization, voice, word choices) or a writing process analysis (e.g., variety of topic and genre selection, planning usage, revision development, proofreading).

There are many instruments for measuring students' perceptions of themselves as readers and writers. When I met with intermediate-grade students in a multi-age classroom at Montview Elementary, I asked the students to respond in writing to the statement, "Describe what a good reader does. Describe what a good writer does." A student who had been at Montview for one day neatly penned: "A good reader is someone that can read all the words. A good writer is someone who writes neat." Another child, who had been at Montview for a much longer period of time, wrote a more complex answer: "A good reader reads good books and knows the right books for him/her. A good reader knows when to read and why they should be reading. A good writer writes what he or she understands. A good writer chooses what's good to write. They know what to write and who to write it for. A good writer doesn't make their writing complicated because they want everyone who reads their writing to understand it." What would an analysis of the responses students make describing the good reader and writer reveal about their understandings of reading and writing? Is there a difference in responses from students based on their length of exposure to the practices in The Learning Network model? Simple pre- and post-tests like these can be analyzed for insights into students' attitudes, understandings, and beliefs about reading and writing. What is collected and used already to analyze what students know and what they need to know can be used to research student growth in a particular area. Many elements of the model already lend themselves to analysis and reflection.

Besides researching the teachers' roles in teaching and the students' roles in learning, studies on the principals' or superintendents' leadership roles in the school community are certainly warranted. A necessary component for success in Learning Network schools is a strong instructional leader. Studies can be conducted at successful Learning Network schools to help articulate and refine leadership roles. If teachers work to change their practices based on sound theory, what roles do administrators need to play to support the teachers, students, and parents? Kussy's research as a superintendent involved in implementing an innovation shows the need for more research on the processes and practices that lead to profound change. One way to do this would be to conduct an ethnographic study that follows a group of administrators from Years 1 to 3 of involvement in The Network. Data can be collected on how each administrator's beliefs match his or her actions and how beliefs and actions change over time.

Most schools collect data on retention, special education and Title I referrals, and suspension and expulsion of students. Not only is it informative to look at numbers of students, but also to look at policy changes that can occur as a result of adopting any innovation. A closer investigation of what, why, and how retentions, referrals, and suspensions change would provide helpful information to those who make decisions about schools and the people in them. One diversely populated Learning Network school has become a model for equity in its district. It is of interest to find out why that is so.

Lurking behind the issue of referrals is the impact on allocation of financial resources within a school. How much does it cost to put a child through the battery of tests that lead to assigning a label? What is the financial impact on a school when teachers see themselves as competent professionals able to support the growth of all children in their charge?

What happens to a community of learners as they seek to take on an innovation is complex. No one piece of research is going to tell the whole story on why or how an innovation is successful. Both qualitative and quantitative studies need to be undertaken by personnel from both inside and outside The Learning Network. Abundant opportunities exist in The Learning Network for poking and prying, seeking and searching.

DARCY BRADLEY teaches children, undergraduate and graduate students, and teachers through Western Washington University in Bellingham, Washington. In the summer she is a facilitator for the Literacy Learning in the Classroom institutes. She has been a classroom teacher and a Reading Recovery® Teacher Leader and holds a Ph.D. from The Ohio State University in Columbus, Ohio.

Epilogue

Zachary

Marilyn Herzog

"When I approach a child he inspires in me two sentiments: tenderness for what he is; and respect for what he may become."

Louis Pasteur

I was surprised to look up and see him in the store. He is now nearly as tall as me. He walks with quiet confidence far ahead of his mother.

I'll never forget the first day I saw him. His eyes held the same fear that one would see in a frightened animal. He came with a history. He had been reprimanded and disciplined in kindergarten more times than anyone could count. The recommended placement was in an emotionally handicapped, self-contained classroom with others suffering from these extreme behaviors.

His mother was his biggest advocate. She was unwilling to accept this placement. Her heart broke for this little boy who didn't seem to fit anywhere. After months of testing and multiple diagnoses, the decision was made to label Zachary as a child who had "high functioning autism."

Zachary was placed in the special education classroom next door to my multi-age classroom. He was six and angry. The teacher in this classroom, for students considered "severe language impaired," asked if he could be mainstreamed into my classroom for "calendar." After explaining the limited time spent on calendar, I invited her to bring him for our language arts block. She assured me the aide would accompany him to keep tabs on his behavior.

I guess I loved Zachary from the start. To be only six and have had such a negative school experience fueled my determination to see that things would be turned around for this little guy.

My classroom was based on the belief that all children would learn. It was based on the understanding that each child came with a tremendous number of strengths. It was my job as a teacher to uncover those strengths and build upon them. With Zack, uncovering them would be a challenge. He didn't have much faith in this system called school and had no trust in those grown-ups called teachers. It was easier to wrinkle his brow and scowl and keep very quiet than to allow someone in to what was locked inside.

I knew that Zachary needed more time in our room. The aide was not needed to control his behavior and it became easier all the time to "forget" to send Zack back to the special education room next door. He was slowly becoming one of us.

Expectations were the same in this community of learners for all of us. Zachary was expected to take responsibility for his behavior and his learning. The good days were beginning to take over. He began to realize that this room was a safe place to be.

Zachary liked the high degree of predictability and structure in this classroom. He liked knowing that when he came in from the bus, he would have some time to quietly adjust before large numbers of kids rolled in. He liked knowing each day that he chose his lunch and found his seat on the floor in order to be read and written to with the rest of the class. He took responsibility for his own planning and methodically planned his language arts block, always being certain that he would have time for exploring books and using the computer.

Many of Zack's fears came with him to school each day. He was terrified of fire engines and anyone in costume. The fire alarm produced terror unlike any I had ever seen in a child. He and I had to formulate plans to deal with these unexpected terrors. If the fire alarm went off, he would quickly find me, hold my hand, and cover his ear with his other hand. Sensitive children in our classroom community would gently lead him to me until he could do it by himself. Each fearful situation was dealt with in the same way: make a plan and stick to it. Like the anger, the fear too began to disappear.

It quickly became apparent that Zachary had a wealth of information about animals. He was the resident expert for the writers in our room involved in research. Once Zachary became a more proficient reader, it was easy to find him tucked in the corner with a nonfiction book. He would report to anyone close enough to listen any new learning he had acquired in his reading. His level of understanding became sophisticated. I remember a conversation prior to reading a book on lizards. Zachary looked at his six-year-old peers who were sharing background information about the geckos that climbed the walls at their houses and quietly asked if any of them were familiar with the Komodo dragon.

Writing provided a vehicle to report this information on Zack's new learning. For a long time, Zachary wrote only about dinosaurs, but provided detailed sketches for planning and meaty information about these prehistoric creatures. His topics shifted to predators in our second year together. We were recipients of endless amounts of knowledge on a vast number of animals. It wasn't until the end of our two years together that Zack gained the confidence to begin to write about himself.

Friendship and social skills were a long time coming for Zachary. He played alongside children, but seemed very confused and equally distressed about what to do with these kids. He was challenged if those interacting beside him would begin to laugh, and was certain that they were laughing at him. His initial response was to lash out physically at his peers, so we had to work slowly through a plan to overcome that behavior. Zachary would practice questions he might ask: "What are you laughing at?" "Can I play with you?" "I don't like it when you say or do that." Over the two-year period Zachary began to understand his role in friendship.

Even with these challenges, our classroom community began to embrace him. One of the most poignant memories of my teaching career occurred one day after lunch. Zachary announced to the class that he had a song to sing to them that they had never heard before. He stood up and proudly and loudly began to sing the "Barney" theme song. I held my breath, but I needn't have worried. This group of children sat and listened as intently to "I love you, you love me" as if they were hearing it for the very first time. As long as I live, I will never forget the look on his face as they burst into applause.

The special education team, Zack's mother, and I met continually over these two years with the child study team to update Zachary's IEP and monitor his progress. Special education conferences didn't often begin with all that the learner knows and can do, but as time progressed more and more evidence was pointing to the fact that Zack was requiring less and less of these services.

Humor alluded Zack. He didn't understand when his peers would laugh at the funny parts in a picture book. He would yell, "Don't laugh at Mrs. Herzog!" He was sure they were hurting my feelings. We would methodically explain to him what was so funny. I made it part of my practice to talk out loud as a reader, saying, "Ohhh, I think this is going to be the funny part," to help his serious little brain get ready for the adjustment.

Zachary's mom spent lots of time in our room. She was suspicious of our stories of success and found it easier to see it for herself. She and I worried about the challenge of change for Zachary and began to plan far ahead of time how we could transition Zack successfully into a third-grade classroom. It became vitally important to both of us that his success reach far beyond the four walls of my classroom.

Zachary found life outside those walls more challenging. Being confronted in the cafeteria by an unknowing adult would send him into a tailspin. Being teased on the playground would bring back the physical reactions we were trying so hard to eliminate. Zack and I immediately began to apply the strategies that were working so well in the classroom to the challenges that would lie outside the classroom. If someone said to him, "What are you doing here?" instead of replying with a negative "nothing," he was encouraged to think, then talk. "I forgot my milk and I need to go get it." Being reasonable at all levels was of utmost importance. I talked at length with additional teachers with whom he worked to share the best strategies for supporting Zachary. Treat him with kindness, fairness, and respect. Explain yourself clearly and he'll be just fine. Zachary deserved no more or less than any child deserves.

I learned the true meaning of knowing each child as a learner in my two years with Zachary. I learned the power of the teaching and learning cycle. As I would assess and evaluate, not just in academic areas, but in all areas of Zachary's life, I would be equipped with the information to better formulate a plan—whether it be to build on his skills to become a better reader, writer, or mathematician, or to build on Zachary's skills for life. When teaching and learning occurred for Zachary, I saw first hand what was meant by the statement, "Self-esteem comes from knowing today what you didn't know yesterday." The more learning that occurred for Zachary, the more he began to see what he was capable of and the more control he began to have over his life.

Ending our two years together was hard for me, but writing this narrative to him and his mother was a joy.

June 2, 1995

Dear Mrs. Seel and Zachary,

It is with great pleasure and pride that I take this opportunity to share the growth and successes that I have seen in Zack during the past two years. Zack has grown from a quiet, tentative child to a verbal child filled with lots of confidence. He is delightful. Zack is smart and he knows it. He possesses a tremendous amount of information. He is able to share that information with others and is valued by others for what he knows. He has learned over the past two years how to have friends and how to be a friend. He has learned not to be afraid (of lots–including fire alarms and clowns) because someone will always be there to care about him. He has learned that it's fun to laugh and listen to others laugh. He has learned that in order to be successful, you must be responsible.

Zack is a very proficient reader. He expects that reading will make sense and uses the strategies that he has learned in order to ensure that reading will make sense. Zack values reading for information. Zack is good at sharing information with his peers and others. Because of his continual quest for knowledge, he has a tremendous amount of background knowledge. He willingly uses that knowledge in small and large group discussions.

Zack is also a good writer. His topic selection is usually limited to the nonfiction concepts that interest him. The content of Zachary's writing is excellent and interesting. His writing has voice. Zachary's control over the surface features of writing (spelling, grammar, punctuation, handwriting) continues to grow. Once these things are under his belt, he should be a writer with control.

Mathematics has provided more challenges for Zack, but he is rising to these challenges. Zack is continuing to strengthen his understanding of how numbers work. He is beginning to mas-

ter computation facts. Problem solving is still challenging for him. Understanding how to figure out the strategies he can use to solve mathematical problems is difficult for him. You might assist in his growth by using real-life situations for him to solve (e.g., We have driven 34 miles to Prescott and have another 42 to go. How far is it from our house to Prescott? How did you figure that out?). By asking him to articulate these strategies, he will come to better understandings about the purpose of computation.

I will really miss Zack. I will miss the twinkle in his eyes when he is feeling ornery. I will miss the passion in his voice when he learns something new about an animal. I will miss watching him grow on the playground as he has begun to understand what friendship is all about. I will miss his hugs. I look forward to hearing of Zachary's successes as he grows older.

Thank you for all of your support in the past two years. Thanks for all of the time and effort you have given to us in this classroom. And most of all, thank you for sharing your wonderful son with me.

Fondly,

Marilyn Herzog

As I reach to hug Zack's mother in the store, she smiles and tells me how well he is doing. He is back at his neighborhood school. She reports that they were initially hesitant about taking him back, but once they saw that he was a regular kid, everything was fine. "He has been on the honor roll every grading period," she reports. "He has lots of friends and relates well to them and his teachers." She proudly shares that Zachary is no longer in need of or receiving any special education services.

She calls Zachary over to me and I see a flicker of recognition in his eyes. She asks if he remembers me. He nods and smiles and softly says, "Hi, Mrs. Herzog." I tell him how pleased I am to hear he's doing so well. I also tell him that I'm not surprised because I know how smart he is. He looks at me, smiles again, and says, "I know," then slowly walks up to me and puts his arms around my waist just like he did when he was two feet shorter. He turns to rejoin his brother. His mother and I hug and she whispers, "Thank you for saving Zachary's life."

I walk to my car, but can't drive for a bit because my eyes are quite blurry. I realize the warmth I am feeling is not from the Arizona sun, but from knowing that we can never leave the heart out of education. Each child who comes to us requires in us a huge investment in time: time for knowing who they are and what they are capable of doing, time for planning what they need to learn, time for teaching so learning will occur, and time for rejoicing in their successes.

Congratulations Zachary.

Bibliography

Ascher, Carol. 1993. "Changing Schools for Urban Students: The School Development Program, Accelerated Schools, and Success for All." Bloomington, IN: ERIC Clearinghouse on Urban Education. ED355313.

Atwell, Nancie. 1987. *In the Middle: Writing, Reading, and Learning with Adolescents*. Portsmouth, NH: Boynton/Cook.

Barth, Roland. 1990. *Improving Schools from Within*. San Francisco, CA: Jossey-Bass.

Beckhard, Richard and Wendy Pritchard. 1992. *Changing the Essence: The Art of Creating and Leading Fundamental Change in Organizations*. San Francisco, CA: Jossey-Bass.

Bedrova, Elena and Deborah J. Leong. 1996. *Tools of the Mind: The Vygotskian Approach to Early Childhood Education*. Englewood Cliffs, NJ: Prentice Hall.

Billig, S.H., A. Foxworth, D. Hoffman, and J. Lurie. 1996. "The Balanced Literacy Approach in Aurora: Evaluation of the Implementation in Four Schools." Final report. RMC Research Corporation, Denver, CO.

Boland, Janice. 1996. *The Strongest Animal*. Books for Young Learners. Katonah, NY: Richard C. Owen Publishers, Inc.

Bradley, Darcy. 1993. *The Running Record: A Newsletter for Reading Recovery® Teachers*. Volume 5, number 3, pp 2–3.

Bradley, Darcy and Kathryn Button. In process. "Comparing Children's Writing Development in Two Models of Early Literacy Kindergartens." Report.

Britton, James. 1970. *Language and Learning*. Gretna, LA: Pelican Publishing Co., Inc., p 164.

Brown, Judson. 1994. "Teaching that Puts the Learner at Center Stage." *Northampton Gazette*, February.

Brueggemann, Walter. 1995. "Psalms and the Life of Faith: A Suggested Typology of Function." In *Psalms and the Life of Faith*. Minneapolis, MN: Fortress Press.

Bunyan, John. 1988. *Pilgrim's Progress*. London, England: Marshall Cavendish Ltd. Originally published in 1678.

Burns, Brendon. 1991. "In New Zealand, Good Reading and Writing Come 'Naturally.'" *Newsweek*, December 2.

Bussis, A., E. Chittenden, and M. Amarel. 1976. *Beyond Surface Curriculum*. Boulder, CO: Westview Press.

Calkins, Lucy McCormick. 1986, 1994. *The Art of Teaching Writing*. Portsmouth, NH: Heinemann.

Cambourne, Brian and Jan Turbill, editors. 1994. *Responsive Evaluation: Making Valid Judgements About Student Literacy*. Portsmouth, NH: Heinemann.

Cambourne, Brian. 1988. *The Whole Story*. Auckland, New Zealand: Ashton Scholastic, p 33.

Clay, Marie M. 1975. *What Did I Write? Beginning Writing Behavior*. Portsmouth, NH: Heinemann.

—. 1979. *The Early Detection of Reading Difficulties*. Portsmouth, NH: Heinemann.

—. 1991. *Becoming Literate: The Construction of Inner Control*. Portsmouth, NH: Heinemann.

—. 1993a. *An Observation Survey of Early Literacy Achievement*. Portsmouth, NH: Heinemann.

—. 1993b. *Reading Recovery: A Guidebook for Teachers in Training*. Portsmouth, NH: Heinemann.

Cox, Rhonda. 1996. *Pigs Peek*. Books for Young Learners. Katonah, NY: Richard C. Owen Publishers, Inc.

Dana, John Cotton. 1912. King College, NJ motto.

Darling-Hammond, Linda. 1993. "Reframing the School Reform Agenda: Developing Capacity for School Transformation." *Phi Delta Kappan*, June, pp 752–761.

—. 1994. "The Current Status of Teaching and Teacher Development in the United States." Background paper for the National Commission on Teaching and America's Future, November.

Davis, Kent. 1991. Staff Development Inservice, Desert Sage School, August, Phoenix, AZ.

Deal, Terrence. 1987. "The Culture of Schools." In *Leadership: Examining the Elusive*, eds. Linda Sheive and Marian Schoenheit. Alexandria, VA: Association for Supervision and Curriculum Development.

Dixon-Krauss, Lisbeth. 1996. *Vygotsky in the Classroom: Mediated Literacy Instruction and Assessment*. White Plains, NY: Longman.

Duncan, Peter. In process. "A Survey to Explore the Consistency of Teacher Perceptions about Teaching and Learning in Literacy." Report.

Evans, Robert. 1995. "Professional Development." Building Professional Culture Conference, keynote address, May, Worcester, MA.

Ford, Carolyn. 1996. *Nothing in the Mailbox*. Books for Young Learners. Katonah, NY: Richard C. Owen Publishers, Inc.

Fullan, Michael. 1991. *The New Meaning of Educational Change*, 2/e. New York, NY: Teachers College Press.

—. 1993. *Change Forces: Probing the Depths of Educational Reform*. Bristol, PA: Falmer Press.

Gentry, J. Richard. 1982. "An Analysis of Developmental Spelling in *GNYS AT WRK.*" *The Reading Teacher*, November, pp 192–200.

Gibilisco, Stan. 1993. *Concise Illustrated Dictionary of Science and Technology*. Blue Ridge Summit, PA: Tab Books.

Goodman, Kenneth S., Patrick Shannon, Yvonne S. Freeman, and Sharon Murphy. 1988. *Report Card on Basal Readers*. Katonah, NY: Richard C. Owen Publishers, Inc.

Graves, Donald. 1983. *Writing: Teachers and Children at Work*. Portsmouth, NH: Heinemann.

—. 1989. *Writing: Teachers and Children at Work*. Exeter, NH: Heinemann.

—. 1994. *A Fresh Look at Writing*. Portsmouth, NH: Heinemann.

Gray, Libba Moore. 1993. *Dear Willie Rudd*. New York, NY: Simon and Schuster.

Harvey, Olive. 1985. *Blackbird's Nest*. Ready to Read. Wellington, New Zealand: Learning Media for Ministry of Education.

Hersey, Paul and Kenneth H. Blanchard. 1978. "The Management of Change." In *Organizational Behavior and Management: A Contingency Approach*, eds. H.L. Tosi and W.C. Hamner. Chicago, IL: St. Clair Press.

Holdaway, Don. 1979. *The Foundations of Literacy*. Portsmouth, NH: Heinemann.

Itterly, Kathleen C. 1995. "Collegial Mentoring: Fragile Relationships." Paper presented at the First Annual Learning Network Conference, July 8, Stamford, CT.

Jinkins, Michael and Deborah Jinkins. 1991. *Power and Change in Parish Ministry*. New York, NY: Alban Institute.

Johnston, Peter H. 1987. *Constructive Evaluation of Literate Activity*. White Plains, NY: Longman.

Joyce, Bruce and Beverly Showers. 1980. "Improving Inservice Training: The Messages of Research." *Educational Leadership*, Volume 37, number 5, pp 379–385.

—. 1995. *Student Achievement Through Staff Development: Fundamentals of School Renewal*, 2/e. White Plains, NY: Longman.

—. 1996. "The Evolution of Peer Coaching." *Educational Leadership*. Volume 53, March, pp 6, 12–16.

Joyce, Bruce, Carlene Murphy, Beverly Showers, and Joseph Murphy. 1989. "School Renewal as Cultural Change." *Educational Leadership*, Volume 47, number 3, pp 70–77.

King, J.A. 1994. "Meeting the Educational Needs of At-Risk Students: A Cost Analysis of Three Models." *Educational Evaluation and Policy Analysis*, Volume 16, number 1, pp 1–19.

Kussy, Katherine. 1994. "Living with The Learning Network." *Teachers Networking: The Whole Language Newsletter*, Volume 13, number 3, pp 14–15.

—. 1995. "The Role of the Superintendent in Transforming Instruction." Ed.D. diss., Columbia University Teacher's College, New York, NY.

Lieberman, Ann. 1995. *The Work of Restructuring Schools: Building from the Ground Up*. New York, NY: Teachers College Press.

Little, Judith W. 1989. "The Persistence of Privacy: Autonomy and Initiative in Teachers' Professional Relations." Paper presented at the American Educational Research Association.

Marris. 1975. *Loss and Change*. New York, NY: Anchor Press/Doubleday.

Millar, J.K., project evaluator. 1992. "Achieving Charter Curriculum Objectives." Teacher development program implemented and evaluated by Wellington, Christchurch, and Dunedin Colleges of Education for the Ministry of Education of New Zealand, October.

Ministry of Education. 1985. *Reading in Junior Classes*. Wellington, New Zealand: Learning Media for Ministry of Education.

—. 1992. *Dancing with the Pen: The Learner as a Writer*. Wellington, New Zealand: Learning Media for Ministry of Education.

—. various years. *School Journals*. Wellington, New Zealand: Learning Media for Ministry of Education.

Mirman-Owen, J. 1995. "The Only People Who Like Change are Wet Babies." Symposium conducted at the Massachusetts Field Center for Teaching and Learning Professional Development Conference: Building Professional Culture, May, Worcester, MA.

Mooney, Margaret. 1987. "A Good Book is a Good Book Anywhere." *Teachers Networking: The Whole Language Newsletter*, Volume 8, number 2, December, p 15.

—. 1988. *Developing Life-long Readers*. Wellington, New Zealand: Learning Media for Ministry of Education.

—. 1990. *Reading To, With, and By Children*. Katonah, NY: Richard C. Owen Publishers, Inc.

Murray, Donald M. 1989. *Expecting the Unexpected: Teaching Myself–and Others–to Read and Write*. Portsmouth, NH: Boynton/Cook.

—. 1984. *Write to Learn*. New York, NY: Holt, Rinehart and Winston.

O'Brien, John. 1993. "Never Ending Teeth." *School Journal*, Part 2, number 2. Wellington, New Zealand: Learning Media for Ministry of Education, p 22–23.

Richard C. Owen Publishers. 1994. *Books for Ready to Read Classrooms*. Katonah, NY: Richard C. Owen Publishers, Inc.

—. 1995a. "The Selection of Teacher Leaders." *The Learning Network Program Coordinator Manual*. Katonah, NY: Richard C. Owen Publishers, Inc.

—. 1995b. "Benchmarks and Indicators for Teachers." *The Learning Network Program Coordinator Manual*. Katonah, NY: Richard C. Owen Publishers, Inc.

—. 1996a. "Cycle for Individual Growth and Development." *Understanding The Learning Network*. Katonah, NY: Richard C. Owen Publishers, Inc., p 10.

—. 1996b. "Characteristics of a Learning Network School." *Understanding The Learning Network*. Katonah, NY: Richard C. Owen Publishers, Inc., p 4.

—. 1996c. "Highlights." *Understanding The Learning Network*. Katonah, NY: Richard C. Owen Publishers, Inc., p 2.

—. 1996d. "Principles of The Learning Network." *Understanding The Learning Network*. Katonah, NY: Richard C. Owen Publishers, Inc., p 5.

—. 1997a. "The Skillful Teacher." *Literacy Learning in the Classroom Resource Book*. Katonah, NY: Richard C. Owen Publishers, Inc., p B-5.

—. 1997b. "Principal's Declaration of Support." Katonah, NY: Richard C. Owen Publishers, Inc.

—. 1997c. "The Change Process." *Literacy Learning in the Classroom Resource Book*. Katonah, NY: Richard C. Owen Publishers, Inc., p B-6.

—. 1997d. "Reading Process Diagram." *Literacy Learning in the Classroom Resource Book*. Katonah, NY: Richard C. Owen Publishers, Inc., p B-32.

—. 1997e. "Reading Process Terminology." *Literacy Learning in the Classroom Resource Book*. Katonah, NY: Richard C. Owen Publishers, Inc., p B-33.

Ricoeur, Paul. 1970. *Freud and Philosophy*. New Haven, CT: Yale University Press.

—. 1971. *Conflict of Interpretations*. Evanston, IL: Northwestern University Press.

—. 1976. *Interpretation Theory*. Fort Worth, TX: Texas Christian University Press.

Schlechty, Phillip. 1990. *Schools for the Twenty-First Century: Leadership Imperatives for Educational Reform*. San Francisco, CA: Jossey-Bass.

Seagar, A. and W.J. Graham. 1996. "Evaluation of the Implementation and Impact of The Learning Network at the Readsboro Central School for the 1994–1995 School Year." Final report. RMC Research Corporation, Portsmouth, NH.

Senge, Peter. 1990. *The Fifth Discipline*. New York, NY: Doubleday.

Sergiovanni, Thomas J. 1987. "The Theoretical Basis for Cultural Leadership." In L.T. Sheive and M.B. Schoenheit, eds., *Leadership: Examining the Options*. Alexandria, VA: Association for Supervision and Curriculum Development, p 121.

—. 1994. *Building Community in Schools*. San Francisco, CA: Jossey-Bass.

Sizer, Ted and Richard Elmore. 1996. "Changing the Conversation." *Education Bulletin*, Volume 41, number 1, December, pp 4–7.

Stewart, David, Tom Prebble, and Peter Duncan. 1997. *The Reflective Principal: Leading the School Development Process*. Katonah, NY: Richard C. Owen Publishers, Inc.

Temple, Charles, Ruth Nathan, Nancy Burris, and Frances Temple. 1988. *The Beginnings of Writing*, 2/e. Newton, MA: Allyn and Bacon.

Trussell-Cullen, Alan. 1996. *Inside New Zealand Classrooms*. Katonah, NY: Richard C. Owen Publishers, Inc.

Vygotsky, Lev S. 1978. *Mind in Society: The Development of Higher Physiological Processes*. Cambridge, MA: Harvard University Press.

Wargar, C.L., C.F. Moffett, B. Schweinefuss, and C. Fuscellaro. 1988. *Human Resource Development Handbook*. Alexandria, VA: Association for Supervision and Curriculum Development.

Wells, Gordon. 1990. "Creating the Conditions to Encourage Literate Thinking." *Educational Leadership*, Volume 47, number 6, March, pp 13–17.

Index